THE CONFLIC

Human beings are paradoxical. We think of ourselves as positive and fair-minded, but our behaviour lets us down. We are health conscious, yet we still continue to smoke. We love our family, but say terrible things to them. *The Conflicted Mind* explores how the conflicting subsystems of the human mind, one slow, deliberate and conscious, one fast, automatic and unconscious, operate together to such telling effect.

This unique book examines classic social psychological research in this new light, including Allport's research on conflicted racial attitudes, Festinger's research on cognitive dissonance, Milgram's obedience experiments, Bateson's research on conflicted communication, Pennebaker's work on emotional disclosure to resolve conflicting memories, and Dichter's clever manipulation of the conflicted mind to sell cigarettes.

Geoffrey Beattie shows that these classics of social psychology, although imaginative, were flawed, which social psychology must remedy if it is to make the kind of impact it aspires to. Written in the author's distinct open and engaging style, *The Conflicted Mind* offers a groundbreaking perspective on why we act in the way we do, and is a fascinating resource for researchers, specialists, and students in the field, as well as the general reader.

Geoffrey Beattie is Professor of Psychology at Edge Hill University and in recent years a master's supervisor on the Sustainability Leadership Programme at the University of Cambridge and Visiting Professor at the University of California–Santa Barbara. He was Professor of Psychology at the University of Manchester from 1994 to 2012. He has a Ph.D. in psychology from the University of Cambridge and has been awarded both the Spearman Medal by the British Psychological Society for 'published psychological research of outstanding merit', and the internationally acclaimed Mouton d'Or for his work in semiotics.

'Geoff Beattie's *The Conflicted Mind* is fascinating and beautifully written. Bold and original, it adds a new dimension to a conception of mind being developed now across psychology – to relate the conscious, purposeful, self-aware, slow-to-act mind to something else, a mind not conscious, not purposeful not prone to self-awareness, and quick. The two aspects, coexisting in every person, come into conflict by their nature. To reveal the conflict in its many forms is the topic of Beattie's book. Most fascinating are the rich, nuanced discussions of the six 20th Century social psychology giants he has chosen, each with his own chapter, who touched the conflicted mind but never fully grasped it.' – **David McNeill, Professor Emeritus of Psychology and Linguistics, University of Chicago, US**

'Psychology has been influential in providing effective aid in alleviating many mental afflictions that confront contemporary humans; but it has hardly offered answers, or even explanations, to the "conflicted mind," which is a product of cultural and environmental factors – not purely cognitive ones. This book deconstructs psychology brilliantly, but also offers an in-depth and powerful assessment of the sources and outcomes of confused and inconsistent emotions. This is a brilliant book and highly recommended for everyone – psychologists and general public alike.' – **Marcel Danesi, Ph.D., Full Professor of Anthropology, University of Toronto, Canada**

THE CONFLICTED MIND

And Why Psychology Has Failed to Deal With It

Geoffrey Beattie

Routledge
Taylor & Francis Group

LONDON AND NEW YORK

First published 2018
by Routledge
2 Park Square, Milton Park, Abingdon, Oxon OX14 4RN

and by Routledge
711 Third Avenue, New York, NY 10017

Routledge is an imprint of the Taylor & Francis Group, an informa business

© 2018 Geoffrey Beattie

British Library Cataloguing-in-Publication Data
A catalogue record for this book is available from the British Library

Library of Congress Cataloging-in-Publication Data
A catalog record for this book has been requested

ISBN: 978-1-138-66578-1 (hbk)
ISBN: 978-1-138-66579-8 (pbk)
ISBN: 978-1-315-61970-5 (ebk)

Typeset in Bembo
by Saxon Graphics Ltd, Derby

For Carol

A light
Back then
In the darkness
For this
Terrible
Conflicted Mind
...and always.

There is a place where Contrarieties are equally True;
This place is called Beulah. It is a pleasant lovely Shadow
Where no dispute can come, Because of those who sleep
William Blake (from Milton,
A Poem in 2 Books. 'To Justify the Ways of God to Men')

CONTENTS

ACKNOWLEDGMENTS

I have a truly wonderful literary agent, Robert Kirby from United Agents, and he and I have discussed some of the ideas in this book over a number of years. He is eternally enthusiastic and receptive to new ideas and I would like to thank him profusely for his wholehearted encouragement, even though in the end I did go in a slightly different direction. Some of the observational writing in this book first appeared in the *Guardian*, the *Observer* and the *Belfast Telegraph*, three publications that have always meant a great deal to me, and I thank the respective editors and feature editors of these fine newspapers for their interest in a certain type of writing, and for their support. I work in the Department of Psychology at Edge Hill University, a really lovely department in a really lovely university, and the Vice-Chancellor, John Cater, has been extremely positive about my work since I started, and has given me the freedom and encouragement to allow me to develop my ideas in (hopefully) interesting and novel ways. I thank him for that support. I would also like to thank my family who have always been there for me (and when times get tough, or really tough, as they can do, sometimes through no fault of your own, you do appreciate how important this is). They are my rock and have been forever.

1

INTRODUCTION

I blame Shakespeare. The concept of the 'conflicted mind' is everywhere in psychology, in one form or another, and critical, I would say, to many of the core areas – attitudes, habits, communication, cognitions, roles and even memories. In each of these areas, many of the main protagonists have built an edifice around the concept, either very explicitly or sometimes less so (but it is still there), be it Gordon Allport's consideration of conflicted attitudes, and his concept of the 'inner conflict' with regard to racial attitudes in the 1950s in the United States; Ernest Dichter's use of 'depth psychology' to produce conflicted habits in the promotion of smoking; Gregory Bateson's attempt to identify conflicted communication as a potential precursor of mental disorder; Leon Festinger's identification of the importance of conflict in cognitions, which he termed 'cognitive dissonance', as a driver of attitude change; Jamie Pennebaker's work on emotional disclosure as a way of dealing with trauma and negative emotional experience, with any conflicted memories somehow dealt with through this disclosure process as the memories become coherent narratives; and Stanley Milgram's investigations of conflicted roles in his work on obedience to authority (the experimental participants did, after all, have to play a role that they were not at all happy to play). And yet, when you mention the 'conflicted mind' to people, they usually come back with the same response. 'You mean Hamlet?' 'No, I don't,' I say, 'Well, not necessarily,' and I'm already on the back foot. That's why I blame Shakespeare. Hamlet's soliloquy is just so powerful, so dramatic and well so memorable – and yet, I will suggest, so inaccurate regarding conflicted minds in general, and how they operate.

I confess that I toyed with a number of possible titles for this book: 'The Janus Effect: Why we say one thing and do another', which came to me in a highly visual and disturbing dream, which may well be one aspect of the functioning of the conflicted mind, but I didn't want to constrict consideration to just the conflict between what we say and what we do. I also considered 'The Light and Shade of the Conflicted Mind'. This title had many attractions because I think that in many ways Daniel Kahneman, the Nobel laureate, is right when he talks about the two 'systems' of the human mind (hypothetical concepts, he is keen to point out), System 1 and System 2, the first a good deal more in the shade than the second, quicker in terms of its operation, more automatic, more unconscious, the stuff of habits. But as I started working on the book, I became more and more interested in potential shortcomings of the work on this topic by some of these greats of our subject (well, maybe not Ernest Dichter, but he's included because of the magnitude of his legacy), although such a judgement is always easier with the benefit of hindsight (and the development of new approaches to the subject). My subtitle thus more or less suggested itself, so I needed something short and simple for the main title.

The response to the title *The Conflicted Mind* was very interesting, as I have indicated, but actually there were two main responses. Both groups of respondents were equally confident in their reaction. 'Got it,' they said, as if it was a test. The commonest response was indeed Hamlet's conflicted mind: sometimes the memory was couched in the form of a visual image of Sir Laurence Olivier's Hamlet with his melodious tones (rather than say those of Gielgud, Gibson or Branagh). It was Olivier, in black-and-white, on the castle walls peering into the crashing waves below, peering into the abyss (in a very literal visual metaphor).

> To be, or not to be: that is the question:
> Whether 'tis nobler in the mind to suffer
> The slings and arrows of outrageous fortune,
> Or to take arms against a sea of troubles,
> And by opposing end them? To die: to sleep;
> No more; and by a sleep to say we end
> The heart-ache and the thousand natural shocks
> That flesh is heir to, 'tis a consummation
> Devoutly to be wish'd.

This is Hamlet's conflicted mind in action, they would tell me, reflecting on life and death, contemplating suicide, balancing both sides of the argument. It is a reflection on the powerlessness of life, where we have to suffer 'the slings and arrows of outrageous fortune', where the only power that we have some say is to take our own life and 'end the heart-ache and the thousand natural shocks that flesh is heir to'. Hamlet's first thought is that suicide is empowering, we finally can take control and take action against the outrageous nature of life itself. Death is to be welcomed, an escape, a sleep, and in this sleep we end 'the heart-ache and the thousand natural shocks that flesh is heir to'. It is a final answer to all of our problems, 'a consummation, devoutly to be wish'd'. But, of course, it's not that easy:

> To die, to sleep;
> To sleep: perchance to dream: ay, there's the rub;
> For in that sleep of death what dreams may come
> When we have shuffled off this mortal coil,
> Must give us pause: there's the respect
> That makes calamity of so long life.

Hamlet realises that there is a catch, there is often a catch to every simple solution. What happens if death is a long interminable *sleep*? Sleep, after all, is the metaphor that we most often use about death ('sleep well, my friend'), and like all metaphorical frames, according to Lakoff and Johnson (1980) they can affect our cognitions. And aren't dreams an integral part of sleep? What dreams 'may come' then? We may be masters of our own destiny, but not masters of our dreams. We do not, after all, control the course or content of our (sometimes inexplicable) dreams in life, my friends explain. I mention my dream from the previous night to them – 'I look at my new book in a Victorian bookshop and the words on the cover in gold lettering tumble to the wooden floor and become dust.' 'Just your acute status anxiety again,' they say. 'You do know that you are a very insecure person.' So why should our dreams be any less frequent or any less inexplicable in death? Who can guarantee that they will stop? What dreams might invade our sleep in that strange and unknown territory that we now occupy? How terrifying will they be? Hamlet muses that we are not in control in life, but we might not be in control in death either.

> Who would fardels bear,
> To grunt and sweat under a weary life,
> But that the dread of something after death,
> The undiscover'd country from whose bourn
> No traveller returns, puzzles the will
> And makes us rather bear those ills we have
> Than fly to others that we know not of?

And then, of course there are the moral considerations underneath it all, interwoven throughout the entire discourse. Suicide is a mortal sin without any opportunity for repentance, it is contrary to the love of God. It is perhaps worth remembering that in 1533 those who committed suicide whilst accused of a crime were not permitted a Christian burial. So, what torments of hell, in the form of 'the dreams that come' await those who commit suicide? And this is not the only moral consideration here. The soliloquy is not just a contemplation of the conflicted mind considering the killing of oneself, but a contemplation of other acts of killing that may also prick the conscience and might also be condemned by God. Hamlet has to avenge his father's death by killing Claudius, his father's murderer. Throughout the play he makes excuses for not killing him and does not proceed when he has the chance. 'Conscience does make cowards of us all', can apply to more than one situation. At the end of the soliloquy he finishes this contemplative way of thinking by concluding that too much thinking can prevent the very action that he has to carry out.

> Thus conscience does make cowards of us all;
> And thus the native hue of resolution
> Is sicklied o'er with the pale cast of thought,
> And enterprises of great pith and moment
> With this regard their currents turn awry,
> And lose the name of action.

This is one possible description of the conflicted mind, the conflicted mind engaged in rumination, the balancing of pros and cons, the mind allowing the imagination to fill in the details. It is multi-layered, with deeper unconscious considerations infusing the argument (we will consider in other domains how important this might be), deeper considerations that need to be teased out, by an audience or the enlightened protagonist himself, therefore making the conflicted mind sequential in its organisation, unfolding over time. It is extremely articulate, as literature has to be. Of course, despite this being the work of the imagination, most of us can instantly recognise what Shakespeare was describing in our own lives, and report instances of being conflicted in some way and going through these sorts of processes. I can remember to this day, sitting on Divis Mountain overlooking Belfast, in a mild drizzle, trying to decide between Biology and Latin 'O' level (hardly Shakespearian in its scope or significance), weighing up the pros and cons of both subjects on a soggy sheet of paper with two lists, balancing, imagining, before finally opting for Latin, which, given my eventual profession, was certainly the wrong decision (I just got too wet in the end and gave up). My rumination and balancing was considerably less articulate and nuanced than that of Hamlet, it was 'greyer', more diffuse, more emotional, in the sense that the two options had a certain emotional valence, which I found hard to describe verbally (to me Latin represented grammar schools and learning, the world I was aspiring to from my working-class Belfast roots). We may recognise Hamlet's dilemma but the conflicted mind is a great deal broader than this, it operates in many other ways as well.

The alternative audience response to my proposed title, when I presented this to friends and acquaintances, was a more philosophical one. 'The mind is always conflicted,' some said. 'Tell me when there isn't some sort of conflict going on in the mind? Decisions or actions are never straightforward. There's always approach and avoidance, leading to a degree of conflict. Only a fool would think otherwise.' And they look at me knowingly. There is some truth in what they say, of course (and I don't mean in the illocutionary force of the communicational look), but this makes the topic very broad indeed – impossibly broad. It is *all* mental and physical action.

I wished to steer some middle path between Shakespeare and his overly reflective and ruminative version of the conflicted mind (which may or may not in the end connect to any resultant behaviour, including the decision *not* to engage in the behaviour in question, i.e. not commit suicide), and the alternative *very* broad view of the conflicted mind which holds that, in effect, it is indeed everywhere and everything. I want to consider the conflicted mind by considering how it pops up in some of the most important research in social psychology, which has often focused on the conflicted mind, in one form or another, and its operations. A number of the most influential social psychologists of the past sixty or seventy years, whose work has shaped, indeed defined, our social psychological thinking, have focused on situations and behaviour where some form of real or manipulated conflict is present. How such conflicts were developed, maintained and resolved was at the very core of their research, and they have informed how we think about the conflicted mind in our everyday lives. I want to see how they conceptualised the conflicted mind, and observed it operating in a number of different guises. I am thinking (perhaps most obviously) of Leon Festinger on cognitive dissonance and conflict in cognitions, Gordon Allport on prejudice and 'the inner conflict' in attitudes to people of different races, Stanley Milgram on obedience and conflict in roles, Gregory Bateson on double binds and conflict in communication, Ernest Dichter on the marketing of brands of cigarettes and conflict in habits, and Frederic Bartlett on the constructive nature of human memory, and conflict in remembering and retelling, but perhaps more specifically here in the work of

Jamie Pennebaker on emotional disclosure and why talking about negative events is good for you, as we rework our autobiographical memories and articulate our emotional traumas, and inevitably iron out some of the apparent conflicts in what we remember. These theorists have shaped the discipline of social psychology and I want to reconsider and reappraise their work. I note that many of these did their most influential work in the 1950s (although some started earlier) and early 1960s, often thought of as the golden age of social psychology, before the experimental revolution in social psychology took place that then shaped and constrained the discipline so much. Their work was essential to the emergence of our discipline.

I began this introduction by mentioning Shakespeare, partly because Hamlet immediately sprang to mind when I mentioned my proposed title to others, but partly to remind us all, if we needed reminding, that psychology is not alone in trying to understand the conflicted mind. It doesn't belong to us, and I sometimes think that we, as psychologists, need reminding of this. Psychology is very good at kidnapping core concepts and holding them ransom. The conflicted mind (in whatever instantiation) is part of our general self-knowledge and self-awareness, approached cautiously for centuries. Psychology merely brought new methods and approaches to the problem. The question is whether these new methods and approaches did cast new light on the subject or whether, as my subtitle suggests, they have failed to deal with it. If they have failed to deal with it, what else could they have done? What else could we do in future? What lessons are there to be learnt?

When it comes to the 'conflicted mind,' psychologists, of course, have most often been concerned with thoughts, or 'cognitions', and their relationship to behaviour, rather than detailed descriptions of mere ideation (or the content of ruminative thought) for the sake of it. And a core issue for psychology generally has been the conflict between our cognitions and our actions, although, of course, it is not the only issue that we are interested in; conflicts in what we think, in what we say or in what we do are also of critical importance. However, the conflict between what we say and what we do would be identified by many as one of the greatest paradoxes of life. Why do we say one thing and do something completely different? The image of the smoker, standing in the cold air, puffing away, saying 'disgusting habit' springs immediately to mind here. This book, in addressing the issue of the conflicted mind, will explore why our everyday behaviour sometimes surprises us so much, but only as part of a more general set of issues. We do think of ourselves as positive and fair-minded, caring about other people and the environment, putting our family first, good in relationships, but our behaviour lets us down time and time again. Part of the reason, according to Daniel Kahneman, for why we say one thing and do another is because we really do have two separate 'selves', a genuine dissociation between two separate mental systems, one conscious, reflective and rational and one whose motives and instincts are rooted in the unconscious and whose operation is not open to reflection (merely observation), no matter how hard we try. When it comes to many aspects of life, one system seems to make very different sorts of 'judgements' to the other, and is subject to distinct, hidden biases. This system often controls our behaviour. This book will explore how and why this operates in the way that it does and what we can do about it, in the context of some classic research from the past.

Malcolm Gladwell, in *Blink*, wrote a bestseller in 2005 about the '*adaptive* unconscious', 'the power of thinking without thinking', but this is, in my view, incorrect. It is not adaptive in the way that Gladwell seems to think. This book will attempt to show how non-adaptive it really can be, and explore the implications of this basic conscious/unconscious dissociation even in those first five seconds when we make so many important decisions in life, when selecting a potential work colleague or 'deciding' what to buy in the supermarket. It will suggest why we might all suffer from a potential bias and how this shapes our everyday worlds.

Gladwell's book generated a lot of interest. Indeed, one might suggest that over the past ten years or so there has been almost a new cultural revolution, both within psychology and in our culture more generally, on the significance of rapid cognition guided by this so-called 'adaptive unconscious'. Gladwell argued that these unconscious processes that operate within us allow us to arrive at the 'correct' conclusion without any apparent consciously controlled thinking on our part. Gladwell tries to persuade us that 'there can be as much value in the blink of an eye as in months of rational analysis'. Gerd Gigerenzer from the Max Planck Institute for Human Development in Berlin in his popular book *Gut Feelings* describes how 'the best pops up first' and that 'experiments demonstrate the amazing fact that less time and information can improve decisions'. This notion of 'the efficacy of decision in the blink of an eye' and the 'adaptive unconscious' has now entered our culture. These days, we are told to trust our gut instincts, to be more spontaneous in our decision making, to go with what feels right. Whole courses have been designed to teach us this art of rapid cognition. I will argue that this may be fundamentally wrong. There may well be unconscious processes within us all but they may well lead to conclusions that are far from adaptive (we will see this in Chapter 2 with research on implicit racial attitudes). The adaptive unconscious can be an incorrect and dangerous notion when it comes to many aspects of everyday life, like race, the environment, habits like smoking, who or what we are attracted to, choosing a partner, relationships, what we remember and what we forget, following a group or political leader – many of the things that are really important to us as individuals and crucial to the workings of society more generally. In each of these domains we can rationally and consciously identify what might work and what we should do, and yet our unconscious impulses provoke us to do something completely different in a completely *non-adaptive* way.

The implication of this part of the argument for society as a whole, therefore, is not to persuade people to trust their gut instincts and to surrender their decision making to their 'adaptive unconscious', as Gladwell and Gigerenzer suggest, but to understand these unconscious processes, identify them, recognise them, and control them. There is, whether we like it or not (this book will argue) a darker side to all human beings; a side that we do not know very well, if at all. We catch glimpses of it sometimes, but we dismiss it quickly, saying things like 'I just wasn't being myself', 'I don't know why I did that', 'I don't even like blondes, burgers, cigars … vodka martinis', 'it will never happen again'. But it does. This darker side 'thinks' differently to the side we know well, it makes different kinds of judgements, judgements that have their own logic, alien to our rational self. We do surprising things, things that sometimes shock us, but we shouldn't be that surprised because it keeps happening, despite our best intentions.

We think that we are fair and decent and that we treat all men and women equally; we say that we care about the environment and the future of our planet. But deep inside, there might well be unconscious processes that control much of our everyday behaviour; there are other priorities, other values (Beattie 2010). We will see, for example, in Chapter 2 that there is evidence that many of us do suffer from distinct racial biases, regardless of what we say (Beattie 2013). It seems that there is a strong unconscious preference for the familiar, for members of our own racial or ethnic group, and this unconscious own-group preference leaks out in many ways, including when we consider people for jobs and end up selecting people just like ourselves, from the same racial group. Indeed, it has been argued that one of the most primitive parts of the brain, the amygdala, the alarm system of the brain, fires differently and habituates differently to people from other racial groups, and this affects the behaviour over which we have least control, like the subtler forms of body language that we have least feedback from and that we can't quite override.

We say that we care about the environment and that we are prepared to adjust our shopping habits to reduce the effects of climate change, and yet when we are out shopping, our eyes seem to unconsciously skip over the carbon footprint information on products (measured and included on the product by multinational retailers at considerable expense), without ever processing it (Beattie et al. 2010; Beattie and McGuire 2015). So that when we buy products we do so blindly with regard to the environmental impact of what we are buying. We literally do not see the carbon footprint on the packaging because, it seems, our unconscious self doesn't really care enough (brand and status are much more important to it). In collaboration with a number of colleagues, I have studied people in detail in our lab who *say* that they care deeply about the environment and who *say* that they feel very positively about low carbon footprint products like low energy light bulbs compared with their high energy competitors. We have projected images of these products, and others, with carbon footprint information in front of them, and monitored the exact fixation points of their eyes twenty-five times every second. These individual fixation points reflect the attentional focus of the individual; these fixation points tell us what they really care about. We have found that the eyes fixate on many other features of products, the brand, the price, the value deal, the calories, the fat content, rather than the carbon footprint, even though many of the people in that lab reported that they cared more about the carbon and environmental impact than all of these other things, and they were clamouring for relevant information, through various consumer surveys, to help them assess the environmental impact of what they were buying in supermarkets.

Or consider a different area. Why, despite saying that we want a quiet, harmonious life, do we find ourselves regularly arguing with our partner? Is it just lack of compatibility, or boredom, or something different? Is it, for example, our unconscious testing them in some way? In desperation, we accuse our partner of orchestrating the argument, and yet this might be even further from the truth. Nobody, in fact, is controlling it; no whole person that is, perhaps it is just being controlled by part of ourselves. Or take our diets. We all understand these days what healthy food is, so why do we stop off at McDonald's on the way home from work and gorge ourselves with convenience food, dangerously high in fat content, and then feel sick afterward because our rational self tells us that this is bad? What is the psychology behind all of this? Why don't we know ourselves better? What affects what we do despite all of our best intentions? What are these dark processes within? Where do these processes come from and how do they work? And significantly, what does classic social psychology have to say about these and similar processes and the conflicts that emerge from them?

I will suggest in Chapter 2, where I write about conflicted attitudes to race, building on Allport's concept of the 'inner conflict', that there may well be two separate 'systems' within each human being, each with a different mode of operation. Part of the reason why we say one thing and do another is because we really do have two sets of processes: one conscious, reflective and rational, and one whose drivers are based in the unconscious and whose operation is simply not open to conscious reflection. When it comes to many aspects of life one system seems to respond differently to the other, and is subject to distinct, hidden biases and this system is often in control of our behaviour. Race may indeed be one of these areas. No matter what we say, it seems that many people do have an unconsciously held racial or ethnic bias. We can now attempt to measure this implicit bias more objectively, using a technique called the Implicit Association Test (or IAT), where the results (based around speed of response in a computerised test) cannot be faked quite so easily as self-report measures, and are not subject to the normal constraint of social desirability (although this test is certainly not beyond criticism, see McGuire and Beattie 2018). Most White people, it turns out, are unconsciously strongly racist, and a significant proportion of Black people in the US have an implicit bias, but against their own race. This implicit bias has a significant effect on behaviour. In research with some colleagues (Beattie et al. 2013), I found that when White people were shortlisting candidates for jobs, they were ten times more likely to select two White candidates than two non-White candidates (despite the White and the non-White candidates having identical CVs; the CVs were rotated in ways that people could not notice) and, in addition, using remote eye tracking to monitor the individual gaze fixation points twenty-five times per second, we found that those doing the shortlisting unconsciously fixated on the weaker parts of the CVs of candidates from different racial backgrounds to themselves. This difference in pattern of fixation can happen by the twenty-fourth fixation point, in other words, within the first second of looking at the CV. One consequence of this selective attention, possibly directed by the unconscious system, is that the final outcome might appear quite reasonable and might well satisfy our conscious and rational self. 'But didn't you notice that …' The unconscious, in other words, is providing our rational mind with the information it needs, and this information is highly biased and selective, but our rational selves fail to notice this. These two systems, the conscious and the unconscious, operating within each person, seem to interact in complex and telling ways. Of course, if we want to do anything about racism, and if we really do want a fairer society, then we need to understand these implicit, unconscious processes and how to combat them. This book will explore the psychological origins and consequences of this great divide within each human being, amongst other things.

The book could help people understand themselves and those around them a little better, and perhaps persuade us that although we are all flawed creatures, who fall well below our rational ideals, crucially we are not alone. It should teach us not to be too naive about possible utopian futures and the human mind because after all there is something more primitive inside just waiting to get out. This is not necessarily about revisiting the unconscious of the great psychoanalysts (although at times it might be); this is contemporary psychology at last discovering that there may be a system inside us all, shaped by evolutionary pressures but potentially understandable and knowable.

The book will also attempt throughout to situate any insights from psychological research in observations of everyday life, because that's what social psychology is designed to explain (surely?). In my view, social psychology cannot be remote and abstract; it needs to be related to real experiences. Our own experiences are relevant to our psychological theories; they always provide the backdrop, sometimes implicitly, of course, when we consider accounts of human behaviour. And if those theories don't quite measure up to what we ourselves have experienced and 'know' about the world, then I would suggest that we might at least pause to think why.

Our own experiences also, of course, remind us of why these theories are so important. When I consider the theory of the 'double bind' proposed by Gregory Bateson and the argument that 'conflicting' communications from a mother to her child can be pathogenic in Chapter 4, I consider my own familial communications, and what was said by my mother to me, and what was meant, and what I now believe (with the benefit of hindsight) was going on at that time. When I discuss how 'depth' psychologists manipulated the unconscious to make smoking glamorous and sexy to produce this harmful conflicted habit (in Chapter 3), I travel back to my condemned mill house in Belfast where the air in the front room at nights was thick with tobacco smoke, as my mother and her friends gossiped about the world they knew, whilst inhaling dreams and images of sophisticated lives elsewhere, lives more Hollywood than Holywood (Holywood, for those who don't know, is a little seaside town just outside Belfast, a dreary enough place, which meant a great deal to the children from the streets of Belfast; it is pronounced 'Hollywood'). My mother and her friends would sit in our front room and dream of the other Hollywood, as the cancerogenic smoke was drawn deep into the lungs from the brown-stained tipped cigarettes ('they're good for your health', my mother would say, 'stop tutting'). When I consider Leon Festinger's work on cognitive dissonance (in Chapter 4), I am reminded of other situations where people are required to say things publicly that they do not believe. I spent years in a gym in Wincobank in Sheffield, training, sparring, observing, as I watched young boxers start that unpredictable and fretful journey in the fight game, some from the age of seven onwards, standing in a circle, at the end of the day's training, covered in the greasy, layered sweat, telling their pals that one day they would be the champion of the world just like the Naz fella over there, and saying out loud and clear that their next opponent, even with that unblemished record of his, was in reality a nobody, a stepping stone to their own greatness. I wanted to see whether Festinger was really correct, and whether with small incentives to comply, to say out loud these things, with just a gentle nudge by the trainer and no more, no threats, no promises, no rewards, just faint praise, whether attitudes do really change so quickly and so conclusively in this 'forced compliance' situation. I wanted to bring Milgram's ideas in Chapter 7 about the psychology of obedience, and conflicted roles, to the gang from my street when I was growing up in Belfast to see if we really do always follow orders to inflict harm on others, and under what conditions we desist. I talk to Tracey Emin about her life in Chapter 6, and she tells me all about those nasty little brutalising experiences associated with growing up in unfashionable Margate, the experiences that infuse her art. I want to see how she translates her sometimes inconsistent and conflicting memories of childhood trauma into words, through this great process of emotional disclosure. I try to determine what this great translation process involves, and whether Jamie Pennebaker has actually got it right in his classic research on the subject. For me, the social psychology of the conflicted mind cannot be something out there, beyond Holywood, Margate, Sheffield and the damp little mill houses of North Belfast, where we sat with no wallpaper on the damp walls and the air full of smoke and the streets full of dread; it needs to work there as well.

Some fifty years ago R. D. Laing published *The Divided Self*, but we now know that human beings are sometimes 'dissociated' in quite specific ways, and this dissociation is greater than anything previously envisaged, and more central to our everyday functioning. The book will explain why this is so and what the likely consequences are. Too many naive assumptions are continually made about the drivers behind human behaviour; this book will show how some sort of conflict, and sometimes dissociation, is at the very heart of what it is to be a human being. But the unconscious does not simply reside within; it guides us to focus on and select certain features of our environment, and adapt our behaviour accordingly, which adds further layers of complexity to the direction and operation of our everyday conduct. This book will show exactly how this all happens, and also how the unconscious can, and is, targeted by skilful marketeers to sell us things that we *really* do not need (like cigarettes), with disastrous effects.

But this is only part of the overall enterprise here. The 'conflicted mind' is a broader concept than just the clash between potential systems of thinking, because in one form or another it forms the very pillars on which the edifice of social psychology is built. Conflict in cognitions, through Festinger's concept of cognitive dissonance, is a core part of our psychological, and cultural, knowledge. Milgram's obedience experiments, where ordinary individuals were apparently given roles to play and were soon displaying behaviour at odds with their beliefs and attitudes, were said to tell us a great deal about the nature of human obedience, and power and influence. Bateson's description of conflict in communications in the form of double binds was meant to revolutionise how we thought about social processes and the ontogenesis of certain psychological disorders. And it did for many, including R. D. Laing himself. Bartlett's explorations of the constructive nature of human memory with its 'effort after meaning', in which the mind works with and changes the sense material, has echoed through the work of Jamie Pennebaker and the thesis of the power of emotional disclosure (and our cultural understanding of the fact that it's good to talk). What types of disclosure work and why? Do they have to be factually correct narratives or just compelling narratives? Compelling to whom?

This book is an exploration of core social psychological research centred on a particular theme. I explore the 'conflicted mind' in the works of the greats who established our discipline, and to whom we owe an enormous debt of gratitude. But I'm not at all sure they got it right. This is my personal voyage of discovery, as I suffer the slings and arrows of (perhaps) outrageous fortune of those greats of our discipline to see whether their results, conclusions and theories stand up or not, and what they really tell us about our everyday experience of conflict in thought and action.

Chapter summary

- Shakespeare wrote about the 'conflicted mind' in *Hamlet*; much of the operation of the 'conflicted mind' in everyday life is not quite so ruminative, nor so thoughtful.

- The 'conflicted mind' is *clearly* critical to the work and thinking of Gordon Allport on conflicted attitudes, Leon Festinger on conflicted cognition, Gregory Bateson on conflicted communication and Stanley Milgram on conflicted roles, and I would suggest also central to the work of Ernest Dichter on conflicted habits and Jamie Pennebaker on conflicted memories and emotional disclosure.

- One idea about the 'conflicted mind', namely the 'adaptive unconscious', is based on the notion of two systems of thinking, and has now become a significant cultural meme; this view may be misguided.

- Any general psychological accounts of the 'conflicted mind' should at least resonate with what we see in our everyday lives, when we notice the odd paradoxes, contradictions and inconsistencies that make us human beings.

2

CONFLICTED ATTITUDES

They say that you can match the psychologist to the topic they study, in the same way that you can match a dog to its owner: the regal cocker spaniel with the Duke and Duchess of Cambridge; the wary bull terrier, always called Patch, with the bulky young man buried deep in his mud-brown hoodie; and the snarling Shih Tzu, with the pink bow in its teased fringe, all mouth and sharp pointy teeth, in the basket of the stick-thin female celebrity. You can always tell what goes together.

My research on the match between the psychologist and the topic has not been that systematic, but when I was a student at Cambridge I did meet a very famous visiting American psychologist who studied human aggression, and after his seminar talk and a few drinks in the college bar, it struck me that this man was one of the most aggressive people I had ever met. He sat there with his shirt unbuttoned, his thick hairy chest curled out around the folds of the shirt, holding court. He nodded vigorously as others spoke and kept interrupting by talking over them; then he physically tried to stop them from taking the floor by holding out his hand, his flat palm up, like a shield blocking arrows. Minutes later, he did the unimaginable. He slowly pushed down on the gesturing, eloquent hand of the lecturer sat next to him on the vinyl covered banquette. You could see the surprised looks around the little table loaded with beer in this bare, small college bar, as his hand was lowered slowly down onto the wet table, where it was held momentarily, although it did seem, in its inappropriateness, to be held there for an eternity. This young lecturer, prematurely balding and very earnest, stopped talking immediately and the American took the floor. He was louder now, more dominant, and he was sitting more upright, almost crouching on his seat to give him extra height and authority as another button on his shirt popped open so that yet more oily, jet black curls were on view. His opinions had been challenged he thought, so he was just fighting back. A fellow student swore that he heard him mutter, 'you pompous Cambridge fuckers, you can give it but you can't take it' under his breath, as he reached down for his warm English beer. You could see the lecturer shaking the sleeve of his jacket dry, but in a polite, English sort of way, not wishing to upset anyone, looking slightly dejected, as the famous American was momentarily distracted by the warm beer. The young lecturer then smoothed his thin hair, repeatedly, as if he was trying to reassure himself.

I bumped into him on the way back from the toilet, and he smiled at me. 'I can see why he studies the roots of human aggression,' he said politely. 'I think that he may have problems; I think that he's trying to understand himself. Even by his culture's standards he's aggressive in the way he talks.' No doubt the visiting professor would have said that this comment was symptomatic of the passive–aggressive style of the Cambridge academic.

But it did occur to me later that this 'high involvement' style of the visiting American professor might have been an attempt to show enthusiasm rather than exert aggressive control in the conversation. After all there are different kinds of interruptions; there are some overlaps in talk that are very positive, these are overlaps of spontaneous interest. Even the act of taking control of the lecturer's hand might have been culturally conditioned, rather than straightforward manifest aggression, which is how I, and the others present, saw it at the time. I suppose that's the point about how we make judgements: they can be made in an instant and they can potentially radiate outwards from the individual to the group, in this case to all Americans. And simultaneously, of course, we move quickly from behaviour to stable disposition, as in 'he interrupted me repeatedly', 'they are always domineering', 'Americans are aggressors'.

Sometimes the match between the psychologist and the topic might not be so obvious, but you still try to work it out. Why spend your life on that topic rather than any other? What is the deep connection? Sometimes a topic is so vast and the influence of one person so enormous that not only do you wonder what attracted them to it in the first place, but you also ask yourself what personal experiences led them to make their particular contribution and develop one set of ideas rather than another.

Gordon Allport and 'the inner conflict'

There is one individual who made more of a contribution to the study of prejudice than any other – the American psychologist Gordon Allport. According to John Dovidio and his colleagues from Yale University writing in 2005,

> any student of prejudice ignorant of Allport would be rightly considered illiterate … Yet half a century after its publication, *The Nature of Prejudice* remains the most widely cited work on prejudice. The scope and endurance of its influence has been nothing short of remarkable.

So what drew Allport to this topic and what did he see in the operation of prejudice that others hadn't so that he could make his 'remarkable' contribution? I think that he saw clearly for the first time the inner conflict in prejudiced individuals in 1950s America and how people had to learn to deal with it, at a time, of course, of great change in terms of the expression and holding of racist views. But deal with it they did, so they could stay prejudiced and yet simultaneously view themselves completely differently as non-prejudiced, fair-minded and as though they treated all men and women as equals. This is, in many ways, the dark beauty of prejudice and that's why it is so difficult to eradicate. How do you cure something like that (imagining it for a second to be some form of cancer that people don't admit to suffering from)? This was Allport's great contribution. He pointed out the wiliness of prejudice (it must be an odd sort of cancer) and how we protect it with various defensive tricks.

Allport's work was in many ways time-specific, but it is thought to have universal appeal. The 1950s, after all, were a time of great social change in the US in terms of the acceptability of the expression of racist attitudes. In 1942, only 35 per cent of white Americans reported that they would have felt comfortable with a Negro neighbour; by 1963 it was 64 per cent. In 1942, only 42 per cent of white Americans found it acceptable for a black person to get onto a bus with them; by 1963 it was 78 per cent. Paul Sheatsley, the pioneer of public opinion research, concluded in 1965 that, 'By the end of 1963, both forms of integration had achieved majority approval.' This was an extraordinarily optimistic conclusion, formed on the basis of what people told him. However, Allport suggested it might not be quite as simple as that. Racism might not have evaporated overnight, or at least over two decades. It may still lie within the individual and might now be accommodated in various ways within their psyche.

I tend to think that there are a few small details in Allport's early life that hold the key to why he made his particular intellectual journey in the first place. Allport was, on the surface, a brilliant Harvard student: precocious, competitive, and confident, at least on the surface. He visited Freud in Vienna when he was just 22 years old. Allport later wrote,

> I wrote to Freud announcing that I was in Vienna and implied that no doubt he would be glad to make my acquaintance. I received a kind reply in his own handwriting inviting me to come to his office at a certain time.

Allport had implied that someone of importance was in town, someone Freud should meet. But in the days before Harvard, Allport had been a shy, studious boy from Cleveland, Ohio; the youngest son of a country doctor and a school teacher, who taught him strong moral principles and schooled him in the Protestant work ethic until both were second nature. Despite having three older brothers, he was a very lonely boy, often teased and mocked by his school friends for having only eight toes as a result of a birth defect. As a student, despite his success, he found the culture and morals of Harvard quite alien; this boy blighted by slight physical difference and devotion to the Protestant work ethic, competing in the most prestigious of academic institutions where it was simply not fashionable to be too driven by work or to be too keen. He knew how cruel other boys could be about students who worked too hard or came from lower-class backgrounds, or students with slight physical defects that could be ridiculed by friends. He saw first-hand that friends could be nice to him on the surface but not very nice behind his back and yet they'd think nothing of it. What then was their actual opinion of him? Did they actually like him or not? Were they, fundamentally good people or not? How did they deal with this inner conflict? Did this only happen when they talked about an individual or did it happen when they talked about a group or a whole race as well? Could one make jokes about skin colour or accent in the same way as about someone having eight toes? Could one laugh at people who are simply different? It is not hard to see that these personal experiences of Allport may have been instrumental to his quest to understand the nature of prejudice, and, perhaps more importantly, how it operates within ordinary lives.

William Hazlitt, the great English literary critic and essayist, is often credited as the first writer to define prejudice in an essay first published in 1826. 'Prejudice, in its ordinary and literal sense, is prejudging any question without having significantly examined it, and adhering to our opinion upon it through ignorance, malice or perversity, in spite of every evidence to the contrary.' He put prejudice down to ignorance, which probably made sense with regards to racial prejudice in the comparative isolation of the England of King William IV. But Allport began his analysis differently, by considering 'the normality of prejudgement', in other words, he did not want to consider prejudice as some sort of pathology or product of ignorance, malice or perversity at the outset, but as something that derived from a set of very normal processes. These normal processes often allow appropriate conclusions but sometimes the combination of these processes produces conclusions that are more malignant.

Allport started with a simple question: 'Why do human beings slip so easily into racial prejudice?' He answered this by stating that

> Everywhere on earth we find a condition of separateness among groups. People mate with their own kind. They eat, play, reside in homogenous [sic] clusters. They visit with their own kind, and prefer to worship together. Much of this automatic cohesion is due to nothing more than convenience. There is no need to turn to out-groups for companionship. With plenty of people at hand to choose from, why create for ourselves the trouble of adjusting to new languages, new foods, new cultures, or to people of a different educational level? It requires less effort to deal with people who have similar presuppositions.
>
> (Allport 1954: 18)

In other words, people like to be in familiar territory because it is safe and easy. We have more shared history and we can make more assumptions; we can feel at ease. All our communications are played out against and interpreted in the light of this shared background. He talked about 'automatic cohesion' fuelled by 'convenience'.

It is hard not to read Allport's historic words and detect a certain personal connection, and conclude that his views really did come from the heart. When he wrote, 'It is not that we have class prejudice, but only that we find comfort and ease in our own class', you cannot help but feel that he was talking about himself here and that he sensed the gulf between himself and his Harvard peers. When Allport commented that, 'most of the business of life can go with less effort if we stick together with our own kind', he perhaps revealed his true feelings about how he had been pushed by his ambitions and work ethic into an institution where he no longer could be with his own kind. There is a certain personal longing in his sentence that is unmistakeable. So this, according to Allport, is how prejudice begins. It is a desire to be with your own kind. The familiar is effortless and good, that which is different requires more effort and is therefore not so good. The roots of prejudice are, according to this analysis, separation first and then categorisation (most fundamentally as 'like me' or as 'not like me') with possible emotional attachments pushing one way rather than another.

Allport highlighted the importance of this early stage of categorisation in our everyday lives. He said that human beings call upon categories endlessly to guide their everyday decision making. 'When an angry looking dog charges down the street, we categorize him as a "mad dog" and avoid him.' When we establish categories, we rapidly place things inside them, 'as a means of pre-judging a solution' (Allport 1954: 21). Again, in Allport's words, 'the mind tends to categorize environmental events in the "grossest" manner compatible with the need for action'. In other words, categories start out crude and often stay crude and only later become refined. However, one critical feature of these categories is that they enable us to recognise and identify any personal ideas of the world,

> every event has certain marks that serve as a cue to bring the category of pre-judgement into action ... when we see a crazily swaying automobile we think, "drunken driver," and act accordingly. A person with dark brown skin will activate whatever concept of Negro is dominant in our mind. If the dominant category is one composed of negative attitudes and beliefs we will automatically avoid him, or adopt whichever habit of rejection is most available to us.
>
> (Allport 1954: 21)

The next feature of categories is that there is often a certain feeling 'associated with them'. Some categories can be purely conceptual but many have an emotional valance attached to them. The example that Allport used is one of trees. We know what a tree is, we can identify and describe one, we can recognise a tree quickly and instinctively, but we also know if we like trees or not. Similarly, it is the same with racial categories. Another point that Allport made about categories is that they 'may be more or less rational' in that a category tends to grow from a 'kernel of truth'. This is true of many types of categories, but Allport recognised that some may be quite irrational and that human beings have a whole series of devices to prevent logic or irrationality interfering with the formation and maintenance of the category. For example, there is the simple cognitive device of admitting exceptions, as in 'Some of my best friends are Jews but ...' or 'There are nice Negroes but ...' Allport describes this as a re-fencing device, 'When a fact cannot fit into a mental field, the exception is acknowledged, but the field is hastily fenced in again and not allowed to remain dangerously open' (Allport 1954: 336). These categories persist through time and have an emotional valence attached to them. They can guide our actions.

However, we may think that this is too simple a set of processes for something as important and enduring as prejudice. Surely it can't all be down to a basic mental process of wanting to be with your own kind because you're instinctively drawn to them? Who would ever admit to making judgements in this way? This, I suppose, was the start of Allport's great insight. His view was that the vast majority of us won't admit to it and instead we have to deal with this difficulty psychologically. We have all sorts of defence mechanisms to allow us to cope with this and his contribution was to expose these mechanisms, to show how they work within the individual.

Allport wrote,

> The course of prejudice in a life seldom runs smoothly. For prejudiced attitudes are almost certain to collide with deep-seated values that are often equally or more central to the personality. The influence of the school may contradict the influence of the home. The teachings of religion may challenge social stratification. Integration of such opposing forces within a single life is hard to achieve.
>
> (Allport 1954: 326)

He contrasted this sort of individual who may make uncomfortable attempts to integrate colliding attitudes, with the out and out bigot, whose attitudes seem perfectly reconciled and seems to have no such problem. The example he used of 'prejudice without compunction' was a telegram sent by Governor Bilbo of Mississippi to the mayor of Chicago in 1920. Chicago, in Allport's words, was facing 'a surplus of Negro migrants who had come to Chicago looking for work during the First World War'. The mayor, it seemed, had enquired whether some of them could possibly be sent back to their Southern homeland. The response from Governor Bilbo was clear and to the point and showed no evidence of any difficulty in expressing underlying attitudes:

> Your telegram, asking how many Negroes Mississippi can absorb, received. I reply, I desire to state that we have all the room in the world for what we know as N-i-g-g-e-r-s, but none whatever for 'colored ladies and gentlemen.' If these Negroes have been contaminated with Northern social and political dreams of equality, we cannot use them, nor do we want them. The Negro who understands his proper relation to the white man in this country will be gladly received by the people of Mississippi, as we are very much in need of labor.
>
> (Allport 1954: 326)

Similarly, consider the words of Lord Chesterfield, who in his letters to his son was keen to offer paternal advice, including living one's life by reason rather than by prejudice. Lord Chesterfield, nevertheless, had this to say about women:

> Women, then, are only children of a larger growth; they have an entertaining tattle, and sometimes wit; but for solid reasoning, good sense, I never knew in my life one that had it, or who reasoned or acted consequentially for four and twenty hours together ... A man of sense only trifles with them, plays with them, humours and flatters them, as he does a sprightly, forward child; but he neither consults them about, nor trusts them with serious matters; though he often makes them believe that he does both; which is the thing in the world that they are most proud of ... Women are much more like each other than men; they have in truth but two passions, vanity and love: these are their universal characteristics.
>
> (Allport 1954: 261)

Of course, many people are not like Governor Bilbo of Mississippi or Lord Chesterfield. However, what proportion of people fall into their category (the out and out bigot) is not clear. According to Allport's own research, only 10 per cent of participants in his research in the late 1940s and early 1950s could write about their attitudes toward minority groups in the US and express prejudice openly and without feelings of guilt and conflict. But these estimates were based entirely upon a sample of college students. The vast majority of the college students Allport tested had ambivalent feelings that could cause them some distress, so that they would get angry at themselves for these feelings. They would call themselves 'hypocrite', 'intolerant' and 'narrow-minded'. But they would often appear stuck, unable to change and hardly able to face up to their intolerance. They would write about the split between 'my reason and prejudice'. They would say that they 'try to lean over backwards to counteract the attitude', but ultimately they recognised that they were powerless: 'it is remarkable how strong a hold it has on me.' They may be conflicted in attitudinal terms, but they stayed eloquent to the end. 'My compulsive prejudice is putting up a fight against its own elimination.' This statement is almost too eloquent to be taken as a clear reflection of how such conflicted attitudes feel to the person experiencing them. These were, after all, college students who were studying psychology, trying hard to convey their experience in their essays, maybe a little too hard at times. But they are valuable nonetheless in their own way. Allport commented on these revealed experiences, 'Defeated intellectually, prejudice lingers emotionally', and later, 'Self-insight … does not automatically cure prejudice. At best it starts the individual wondering' (Allport 1954: 332).

So what are the implications of this inner conflict on the experience of prejudice? According to Allport,

> when inner conflict is present, people put brakes upon their prejudices. They do not act them out – or they act them out only up to a certain point. Something stops the logical progression somewhere. In New York City, as E. B. White has pointed out, there smoulders every ethnic problem there

is; yet the noticeable thing is not the problem, but the remarkable control.

(Allport 1954: 332)

Allport argued that such prejudice may be expressed when in the safe bosom of one's own family but not in the presence of members of the target group; prejudice may pop out in the bar or the club but not on the street or the station, in other words where one feels safe and protected, both psychologically as well as physically. But Allport maintained that 'such marked contrast in *situational* behaviour would not occur unless there were *inner conflict* in the person harbouring prejudice' (Allport 1954: 334).

So Allport maintained that most human beings are conflicted when it comes to prejudice and much of everyday life is spent in a battle with this seemingly uncontrollable prejudice. He then identified a number of ways that people try to handle these unruly and 'contrary impulses': repression (denial), defence (rationalisation), compromise (partial resolution) and integration (true resolution). Repression, according to Allport, is so powerful because the alternative, actually admitting that there is an issue,

is to accuse oneself of being both irrational and unethical. No one wants to be at odds with his own conscience. Man has to live with himself. Evidence of repression appears in many forms, but one of the most common is 'I am not prejudiced, but...'

To Allport, 'Psychologically, the mechanism is one of affirming virtue so that the subsequent lapses will pass unnoticed.' However, he argues that repression rarely 'stands alone' and it needs defensive rationalisations to back it up.

Defensive rationalisation, according to Allport, is all about 'selective perception' and 'selective forgetting'. This is where the individual consciously or unconsciously (but in most cases unconsciously) sees or finds 'evidence' 'to bolster a categorical overgeneralisation' and then remembers it clearly but forgets counter-examples. Individual examples are stored in memory to support the overgeneralisation; details are noticed that would otherwise never have been noticed. For example, the Jewish student who borrows the bus fare and never returns it (tight), the black student walking slowly to the lecture theatre (lazy) or the Irish student play-fighting in the Student Union (belligerent). Newspapers and the media are scoured for further support and they are a rich vein for such matter, not just because of the amount of material to be selectively read but because of their own explicit or implicit biases.

But there are other 'defensive tricks' (Allport's term), which are available as well. There is *bifurcation*, which seems to represent differentiation within a category, but it is a differentiation based upon questionable criteria. 'I am not prejudiced against Negroes; some are good. It is only bad niggers that I dislike.' So what, asks Allport, is a 'bad nigger'? Is it a black person who flatters the white man's self-esteem? 'The bifurcation is based on what does and what does not seem to threaten one, not on the merit of individuals.' Another defensive trick is 'rationalisation by making exceptions' as in, 'some of my best friends are black, but ...' As Allport said, 'If one makes a few exceptions, then one can justify holding the remaining portion of the category intact.' The essence of this kind of statement is that if you have good friends that fall into the category then what you are about to say that is very negative, signalled by the 'but', cannot be put down to prejudice.

Then, according to Allport, there is evidence of inner conflict in 'alternation'. 'When one frame of reference is invoked, one set of subsidiary attitudes and habits comes into play; when a contrary frame is invoked, a quite opposite set of dispositions is activated.' In other words, human beings deal with this inner conflict by not being consistent with themselves. Sometimes they display prejudice and sometimes they do not; it depends upon the situation and who they are with. The inconsistency can be in what they say or between what they say and their actual behaviour, and Allport wrote that this is perfectly normal and understandable. Indeed, he said, 'it is the rigid consistency of the fanatic (whether of a bigot or a crusader for equal rights) that is regarded as pathological in our society.'

Allport maintained that the fact that we have multiple roles to play in everyday life assists in this process of not being consistent. Different roles demand different behaviours; we can say things in the football stadia that we would never say at work. Allport finished his comments on alternation with the quixotic, 'To be a conformist under diverse sets of conditions is almost unavoidably to compromise one's integrity as a person.' Here he makes clear the logical necessity of a degree of alternation in everyday life. But the critical point is to what degree this alternation is allowable. If people are aware of an inconsistency in their underlying values, they may find this very troubling and it may lead to a psychological and emotional journey to resolve this, hopefully by getting rid of 'racial bogies' and 'traditional scapegoats'. Allport was not that optimistic about how easy this is to achieve:

> Perhaps few people achieve integration of this type; but many are fairly far along the road ... Such resentments and hatred as they have are reserved strictly for those who actually threaten basic value systems. Only a personality organized in such a manner can be fully integrated.
>
> (Allport 1954: 339)

This was how Allport finished his treatise on 'inner conflict'. It was pioneering and it explained how people can deal with prejudice in a way that allows them to maintain a very favourable perception of themselves. Of course, it left many questions unanswered. His point was that some inconsistency within human beings seems to be unavoidable and that people repress and rationalise much of the time. Some do achieve consistency eventually, but how and why remains unclear. So how does the inner conflict actually feel to a person experiencing it? How does it work? Are we necessarily aware of all our inconsistencies? What are the mechanisms of change? How are the inconsistencies represented in the human mind? Indeed, perhaps the most extraordinary thing about Allport's analysis is that he avoids considering at all whether a major component of prejudice resides wholly in the unconscious. Was Allport only dealing with the conscious cognitions of everyday life and not the unconscious emotions that energise them in the first place?

Is prejudice really all conscious?

To understand why he might have neglected or avoided the more unconscious aspects of this process we may again need to look at Allport's own life and that famous visit to Vienna that he made after graduating (as I did in Beattie 2013). Freud was then at the height of his fame and Allport had just graduated with a bachelor's degree from Harvard, but he had the confidence to write to the great man to set up the visit. On entering Freud's office Allport was greeted with the familiarity of the room, known even then, and an expectant but uncomfortable silence that seemed to open up and engulf them both. Here he was in front of Freud, at last, but he found himself staring down at the red, patterned Berber rug in the famous inner office, the matte walls painted deep red and covered with pictures of dreams with their iconic and provocative symbolism and the whole room reeked of decayed cigar smoke. The heady, stale smell that almost made Allport choke.

Allport coughed briefly. The bookshelf behind Freud's desk acted as a reminder to all who entered the room of his great intellectual journey, with books by Goethe, Shakespeare, Heine, Multatuli and Anatole France, the dramatists, philosophers and poets, who had recognised the power of the unconscious. Allport noted each of these books in turn. He had never heard of a number of the authors. He felt intimidated and in that silence when he dared to lift his head, he had the opportunity to scrutinise some of the pictures hanging around the room such as 'Oedipus and the Riddle of the Sphinx'. He saw the famous couch covered with velvet cushions and a patterned Qashqa'i rug with the three linked octagons symbolising, to some of Freud's followers at least, the uterus' contractions during parturition. But the three linked octagons merely acted as a reminder to Allport of the id, the ego and the superego and the holy trinity of the psyche and the neat packaging of psychoanalytic ideas into a list of three. Allport noticed the plush green armchair where Freud would sit behind his patients whilst they engaged in free association. He was drawn to the famous painting by André Brouillé of Doctor Charcot at work at the Salpêtrière, with the hysterical female patient in full seizure displayed before the staff and medical students. Freud himself had been a student in the audience many years before and the painting may have reminded him of those happier carefree days, or it may have acted as a symbolic reminder of the power of the mesmeric teacher and the effects this teacher was having on his captivated audience and on the frozen, hysterical female patient who was helpless in front of them all, with only the great doctor Charcot or Freud himself capable of understanding her malady. It made Allport very uncomfortable; it was all a bit too *showy* for him as it went against his own implicit beliefs.

Allport had the veneer of Harvard sophistication, of the new international academic in the making, but silences like this made him uncomfortable. It possibly reminded him of who he had been; maybe of who he was. He knew better than most that one's personality never really changes. He needed to say something, so he thought that he would make an observation, a psychological observation of something that he had just witnessed. He described how on the tram car on the way to Freud's office he had watched a small boy of about four who was terrified of coming into contact with any dirt. He refused to allow a particular man on the tram to sit beside him because he thought that the man was dirty, despite his mother's cajoling and reassurance. Allport studied the woman in question and noted how neat and tidy she was and how domineering she was in her approach to her son. Allport hypothesised that the boy's dirt phobia had been picked up from his mother, someone who needed everything neat and tidy and in its correct place. 'To him [the boy] everything was *schmutzig*. His mother was a well-starched *Hausfrau*, so dominant and purposive looking that I thought the cause and effect apparent.'

Freud looked at Allport carefully for the first time, with his 'kindly therapeutic eyes', and then asked, '"And was that little boy you?"' Allport blinked uncomfortably and said nothing, appalled by Freud's attempt to psychoanalyse him on the spot. Allport knew that his observation was driven by the desire to fill the silence, his desire to display to Freud that as a psychologist he, the young man from Harvard, never stopped observing and he desired to connect with the great man, maybe even to feel that he belonged in the room with Freud through this essential connection. These were all clear motives that were open to the conscious mind and should be obvious to all. What it was not was any unconscious desire to reveal his own deep-seated uncertainties and anxieties resulting from problems in potty-training back in Montezuma, Indiana. Allport tried to change the subject but the damage had been done.

> I realized that he was accustomed to neurotic defences and that my manifest motivation (a sort of rude curiosity and youthful ambition) escaped him. For therapeutic progress he would have to cut through my defences, but it so happened that therapeutic progress was not here an issue.

Allport later wrote that the 'experience taught me that depth psychology, for all its merits, may plunge too deep, and that psychologists would do well to give full recognition to manifest motives before probing the unconscious.' This one significant personal experience guided Allport's thinking in psychology, where he avoided introducing any theorising about unconscious processes. This was a clear example, in his mind, of 'psychoanalytic excess', although interestingly psychoanalysts ever since are not necessarily convinced by his argument. Faber, writing in 1970, suggested that Freud had got it exactly right, that Allport had

> practiced a kind of deception in order to work his way into Freud's office. This deception lay in his implied claim that (1) he genuinely wanted to meet Freud as a human being and as an intellectual rather than as an object, and (2) that he (Allport) himself was worth meeting as a human being and as an 'intellectual'.

Faber believes that Freud saw through this deception quickly and that by asking Allport whether he was the little boy in the story, Freud was in fact indicating to Allport that he knew that he was a 'dirty little boy' and that by putting this question to him, Freud was merely trying to restart the conversation in an honest and straightforward way. Elms (1993) attributed even greater analytic power and clarity of thinking to Freud in this meeting. Allport's childhood was characterised in his own words by 'plain Protestant piety', and an upbringing in an environment that doubled as a home and as a hospital, run by Allport's physician father. According to Elms, the question had such a marked effect on Allport because he 'was still carrying within him the super-clean little boy' brought up in that literal and metaphorical sterile, Protestant environment, where patients were to be avoided as they were sources of infection and possible danger.

Allport was convinced of his own explanation of the event and he was determined to do something about this psychoanalytic excess. This meeting encouraged him to develop something different, a new approach to the human mind and one that stayed with us for some sixty years before anyone really dared challenge it in a systematic way. His new approach was based around conscious reflection and the power of language to uncover and articulate underlying attitudes, to bring these attitudes out into the open where they could be studied and analysed objectively and scientifically. His new approach avoided the unconscious. Allport's type of theorising was to characterise the new social psychology that held sway for the next half century or more and gave us our core methods and techniques in social psychology. But was this really the whole story?

The answer is most definitely no. Indeed, we now know that it is more than just convenience that pushes us towards our own kind. Allport hints at this in this short passage: 'Psychologically, the crux of the matter is that the familiar provides the indispensable basis of our existence. Since existence is good, its accompanying groundwork seems good and desirable' (Allport 1954: 44).

There is clearly something psychologically powerful about the familiar. We know this from the decades of research that followed Allport and we also now know a little about how the familiar feeds into other processes and how these processes tend to occur deep in our unconscious. It seems that even three-month-old babies (but not newborns) show a distinct preference for members of their own racial group in terms of the amount of time spent fixating on the face (Kelly et al. 2005). This, it would seem, is not something that needs years of cultural experience. We also know that the first judgement that one human being makes about another when they see them for the first time is how 'trustworthy' they are (Willis and Todorov 2006). Willis and Todorov presented participants with photographs of people and asked them to judge how 'attractive', 'likeable', 'competent', 'trustworthy' and 'aggressive' they were. In some trials, the faces were presented for only 100 milliseconds, in others for 500 milliseconds and the remaining trials for 1 second. Even after being exposed to a picture of a human face for one tenth of a second, judgements about their personality traits were made and these judgements correlated with the judgements made when the test subjects had significantly more time at their disposal. The closest correlations were for judgements about 'trustworthiness'. In other words, after seeing a face for one tenth of a second, people have already made up their mind about how trustworthy a person is and that judgement tends not to change.

This is even quicker than judgements of 'attractiveness', which may surprise many people as most would say that sex is the most basic of all animal drivers. Sex ensures that our genes continue into the next generation and instant judgements of trustworthiness aim to ensure that we will stay alive and have further opportunities to procreate. Human beings make this judgement of trustworthiness very quickly and one of the most primitive parts of the brain responsible for emotional processing, the amygdala, is crucial in this process. Interestingly, the amygdala also seems to be critical in responding differently to images of people from different racial or ethnic groups. It fires and habituates differently to people from different racial groups to our own.

According to Willis and Todorov, the question of why 'trustworthiness' is so critical makes sense in evolutionary terms. In our evolutionary past, you needed to know whether a stranger was a friend or foe, whether they had good intentions towards you or bad intentions and whether you could trust them or not. Your individual survival may have depended upon this. Brain imaging studies show that the detection of trustworthiness is a spontaneous and automatic process linked to activity in the amygdala. The researchers go on to suggest that a tenth of a second may not actually be required for these unconscious judgements to be made; we may do this even quicker than that. Research on object detection seems to demonstrate that objects can be categorised as quickly as they can be detected. In other words, 'as soon as you know they are there, you know what it is.' In the words of Willis and Todorov, 'Maybe, as soon as a face is there, you know whether to trust it.'

The amygdala is also linked to perceptions of differences connected with race or ethnicity. Allen Hart from Harvard University and his colleagues using brain imaging found greater activity in the amygdala to out-group versus in-group faces for both white and black participants. You can easily imagine how our brains have evolved to identify any individual as trustworthy or not, as belonging to our social group or not, or as a serious threat or as a less serious threat. This is how our brains are set up to work to begin the processes of perception of difference and the categorisation that follows from it. The amygdala and the processing of fear associated with the unfamiliar seems to be crucial here. Indeed, in 2005, Andrea Meyer-Lindenberg, director of the Central Institute of Mental Health in Mannheim, Germany, reported that children with a neurodevelopmental disorder called Williams Syndrome, where there is some malfunction in amygdala activity, are as a consequence overly gregarious because they do not show the normal fear of strangers. They also do not develop negative stereotypes about other racial groups. The children, who were aged between 5 and 16 years old, heard stories about people who were either 'good' or 'bad' and the children had to pick which of two pictures went with which set of attributes. Children who do not have Williams Syndrome tend to choose pictures of light-skinned people to match the positive attributes in the story and dark-skinned people for the negative characteristics. The children with Williams Syndrome, however, didn't show this bias. The conclusion of the research was that social fear, which the children with Williams Syndrome did not suffer from, is an essential prerequisite of racial stereotyping. In other words, this fear of the unfamiliar kick-starts the process of prejudice and occurs unconsciously.

Allport wrote, 'Thus most of the business of life can go with less effort if we stick together with our own kind ... It is not that we have class prejudice, but only that we find comfort and ease in our own class.' But we must remember that some very primitive, unconscious processes may be driving the fundamental desire to stick with one's own kind, processes that would have been unknown to Allport in their detail, and possibly their scope.

This new way of thinking about prejudice means that the unconscious is no longer out of bounds. Therefore, I and others have been working for the past few years on developing new ways of measuring it, to see it in action. There are now a number of ways to measure 'implicit' or unconscious attitude, whose measurement requires no conscious reflection at all. One method is the Implicit Association Test (IAT), first developed by Anthony Greenwald, which requires individuals to press a key as quickly as possible when they see an image of a face, or a name, and a word together on a screen. Greenwald found that white people are quicker at associating white faces and names and the concept 'good' than they are black faces and names with the concept 'good'. Similarly, white people were slower at associating white faces and names and the concept 'bad' than black faces and names with the concept 'bad'. In the first web-based experiment of its kind, Project Implicit, 600,000 tests were carried out between October 1998 and December 2000, and it was found that white participants tended to *explicitly* endorse a preference for white people compared to black people but *implicitly* (in terms of IAT score) they demonstrated an even stronger preference for white names and faces (i.e. they were quicker to associate white names and faces with the concept 'good', and this was a very strong effect). Black participants on the other hand, demonstrated a strong *explicit* preference for black people compared to white people and yet, remarkably in the IAT, black participants demonstrated a weak *implicit* preference for white names and faces (i.e. they were quicker to associate black names and faces with the concept 'bad').

In our research, we also found that white people were quicker at associating images of white faces and the concept 'good' than they are non-white faces (black, Asian, Middle and Far Eastern), and slower at associating white faces and the concept 'bad' compared with non-white faces (see Beattie 2013).

This IAT essentially measures associations between two concepts: racial background and the concepts of good and bad; associations that you may well be unaware of. It seems that 'white' and 'good' are more closely associated than 'non-white' and 'good' and this even applies to some non-white individuals who are plugged into broader cultural stereotypes, until they themselves accept this automatically and without reflection. This negative implicit attitude seems to be often at odds with what people express about race and for the first time we can attempt to measure more objectively the 'inner conflict' within each person and work out what the implications are. In fact, in our study we found that over 40 per cent of the participants who explicitly espoused exactly neutral attitudes about race actually held very strong implicit attitudes, which in the vast majority of cases favoured whites over non-whites.

For the past few years, I have been considering in my own research the importance of these unconscious attitudes in one very simple situation: the shortlisting of candidates for certain jobs, particularly university posts, and I have done this for one very good reason. If we are ever to understand possible racial discrimination in job opportunities and social mobility, which do clearly exist, then we need to consider some of the processes involved in selection. An article in the *Guardian* newspaper in 2011 highlighted the issue of possible racial bias in liberal, meritocratic universities. The article was headed '14,000 British professors – but only 50 are black', and continued,

> Leading black academics are calling for an urgent culture change at UK universities as figures show there are just 50 black professors out of more than 14,000, and the number has barely changed in eight years, according to data from the Higher Education Statistics Agency.

Only the University of Birmingham had more than two black, British professors, and only six out of 133 had more than two black professors from the UK or abroad. There was a great deal of hand-wringing in the article about what was going on and what could be done to rectify it. There was a picture of Harry Goulbourne, himself black and a professor of sociology at London's South Bank University, who was quoted as saying that, 'Universities are still riddled with "passive racism".' The chief executive of Universities UK, the organisation for vice-chancellors of British universities, was quoted in the article as saying, 'We recognise that there is a serious issue about lack of black representation among senior staff in universities, though this is not a problem affecting universities alone, but one affecting societies as a whole.' This appears to be an international problem, with a similar picture emerging from the US, where only 5.4 per cent of all full-time academic staff at universities come from a black and minority ethnic background (US Department of Education 2007). According to the *Journal of Blacks in Higher Education*,

> If we project into the future on a straight-line basis the progress of Blacks into faculty ranks over the past 26 years, we find that Blacks in faculty ranks will not reach parity with the Black percentage of the overall American workforce for another 140 years.

So in our research we presented the participants with the CVs of job candidates. What they didn't know was that the apparent race of the candidate was systematically changed, everything else remained the same. We wanted to see who they shortlisted but, before they had come to their final decision, we used a remote eye tracker to see where they looked at the CV on the screen in front of them. We also measured their implicit attitude and their self-reported attitude. The results were, I have to say, astounding. White participants (mostly young, liberal-minded students from a UK university, and staff from the same university, who espoused no negative racial attitudes whatsoever) were ten times more likely to shortlist two white candidates for the lectureship post than two non-white candidates with exactly the same CV. The implicit attitude of white participants significantly predicted the ethnicity of those candidates who were shortlisted for the academic post. The IAT score of those white participants who shortlisted two white candidates (as opposed to one white and one non-white or two non-white candidates) for the lectureship post indicated a strong pro-white bias. Self-reported attitudes towards different ethnic groups, in other words what people say, did not have a significant bearing on the behavioural preferences for shortlisting white candidates over non-white candidates (Beattie et al. 2013).

The race of the participants also affected what sections they looked at on the CVs of white and non-white candidates in the minute before they had to make their shortlisting decision. White participants spent more time looking at good information on the CVs of white candidates and bad information on the CVs of non-white candidates. Non-white participants spent slightly more time looking at the bad information rather than the good information of white candidates but looked at the good and bad information of non-white candidates equally. Moreover, the stronger the pro-white bias of the participant, as measured by the IAT, the more likely they were to fixate on the negative parts of the CV of a non-white candidate as they made their decision.

People may think that they are making rational decisions when shortlisting for university posts, but what they fixate on when they are looking at a CV is affected by both their own race and that of the candidate. Those participants with high IAT scores (strong implicit pro-white bias) spent more time looking at the good information on the CVs of white candidates compared with participants with lower IAT scores (less strong pro-white implicit bias).

In other words, our implicit (and largely unconscious) attitude to people from different racial backgrounds seems to direct our unconscious eye movements when we consider their CVs. Our 'rational' decisions about the suitability of candidates are based on this biased pattern of fixation. I have to say that I found these results extraordinary. Allport may have uncovered the way that the 'inner conflict' regarding prejudice is dealt with cognitively, but this new research shows how the underlying unconscious attitude impacts on behaviour, like eye gaze. Through these gaze fixations we access different information about another person depending upon their racial background and its match to ours. We may think that we are making 'rational' decisions about their suitability for certain posts, but these rational processes and our scrutiny of their CVs are, in reality, dominated by our unconscious. This is the reality of prejudice in action, working away below the level of consciousness, with unconscious attitudes influencing unconscious behaviours to gather the information the conscious mind needs to appear rational, orderly and fair. This is what Allport missed.

A week after we had completed this work I met up with the man who had suggested that I should do this work in the first place and we shook hands. Patrick Johnson had read my preliminary report and thanked me profusely, but I have to say that our greeting suddenly felt very odd for the very first time. There was something in that handshake which made me nervous and, I think, him too. I could see it in his eyes, the eyes of the Head of Equality and Diversity at this university, who just happened to be black. We were standing on some cold, stone steps in this quiet corridor with high gothic arches of Manchester University founded by merchants of the nineteenth century who exported cotton around the world. That cotton had been picked by slaves. We both knew what was implicit and woven into our surroundings. I grasped his hand firmly, perhaps too firmly, as if I was trying to prove a point. I just wanted to make the handshake perfect and natural, like any other non-discriminatory handshake. But I was trying too hard. It now seemed clear to me that at some deep, unconscious level many of us are biased towards people who belong to different racial groups from ourselves and this may be rooted in our evolutionary past. Fundamentally, we trust our own. Difference reflects strangeness, uncertainty and danger. The roots of racism may lie within us all, if we probe deeply enough. We need to recognise this and deal with it, to prevent it from having its sly influence on all of the things around us. But, of course, like everything in life, it can potentially be changed with the right experiences and perhaps some careful thinking to ensure that we and others, from childhood on, have exactly the right kinds of experiences.

Patrick smiled back at me. I felt very little danger. But was there something in that handshake? It seems that unconscious prejudice leaks out in exactly those forms of behaviour over which we have least control. It leaks out in nonverbal communication rather than speech, and it leaks out in those particular forms of nonverbal communication that we are usually unable to control: the unconscious gesture, the multifunctional touch or the edgy foot movement, rather than in the guarded and controlled expressions on the face which, both I and Patrick knew, were perfectly appropriate.

We had considered possible unconscious prejudice in just one domain: selection for various university posts, but a domain of central importance to how society works (equal access to good jobs is, after all, critical to social mobility and selecting the best candidates, irrespective of race or gender, is crucial to the long-term success of any organisation) but we both knew that this work of ours had very general implications. The broad lesson is that sometimes we have to control our unconscious impulses when it comes to race; they are not necessarily 'adaptive' except in the most primitive evolutionary sense. We have to override that primitive part of the brain which 'fires' when it spots racial difference, in order to achieve a fairer society.

In specific domains, the practical implications are clear. We now know that the central task of any selection panel must be to match the characteristics of candidates against specific criteria, rather than to provide a holistic overview of candidates. 'Holistic' overviews are always going to be vaguer and therefore more likely to be biased and draw upon implicit psychological processes. We also now know never to ask for the 'first thoughts' of any selection panel about the suitability of the candidates, as first thoughts will draw heavily on the implicit psychological system. Similarly, we should never use 'gut instincts' as a basis for shortlisting and never conduct any shortlisting meetings under very strict time pressure. The more time pressure, the more powerful the effects of these implicit processes will be.

Gladwell was not correct when he talked about the quick and immediate 'adaptive unconscious'; this can be a dangerous concept. The unconscious is often heavily biased and sometimes it needs to be contained. Sometimes you have to obstruct the whole process using 'implementation intentions', conscious plans to override these unconscious instincts, of the type: 'If I see the application of a candidate from a black or minority ethnic background then, if I am white, I should be careful to scrutinise the best sections of the application once again before I make my final decision.' It sounds clunky and unnatural, but it can work. It makes you think in a deliberate and careful fashion when a major part of your mind wants to resist this at any cost. Part of the brain wants to jump to an immediate conclusion; the use of these implementation intentions can stop this and is worth some momentary discomfort.

This project had produced many shocks along the way for both Patrick and I, and perhaps for the first time we both fully understood the power of this implicit racism buried within us all. We both knew all about these findings and that is why we stood there trying to work out why the handshake took so long and felt so odd, despite our best intentions. Neither of us made any comment on it and it was certainly better knowing than not knowing. However, I suppose, that is the point about new knowledge: it can produce an immediate emotional effect and in time it can change us, for the better, and sometimes without us even thinking about it.

As I left the university that day, I couldn't help reflecting that Gordon Allport might well have laughed at this modern quandary – the inner conflict, which he had identified so clearly half a century ago, had just shifted a notch, or several notches. It really would have been interesting if he had had the opportunity to explore how people could explain this type of inner conflict, coming from deep within their unconscious, and impacting on so much of their everyday lives, including selection for jobs, meeting people for the first time or even greeting old, familiar colleagues. In many ways, I thought, the whole issue of the racism within had suddenly become much more sinister than I'd first thought, and perhaps if Allport had decided not to visit Freud in Vienna all those years ago, he and therefore the rest of us, would now understand this whole thing an awful lot better. Perhaps he wouldn't have been put off studying the unconscious for so long by Freud's crude attempt to psychoanalyse him.

But I suppose that's the point about being a true pioneer like Gordon Allport: you inevitably leave a lot for those who follow on to discover when they start tramping across the fresh, white, unsullied layers of new knowledge.

Chapter summary

- William Hazlitt was the first to define prejudice as 'pre-judging any question without having significantly examined it.'
- Hazlitt thought that prejudice was 'the child of ignorance.'

- In 1954 Gordon Allport stressed that prejudice involves both 'unfounded judgement' and 'a feeling tone'.
- According to Allport, prejudice results from pre-judgement and derives from the fact that we are most at home with people 'like ourselves'.
- Categorisation and separation are, according to Allport, crucial for the development of prejudice.
- Some categories grow from a 'kernel of truth' but some are irrational.
- People have simple strategies for maintaining the categorical distinctions in the face of any irrationality 'When a fact cannot fit into a mental field, the exception is acknowledged, but the field is hastily fenced in again and not allowed to remain dangerously open.'
- People often say things like 'there are nice Negroes, but …' This is an example of such re-fencing.
- Allport avoided considering at all whether a major component of prejudice resides wholly in the unconscious.
- Allport only dealt with the conscious cognitions of everyday life when it came to racial prejudice, but not the unconscious emotions that may energise them in the first place.
- Some psychologists have argued (from an evolutionary perspective) that the first thing people want to know about another person is whether this person is a friend or a foe and whether they are competent or not (i.e. how big a threat they really are).
- This two-dimensional space defined by 'warmth' (friend/foe) and 'competence' (big threat/little threat) is crucial to understanding our emotional and cognitive responses to a range of other social groups.
- The amygdala seems to be critical in responding differently to images of people from different racial or ethnic groups. It fires and habituates differently to people from different racial groups to our own.

- Social fear, which children with Williams Syndrome do not suffer from, seems to be an essential prerequisite of racial stereotyping.
- Fear of the unfamiliar may kick-start the process of prejudice, and this happens unconsciously.
- Emotion often precedes cognition. We may have a feeling state that sets up a predisposition to act. Our cognitions may sometimes allow us to deal with these feelings in rational, or seemingly rational, ways.
- Gordon Allport had written 'The course of prejudice in a life seldom runs smoothly … Integration of such opposing forces within a single life is hard to achieve.'
- Our implicit (and unconscious) attitude to people from different racial backgrounds seems to direct our unconscious eye movements when we consider their CVs in a shortlisting task.
- Our 'rational' decisions about the suitability of candidates are based on this biased pattern of fixation.
- The interaction of these more unconscious and conscious processes might be one way that these 'opposing forces' have to be integrated within the individual.

3

CONFLICTED HABITS

I grew up with smoking; it just seemed to be life back then in the 1960s and 1970s. It was all around me; my clothes stank of it. Both of my parents smoked, and on Saturday nights the smoke hung like a low cloud in our front room. My father would be down in Paddy's Bar at the bottom of Barginnis Street, and my mother, my Aunt Agnes and a few close friends sat with their sherry, port and vodka in our front room, and had a wee fag. The public bar was for the men in those days; the women and their wee drink were largely confined to the house on a Saturday night. They would sip at their drinks in the front room in front of the telly with the sound turned down, 77 *Sunset Strip*, and silenced images of glamorous Los Angeles, and they would pass the fags round, and maybe dream a little of Stu Bailey and Jeff Spencer, the private investigators from the show.

I would sit at the top of the stairs, waiting for my father to come home, needing the toilet out the back of the yard. I would spoil the glamour and the dreaming. 'I need to go out to the yard,' I would rhyme, that was how it was described, as rhyming, and probably how it sounded, until my mother eventually gave in. 'Out you go, then straight back to bed.'

You could feel yourself walking down into this thick cloud of smoke with sharp, visible boundaries that you could trace with your finger, halfway down the stairs. It was like walking into a cloud of acrid gas. The glasses would be pushed behind the settee, and the fags held out of sight, as if there was some shame in it on their part, as I walked past, fanning the smoke away from me. 'Stop breathing it in, if you don't like it,' my mother would say. 'You can stop breathing for a few minutes, if it upsets you this much.'

One of the few photographs I have of my father is of him, down on his hunches, by our front door, feeding the pigeons in the street with a cigarette hanging out of the side of his mouth. He wasn't a big smoker compared to most in my street. My mother liked Humphrey Bogart in *Casablanca* ('Humph' she called him in a familiar sort of way and her eyes would look all dreamy) and she loved how Humph or Bogie would talk with a cigarette in his mouth. She liked my dad with a cigarette hanging out of the side of his mouth; that is what I guessed anyway, as if he wasn't bothered either. Sometimes, I think my father was just trying to look cool and sophisticated for her. He died suddenly at 51 when I was 13. This sudden loss left me feeling numb. I was angry and hopelessly lost, but it was an unarticulated anger about that great chasm of death. My Uncle Terence said that he had never seen a boy so close to his father, but after my father died, Terence said that I just pulled the shutters down and never mentioned him. I couldn't. It would have been far too painful. One night, however, I plucked up the courage and suggested to my mother that maybe my dad shouldn't have smoked and maybe, just maybe, he should have exercised more. However, my mother, inconsolable in her grief, could not bear to listen to any of this. She told me that I didn't know what I was talking about, that he had rheumatic fever when he was a boy, that he had a heart murmur, and that my compulsive running, every day, which I started that same year he died, would do me far more harm than the odd relaxing fag. 'All that bloody sweating, do you think that's doing you any good?' she was crying as she said it, 'that sweating will give *you* rheumatic fever.'

Smoking always seemed 'natural' up our way, built into the very rhythms and patterns of life itself. You smoked when you were laid off from a job and when you were on the bus home at the end of a hard day in the shipyard or the mill, but only on the upstairs deck. You smoked when you had a lot on and when you had nothing on. The fags would be passed around when your friends popped in as a way of starting a social exchange. In houses, there would be an ashtray beside the settee, another beside the cooker, one beside the bed. They had to be handy and the rooms were organised around smoking. In some of my friends' houses there were bottle-thick glass ashtrays, the thick glass stained by smoke, the ashtrays probably lifted from bars at the end of the evening ('they'll never miss them'). Some ashtrays were even more obvious in terms of place of origin – coloured, dented ashtrays with 'Guinness' in bold black letters on the side or 'Harp' in an insipid green. However, these ashtrays had little class, and signalled none of the sophistication of smoking, or none of the glamour of 77 *Sunset Strip*, which my mother and her friends desired. They all wanted to be 'the fella in the big picture', that was the expression then, or at least his female companion.

My mother worked for a while in the 1960s for Ulster Plastics and we had fancy chrome and transparent red plastic ashtrays where you pushed the cigarette through a lid into a smouldering cauldron underneath. The burning ash looked even more volcanic because of the thick red hardened plastic that gave off a Vulcan glow, and then the light chrome lid would jump back into position after you had pushed the butt through, with a little sharp yell, starving the cigarette of oxygen (eventually). It was like a cross between a child's toy and a utensil. I would ask if I could put my mother's cigarette out ('mind your fingers, that lid will cut them off'), and wished that I were old enough to have my own cigarettes to extinguish in this way.

The women from our neighbourhood did a lot of their smoking in their houses, certainly not on the street or on the bus ('too common'), and the fancy ashtrays would come out then. There were plenty to go round; Ulster Plastics never missed them. It was another part of the ritual of that most ritualistic of all habits. 'Pass me one of those lovely ashtrays, Eileen. I bet they were very expensive.'

My friends all smoked, starting at eleven or twelve, at the very beginning of secondary school. It was a rite of passage, like kicking the doors of the old pensioners from Legann Street (but only the ones that could still run after you like Charlie Chuck), and hoofing it back to our street. Or jumping nine feet off that overhang up Harmony Hill into the soggy ground at the other end of the wee millstream, without getting your feet too wet, or breaking your leg. 'Have you done it?' they would ask. 'Have you done the big Harmony Hill jump?' 'Have you had your first fag?'

I never liked smoking but I can recall that first taste in a wee damp hut at the top of our street, egged on by an old night watchman sitting in the hut, there to watch over the new tar going down on the road. Duck, Jackie and Kingo sat huddled around as the old man's stained butt was passed around these young lads sitting on the wooden stools in the light of a paraffin lamp. 'It'll keep out the cold,' he said. 'Suck it right up into your lungs; it'll warm you up. It'll give you a lovely glow.' It was my turn to hold the damp little butt and try to suck it in. I was revolted at the taste, and the wet spit on the end of it, and they were all laughing at me, egged on by the night watchman with the stained yellow teeth.

My friends, too young to buy their own, would ask the bigger boys for their butts, or pinch a fag from the open pack of their parents on the kitchen table. That night it was a wee butt, just about to be discarded, the fingers of these young boys pinched around the stem already brown, already nicotine stained. It looked and tasted disgusting, and whatever was drawing them to it was not enough for me to overcome that most basic of emotions.

My mother smoked fags with filter tips. They were more ladylike in the sense that you didn't have to smoke them right to the end, and hold them in that miserly, manly pinch with hollow sucking cheeks. She always described smoking in a particular way: 'I'm just going to have a wee fag.' It was always 'a wee fag', as well as 'a wee drink.' Just as long as you put the diminutive in front of it, it never seemed that serious or harmful. But I didn't like the smell of smoke and I would fan the smoke away with my hand with these short sharp little repetitive movements even when the house was full of her friends round for their wee fag and their wee drink on a Saturday night. My mother would tell me off for it. 'Our Geoffrey is at it again, always making a fuss about nothing. It's not going to kill you, for God's sake,' she would say. 'It's only a wee bit of smoke.' However, I was sure that it made me cough, it irritated my chest, but it was hard to complain without starting an argument. 'It doesn't do you any harm,' she would say, 'or they'd ban it like everything else.'

On my lunch breaks from primary school, I would be sent down to the shops for my Aunt Agnes when she was on her break from the mill in Ligoniel. She worked in the carding room in Ewarts where the flax was combed and prepared for spinning and the dust from the flax hung in the air. 'You'd have something to complain about if you had to work there,' my mother would say. 'That would make you cough.' My Aunt Agnes was a big smoker. It was always the same order every lunchtime, a half-pound of steak for grilling for my Uncle Terence who was always on a diet and a bone for our dog, Spot, who should have been on a diet but wasn't, and then it was down to the sweetie shop for forty Woodbine for my Aunt Agnes ('and get an extra packet when you're down there, and you can keep the change'). In later years, it was Embassy for the cigarette coupons, which she collected, but the coupons were always collected for other people, and mainly for me. My Aunt Agnes would say that she smoked forty a day, but in reality it was probably sixty or even more (and the third packet would mysteriously come out late at nights). 'Who's counting?' my mother would say, and my aunt had a very loud and very distinctive chesty cough that bent her double and lasted for an eternity, but this was never attributed to the cigarettes themselves, it was always attributed to the carding room and the mill. 'All the girls from the carding room have a cough like that for goodness sake,' my mother would say, 'the dust gets into your lungs. Many people say that smoking clears the lungs, especially the menthol ones. Apparently they are very good for the air waves.' My Uncle Terence hardly smoked at all, and Agnes had to hide the extent of her smoking from him. She didn't bother with the menthol ones in the end.

My Aunt Agnes was my mother's sister; my Uncle Terence was my father's best friend. They were more than an aunt and uncle though; they were more like a second set of parents. They lived at the top of Ligoniel in Belfast, we lived at the bottom. I would be allowed to go to their house on a Saturday night and sleep between the two of them. Her cough would keep me awake. All these years later, I can close my eyes and see her bent double, and I can hear the same hacking sounds.

The carding room, where my aunt worked, was one of the dirtiest jobs in the mill; my mother worked in the twisting room – one of the cleaner jobs. My uncle always said that my mother was a great one for the style, with her clothes and tipped cigarettes. She worked in the twisting room and looked like a film star, 'the best looking girl in Ligoniel', my father always told me. I am now sitting years later reading some British Parliamentary Papers on the subject of the conditions of work in the flax mills of Belfast on the health of the workers. The report mentions the professional opinion of a Dr St George, surgeon to the Antrim Infirmary: 'I find that a large number of hacklers and roughers among males, and carders among females, suffer from phthisis, bronchitis, and asthma due to the irritation caused by the particles of flax being carried into the lungs and causing mechanical irritation.' The hot, damp condition of some rooms in the mills killed many prematurely, but in the carding room it was the dust. James Connolly, the Irish socialist leader, later famously executed in a chair by the British for his part in the Easter Rising, wrote a powerful manifesto to the 'Linen Slaves of Belfast' in 1913, condemning the 'condition of the sweated women of all classes of labour in Belfast.' There were many folk tales amongst the workers as to what would help these sweated women, including the use of whisky 'to clear the pipes', to allow you to breathe, but smoking is still to me at least one of the less probable antidotes, especially in this more modern era.

'Your mother was always fond of style,' my uncle would say, 'she could go to work dressed – your aunt couldn't.' She would come to our house every day for lunch: it was always the same thing, banana sandwiches and a fag. Soon after my father died, my aunt and uncle moved to Bath, just before the Troubles started. My uncle worked for the Royal Naval Stores and he got a transfer because he was a Roman Catholic and he felt that he was being discriminated against in terms of promotion. I would spend all of my long school holidays with them. My aunt was 53 and looked out of place in Bath among the foreign students, French schoolchildren and middle-class matrons who invaded the Pump Room. While my uncle worked, she would wander about Bath in their first year there – the shops mainly, Woolworths and Littlewoods. She didn't think much of the Georgian terraces and, anyway, most of them were at the top of a hill. All those Woodbine and Embassy for the coupons made that hill very difficult to climb. My aunt got a job in the Naval Stores where my uncle worked, after twenty-eight years of inhaling flax dust. 'She couldn't believe her new job,' my uncle said. 'You could go to the toilet whenever you wanted to – and have a fag if you wanted one. If you'd done that in the mill, you'd have been out on your arse.'

They only came home once for a holiday, I think that it was too painful for them, they were far too homesick. However, there were not many holidays left. My aunt's health deteriorated. For two years, she couldn't walk more than a few yards at a time. When she inhaled, her chest made a loud whistle. The carding room, and all that saving for the Embassy gifts, always given to others, had taken their toll. She died in Bath, cardiac arrest, respiratory failure, pneumonia; the grim reaper had made no mistake with this one. But at the time of her death, one strange thing had occurred. My aunt and uncle had come to resemble each other quite closely. They had both gone grey, and old age had bent and shortened my uncle and made him thinner, in a way that the steak for grilling never could; infirmity had made my aunt fatter – her body had filled with fluid, her abdomen had expanded. She had the same skinny legs but massive torso. She resembled a house sparrow at the time of her death.

After the service, we went to the pub and my uncle told anybody who was prepared to listen that he'd 'just buried his wife today', even though she had just been cremated. However, the smoking was never really blamed for this life foreshortened and sad in the end. I always thought that a little odd, even at the time. My uncle and aunt had many arguments about smoking but it was never about the health aspects, more about wasted money and will power. 'It's not money wasted,' my aunt would say, 'What about the wee cigarette coupons?' Sometimes the arguments were about 'giving it up for a while to show who's in charge', arguments about human weakness. However, there was always that strong and resolute defence. 'It's my only pleasure.' It was that argument over and over again, 'It's not that bad for you they say; if I stopped now it would probably kill me.'

Years later this became my mother's refrain as well and then in the end she packed them in 'and I was never as unwell when I did.'

Health warnings that were ignored

This, of course, is just a story of an ordinary family and smoking. Smoking was a part of life, and there must be millions of stories like this. But why was such a harmful activity so deeply ingrained in everyday life, so accepted, so uncontested? It's not as if the scientific evidence didn't exist, even back then. Dr Leroy E. Burney, surgeon general of the US Public Health Service, had warned the public back in 1959 that 'The weight of evidence at present implicates smoking as the principal ... factor in the increased incidence of lung cancer.' However, the public paid very little notice. Boyd and Levy (1963) reported that in the US in 1963, 78 per cent of American men smoked; with the proportion of women smoking significantly increasing. They also reported that deaths from lung cancer in the United States had increased 600 per cent since 1935, paralleling the rise in smoking. They expressed considerable surprise at the fact that the public were clearly failing to see the connection between cigarette smoking and lung cancer. Indeed, the American Cancer Society had reported that only 16 per cent of the American public thought that the two things were related. Boyd and Levy said that

> This may be selective perception at work; that is, because the facts of the situation [smoking] are totally unpleasant and affect a basic habit, the mind rejects the message or, in effect, never receives it. Domestic sales of cigarettes in 1963 hit a record of 512 billion.

They also pointed out that there were decreases in cigarette smoking in only two years since 1935, and they were in 1953 and 1954, which happened to be the years immediately after the negative publicity emanating from the first set of studies suggesting a link with cancer. However, from 1954 onwards the figures started to rise again, 'attributed in part to filters, which now account for over 50% of all cigarette sales.' For Boyd and Levy, this change was not attributable to the 'technical' aspects of the filter tip but the psychological aspects. They say that it allowed smokers, particularly female smokers, 'to rationalise the habit', to feel safe. When I watched my mother and my aunt refuse non-tipped Embassy, I knew exactly what they meant. The cigarette companies guessed that women are the more cautious sex.

Boyd and Levy wanted to address the question of how we can prevent young people starting to smoke in the first place. In the early 1960s, the evidence was that children were starting to smoke at younger and younger ages, with boys starting younger than girls. Boyd and Levy suggested that we have to think beyond the basic facts that smoking is a deeply ingrained habit rooted in biological addiction. These are critical factors but they are only a small part of the story. They argued that we need to understand better the psychology of smoking and here they turned their attention to that guru of the smoking industry Dr Ernest Dichter. Back in the 1940s, Dichter had been the president of the Institute for Motivational Research which had conducted the pioneering research into the 'strong psychological forces' that operate with smoking. He had carried out his original groundbreaking research not to stop people smoking, but to help them get addicted. Given how effective Dichter had been, Boyd and Levy suggested that this might well be a good place to start. 'How else could the habit continue to exist?' they ask, 'when so many smokers classify it as being unhealthy, wasteful, dirty and immoral? Certainly, powerful motivations must be operating to sustain cigarette smoking in the face of these negative attitudes.' Powerful motivations indeed, not just assessed, but manipulated by Dichter and other psychologists using *depth* techniques to probe the human mind and reveal its unconscious motivations and then direct them in certain ways.

How Ernest Dichter used 'depth' psychology to get us all hooked

Ernest Dichter was by training a psychoanalyst, another of that wave of Jewish refugees from Nazi Germany arriving in the US in the late 1930s. He was obviously taken by the entrepreneurial spirit of his adopted country, and he had a simple idea that was to have a profound impact on all of our lives. Psychoanalysis was providing new insights into how the mind works; the emerging (and now somewhat clichéd) metaphor was that the human mind is like an iceberg: most of it is hidden from view. Human beings may be rational creatures, but not rational all of the time, and there are unconscious forces that govern much of our lives. Could marketing tap into these unconscious forces? Dichter decided to turn his attention away from the curing of neuroses using psychoanalytic methods to the application of psychoanalytic understanding to marketing. There were more similarities than differences between the two enterprises, he thought. People say that they are not subject to neurotic complexes and people say that they are not open to manipulation through advertising. However, people say many things; the reality might be quite different. Both enterprises need a clear model of the mind. You need to see below the surface, to *access* the unconscious to cure neurosis and to *manipulate* the unconscious to sell brands. If you want to understand how people think and feel about products, you cannot just ask them directly. Psychoanalysts would never do that, it would be ludicrous ('please tell me about your neurosis'); you need more indirect and more intense methods. You need the psychoanalyst's couch, but on an industrial scale.

His first commercial project was on the marketing of milk. He suggested using more indirect methods for his market research. He interviewed consumers without ever asking them to talk directly about milk. This approach did not impress his employer ('Why is he asking them *that*?'). However, this did not dent either his self-belief or his belief in the truths that psychoanalysis had highlighted. He wrote to six of the biggest American marketing companies introducing himself as 'a young psychologist from Vienna' with 'some interesting ideas which can help you be more successful, effective, sell more and communicate better.' He emphasised his connection with Freud, whose views on the importance of the unconscious were at that time becoming more familiar through the popular press in the United States (although even then often parodied in the press). Dichter had been trained in psychoanalysis in Vienna but not by Freud himself. However, he had lived on the same Vienna street as Freud and he liked to weave this into the conversation whenever he could. Dichter liked to point out a few simple facts from psychoanalysis to the marketers of the day. People do not know themselves well, so there is really no point in asking them, he would say. You cannot ask people why they are neurotic; they have no idea, he would say this over, and over, again. So much of life is unconscious. Similarly, he argued, there is no point in asking people why they choose one brand over another. It is all about unconscious associations and subconscious impulses, repressed desires, defence mechanisms and guilt. That is the stuff of neurosis and the stuff of everyday desire, including the desire for brands. Freud had focussed on one set of applications of psychoanalysis; Dichter was going to focus on a different set. That was his mission; that was what unconsciously drove *him*.

It is important to set all of this within its natural context. A much simpler understanding of the human mind drove market research at the time. The traditional view was that people could report why they preferred some products rather than others. They knew what they liked about certain products and what they didn't. The big market research companies commissioned hundreds of surveys where people were simply asked why they bought one product rather than another. Vance Packard, in his classic 1957 book *The Hidden Persuaders* refers to these methods as 'nose counting'. The problem, according to Packard, was that what people said retrospectively, and in the context of wanting to be helpful to the interviewer, often bore very little relationship to what they actually did. Packard says that informants wanted to appear to the world as 'sensible, intelligent, rational beings.' But how rational are people *really* in their decision making? That was the big question. Dichter said he already knew the answer to this based on his psychoanalytic training; it really was very simple. 'Not very', was his conclusion. Moreover, some new research coming out of the Color Research Institute of America at the time was backing him up on this.

The Color Research Institute of America was another new development in rethinking how the human mind works and applying it to the commercial world. It was founded in the 1930s by Louis Cheskin, another clinically trained psychologist. Cheskin is hailed as the other main contender to be considered as the originator of the 'depth' approach to marketing in the 1930s. He also argued that consumers make unconscious assessments of products and that these are not just based on the product itself but derive from all of the associated characteristics, including the sensory input from the product, all processed automatically and unconsciously. One major sensory feature is the colour of a product, which is rich in both biological meaning (consider the colour 'red', for example, and its unconscious associations in the natural world – lips, blood, sex, etc.) and in symbolic meaning (where 'red' is often associated, again unconsciously, with festivity, danger, and, of course, sex again). These unconscious sensory impressions from the product (or its packaging), Cheskin argued, can transfer directly onto our perceptions of the product itself, including its perceived value, price and quality. It also affects our emotional response to the product. In one market research study, the Color Research Institute tested package designs for a new detergent and housewives tried out three 'different' detergents in three different boxes (which were either yellow, blue, or 'blue with a splash of yellow') on their weekly wash. The verdict was that the detergent in the yellow box was too harsh for their clothes, 'it ruined them', many of the respondents complained, whereas the detergent in the blue box was not strong enough, and left the clothes still dirty. The detergent in the blue box with splashes of yellow was 'just right', they said. 'It cleans my clothes well but doesn't ruin them.' The detergent, however, was identical in all three boxes. The colour of the packaging affected the respondents' perceptions of the effectiveness of the product. Unconscious associations, manipulated by the marketer, could determine our preferences.

Cheskin concluded that asking consumers about products or what influenced their preferences is not a very informative way to understand the processes involved. It is what people do rather than what they say that matters, and we should not underestimate the role of the unconscious in this. Cheskin's company advocated putting Del Monte peaches in a glass jar rather than in a can ('it unconsciously reminded them of their grandmother bottling fruit'). His company suggested putting a sprig of parsley on tinned Spam to signify 'freshness'. It was the research of this company that found that when you changed the colour of the 7-Up can, with a 15 per cent increase in the amount of yellow on the can, it led to serious complaints about a change in flavour. Too 'lemony', consumers protested about the drink whose flavour, of course, had not been touched. It now tasted 'lemony' because consumers had been unconsciously primed with that lemon association through the colour of the can. This research was starting to question the more rational model of consumers, and how the human mind works.

Ernest Dichter was now at the forefront of this, and he developed a completely new approach to uncover the more irrational and unconscious side of consumer behaviour. Dichter said that we need to start at the very beginning, indeed with our first point of contact with the consumer. Interviews can be revealing for market research, he argued, but these interviews need to fundamentally change. He suggested that much smaller numbers of respondents should be interviewed (after all many of the great insights of psychoanalysis were based on single case studies). But these interviews needed to be much longer and much more in-depth, on the assumption that if you let people talk long enough, you may be able to find something interesting in the associations between concepts that come tumbling out in spontaneous speech often in unguarded moments when the ego is less in control. You also need to get respondents to talk indirectly (rather than directly) about the product. You need to get them to verbalise their feelings, you need to listen carefully, you need to check and crosscheck, and you need to listen for inconsistencies. You do not take what they say at face value, you need to understand instead the symbolic importance of products in people's lives, and you need to interpret what they say. You need to look out for defence mechanisms and projection. His approach clearly owed a lot to some of the basic processes of psychoanalysis, and it relied heavily on a number of its core concepts.

In a retrospective account of the first part of his career, Dichter outlined the principles underpinning his approach to understanding and measuring human motivations (Dichter 1960). His explicit goal in publishing this retrospective book in 1960 (and this is an interesting admission on his part) was 'to set the record straight.' He thought that many misunderstandings had developed about how 'shrinks' like himself were manipulating the American public. 'I think the time has come for a little factual and unemotional clarification', he wrote (Dichter 1960: 33). In an attempt to do this, he said that he needed to explain his fundamental understanding of the basis of human motivation.

He argues that 'most human actions are the result of tensions. Whenever tension differentials become strong enough, they lead to action' (Dichter 1960: 38). The example he uses here is buying a new car. The typical 'tensions' in a family derive from one's children complaining about the old model, their friends' dads having better cars, ads that tell you how good other cars are, your old car breaking down, etc. He says:

> We are dealing with a series of events, some coming from the inside, some from the outside, some from technical factors, others from psychological factors, all building up to a tension which results in action. The tension differential ... has become so great that the action is finally triggered off.
>
> (Dichter 1960: 38)

And notice the way that he stresses the role of the children in the family as being important, indeed critical elements in producing this 'tension' and thereby acting as instruments of change.

Underpinning his approach, he says, there are three very basic principles. The first is the 'functional principle'. He argues that we cannot explain why somebody buys the same make of car each time or chooses a particular brand of cigarettes unless we know why they buy cars or smoke in the first place. We need to understand car buying and smoking in their natural context. For example, he says that in the case of smoking we need to 'analyze smoking in a way that will not disturb its natural ties with all its related activities and phenomena such as working habits, leisure time, occupation, health etc.' (Dichter 1960: 39). He says that there is nothing new in this approach, this is really just applied cultural anthropology (rather than primarily psychoanalysis in action) and he quotes Margaret Mead, who wrote 'Anthropological science gains its importance from the fact that it attempts to see each individual which shares a common culture in its natural context' (cited by Dichter 1960: 39).

The second core principle that Dichter identifies is the 'dynamic principle'. He argues that human motivations change during a lifetime as a function of aspiration. Motivation and consumer choice are influenced by previous experience and where the individuals concerned are hoping to end up. In other words, one needs to take a longitudinal perspective on the nature of the behaviour in question. A major focus for Dichter was the first experience of any product – the first car (always the most important symbolically), the first cigarette (for example, mine in that watchman's hut), the first fur coat (these were, after all, different decades). He would get his participants to talk at length about these first experiences in order to understand their current motivations and how these motivations had changed with time. I laugh when I think of what he might have made of my first experience of smoking, sucking on the night watchman's old dirty cigarette butt and feeling nothing but revulsion. At least it put me off smoking; I am thankful for that. What other associations might *he* have seen?

The third of Dichter's core principles was 'the principle of fundamental insights'. He says that the point about human motivation is that we, as actors, have no real idea why we do one thing rather than another.

> In practising research on human motivations, we feel it to be our duty to get down to fundamental insights, to accept the fact without fear or embarrassment that quite a number of human motivations are irrational, unconscious, unknown to the people themselves. This principle means that most human actions have deeper motivations than those which appear on the surface, motivations which can be uncovered if the right approach is used.
>
> (Dichter 1960: 45)

Of course, if you ask people why they do something, they will give you an answer ('we are not allowed by our culture to admit true irrationality as an explanation of our behaviour'), so he avoided asking them. Instead, he allowed them to talk indirectly and in depth ('tell me about your first cigarette'). He encouraged them to disclose their emotions and to talk about the extremes ('tell me about the best beer you ever had and the worst beer you ever had'). The reasoning here was to mobilise 'true feelings' and 'real experience' and to move away from 'considered opinions'. He encouraged them to be specific. When people talk in terms of generalities, it is easier for them to present a 'rational' and considered view of things. However, perhaps most importantly of all, he encouraged them to be spontaneous and then he analysed them carefully to work out their true feelings and intentions. In other words, this was an approach that did not take what people said at face value.

> Many of the aspects of depth interviewing are borrowed from the approaches used in psychiatry, where the problem often is to understand the real reason for a person's behaviour. We employ these techniques continuously in our daily lives. When the hostess keeps urging us to stay a little longer, but yawns at the same time, most of us don't need any knowledge of depth interviewing or of psychology to detect a discrepancy between her statement and her actual feelings. We leave.
>
> (Dichter 1960: 285)

He filmed his respondents interacting with various products (women were often surprised by how much time they spent sliding their fingers over a bar of soap to test its smoothness). He used psychodrama where they acted out their relationship with the product (the sound of the fist on the glove is a crucial dimension for baseball gloves). He used various projective techniques ('imagine that you are a little boy looking through a keyhole into a kitchen ten years from now. What do you see?').

Washing your sins away

His first major professional success was with the Compton Advertising Agency to promote Ivory soap, whose sales had significantly slumped at that time. 'The soap that floats' had been discovered by accident in 1879; it had been performing extremely well for many years. The standard market research approach had been to ask consumers why they chose this particular product, or why they didn't. Dichter wanted to apply his 'functional principle'. He said that there was no point in trying to promote a brand of soap before you understood more about the psychology of bathing so he began by interviewing one hundred people at various YMCAs around the country, in his usual non-directive way. 'I decided to talk to people about such things as daily baths and showers, rather than to ask people various questions about why they used or did not use Ivory Soap' (Dichter 1960: 33). Bathing, he discovered, had all kinds of hidden psychological significance. It was not just to do with washing dirt away for some people; rather it was a process of psychological cleansing as well. As he himself put it, 'You cleanse yourself not only of dirt but of guilt.' The slogan that he came up with was 'Be smart and get a fresh start with Ivory soap ... and wash all your troubles away.' 'Troubles' was used here to represent implicitly all of those guilty secrets that could be washed away with the right type of soap. It might sound implausible or far-fetched. How can soap wash away guilt? However, Ivory soap had a whole series of *pure white* connotations helping you to bathe, to look forward to getting dressed and going out, helping you to focus on what lies ahead rather than what lies behind. It represented a cognitive focus on the future rather than the past. If you can use ritual to shape your cognitive focus then you can start to deal with the emotions that attach to thinking too much about what you have done, like guilt. This all made some intuitive sense to Ernest Dichter. However, much more importantly, the campaign was a great success.

But bathing cannot just be about ridding oneself of guilt. That would be ridiculous. It would be like suggesting that a cigar *always* has some sort of sexual significance regardless of context. After all, did Freud not once say that a cigar is sometimes just a cigar? (Although interestingly this quote is often attributed to Freud, it turns out that he himself may never have actually used these words, see Elms 2001, but the point still stands.) Every instance of bathing could not possibly represent an attempt to deal with guilt (is there that much guilt in the world?), so Dichter also suggested that bathing sometimes has quite a different psychological function. He says that bathing is 'one of the few occasions when the puritanical American [is] allowed to caress himself or herself while applying soap.' It's not about getting rid of guilt any more, it is about possibly enjoying the sins of the flesh. If you are going to market soap, the importance of the guilt-free caress could also be very important, Dichter argued. That was another starting point for his thinking, and then his psychoanalytically trained marketing brain took over. There are very different kinds of caress, depending upon who is doing the caressing and who is being caressed. The touch, after all, is one of the most powerful and ambiguous forms of communication, which requires careful consideration (Beattie and Ellis 2017). The caresses of, for example, a mother or a lover are very different things and Dichter argued this sort of distinction has to be considered carefully in the marketing process. Some soaps (like Camay) could be constructed as sensual, the caress of an indulgent 'seductress'. For other soaps, like Ivory, the caress is maternal and caring. Thus, back in 1939 he was developing the concept of the 'personality' or the 'image' of the product. This is something that we take more or less for granted now, but was very original at the time, groundbreaking even. Dichter argued that marketing campaigns could be built around these personalities of products, uncovered in the first instance through the depth interviews and then systematically developed in the campaigns themselves. The 'personalities' of some products, originally identified by Dichter, stayed in place for the decades that followed; they became the products that we all know and recognise today.

One Camay ad from the 1950s shows a fresh-faced bride carried across the threshold by the young groom. She has bright red lipstick that draws the eyes. Her lips are slightly apart, exposing bright white teeth. The groom is holding her tight around the waist; she is pulling him towards her. The copy reads 'Your skin has a fresher, clearer look with your First Cake of Camay!' 'First Cake' is capitalised and underscored with a red line, drawing the eyes between the red lips and the red line. Camay is described as 'cake' (as some other soaps are), indulgent and to be enjoyed; it is sensual rather than functional. 'First' cake connotes the first time, unconsciously signalling that it is the first time for the young wholesome bride; in other words, she is a virgin. There are red roses around the packet of soap and the 'undressed' bar of soap in the image beneath the main picture. That is the third use of red in the ad. Of course, red roses communicate romance but at the same time, roses are associated with the wooing process. The man sends the woman red roses before a date, it is the will she or won't she phase, the wait. Tonight is the end of that long wait. The caress is sensual, like the soap itself.

Another ad from the same era shows a woman in a bath, bubbles cover her modesty. Again, she is fully made up, with bright red lipstick unblemished and expertly applied, and a mouth slightly open. Her hands luxuriantly stroke each other with a white bar of Camay caressed in-between them. She looks dreamy, her eyes half-closed, but in the reflection in the mirror beside the bath her eyes look fully closed. She looks as if she has just been sexually satisfied. The copy reads 'You'll be a little lovelier each day with fabulous pink CAMAY'. However, there is more text on this one. There is little ambiguity about the message. 'When you surrender to this luxurious caress … feel Camay's gentle lather enfold you.' This is seduction and beyond, it is surrendering to the caress of a seducer, it is guilt-free sex with a bar of soap in the bath.

Ivory soap was not like that; it was never a seducer. It was pure white, and 'pure' was its main associative connection. Therefore, it needed to be marketed differently. It was more maternal and comforting; it was a different kind of caress. 'Wash your troubles away', the way a mother might comfort you (and forgive you for the things that you've done, thus dealing with feelings of guilt). The ads built on this maternal image. They often showed a baby with 'that Ivory look' ('what is the first thing that comes into your mind when I say, "mother" … "baby"'). The copy reads 'Babies have That Ivory Look … Why shouldn't you? … doctors chose it ahead of all other soaps for today's complexion and for yours.' Another reads 'Imagine this! Best costs less than all the rest'. Again, there is a picture of a baby. This will be the housewives' choice, doing the best for her family, careful with cost and family finance, taking advice from the family doctor, staying young to hang on to her husband, washing your anxieties about this away in the bath (regaining your baby-faced complexion with soap), allowing you to wash any guilt away. Two bars of soap whose prototypic 'personalities' are borne out of psychoanalytic theory – the wife as whore and the wife as mother. You could not ask consumers directly about these things; they would laugh in your face or punch you ('Who are you calling a whore?').

Of course, you can easily criticise this type of approach, taking the unconscious and trying to manipulate it, but Dichter argued that there was hard data to evaluate the hypothesis. Not necessarily scientific data per se, of course, but the sales figures, in black and white, to see whether the idea was working or not ('better than any laboratory experiment', Dichter said). Sales of Ivory soap shot up. By 1979, according to *Advertising Age*, Ivory had sold more than 30 billion bars. I do recall that when my mother's old mill house was demolished in the 1980s and she got her first house with a bathroom in North Belfast, her very first purchase was a 'cake' of Camay soap. She deserved a little luxury and a little indulgence, she said, after all those years in an old condemned mill house. She had forty years of advertising firmly entrenched in her head. She knew the personality of Camay soap inside out.

Dichter now turned his attention to cars. The brief here was to understand why the new Chrysler Plymouth had not taken off in the way that had been anticipated by the company. The report from Chrysler's own marketing agency, J. Stirling Getchell, makes fascinating reading.

> Dr. Dichter proposed the use of a new psychological research technique to get beyond the limits of current statistical research in an understanding of the factors which influence the sale of cars. Quite frankly, we were at the onset as skeptical of the practicability and value of the proposed study as, we learned later, executives of the corporation had been when first approached.
>
> (Dichter 1960: 289)

Chrysler were interested in two main questions: why do most car buyers buy the same make of car as their previous vehicle (estimated to be around 70 per cent at the time), and what influence do women have on the purchase of cars? The feeling amongst marketers at the time was that all previous answers to these two questions, based on the standard surveys, were not entirely satisfactory. The standard answer to the first question was that we tend to buy the same make of car out of 'habit' or 'loyalty'; marketers had no answer at all to the second question. Dichter was particularly scathing especially about any attempt to explain behaviour in terms of habit –

> They are similar to the type of pseudoscientific facts assembled over many decades by psychiatry which explained the fear of narrow places as being the result of claustrophobia. Translating this into simple language, the statement would read, 'He's afraid of narrow places because he has a fear of narrow places.'
> (Dichter 1960: 45)

Dichter used his depth interviews and offered new answers to these questions, answers of a type that they had never seen before. He said that cars (like soap) have personalities ('the more you live with, or experience your car, the more personality it has'). He also said, on the basis of his psychoanalytic training of course, that cars clearly project our innermost fantasies. Convertibles, he said, symbolise freedom and they project the fantasy of being young, free and single again. For this reason, Dichter argued, wives will rarely allow their husband to buy a convertible. This has nothing to do with economy or appropriateness or even (in those sexist times) 'what a convertible might do to their hair', rather the women respond negatively to the symbolic significance of the convertible for their husbands (although they would never allow themselves to think such thoughts explicitly in those terms; such thoughts would be far too threatening). Women unconsciously and implicitly understand the danger that a convertible poses to their marriage. Dichter reasoned, therefore, that car dealerships should put convertibles in the front windows of their showrooms to draw in the middle-aged men, racked by desire for wish fulfilment, yearning to be young, free and single again. However, in addition to this, the car dealers had to ensure that there were plenty of attractive sedans just behind the convertibles, so that husbands and wives (driven there by differing desires and motivations, explicit and implicit) could make harmonious joint (compromise) decisions. Women, he asserted, have a critical economic decision making role in the family, and the final decision, one way or another, is always going to be a joint decision.

Dichter's overall view on the role of women in car buying was that 'Women influence car buying directly or indirectly in about 95 per cent of all car purchases' (Dichter 1960: 310). Once you recognise this fact then there are certain logical consequences. According to Dichter, women are 'the economic conscience of the family of the average income bracket', and, therefore, you have to give them 'moral permission' for the 'sinful extravagances' of the new car. At the time (1939), many women still considered cars to be a luxury; the goal was to persuade them that they were a necessity.

Then Dichter turned his attention to the question of why most car buyers go for the same make repeatedly. It is not habit, he said, 'that's too easy and it's not even a proper explanation; the real reasons are separation anxiety and fear.' He argued that we have a degree of psychological attachment to the old car and we suffer from 'separation anxiety' when we think about getting rid of it. According to Dichter, 'People do not buy new cars as much as they sell their old cars.' We cannot bear to part with the old car despite all the 'tensions' that have built up – 'The old car has become a part of our personality. To give it away is like giving part of our personality away.' He referred to this as a form of 'separation anxiety', but it is an odd sort of 'separation anxiety', it is more like a form of splitting of the ego with a part of ourselves given away. So, Dichter argued, we essentially compromise, we buy a newer model, but the same make to decrease the separation anxiety. This is one major factor in sticking to the same model. Then there is the fear of embarrassment. Men feel 'more comfortable buying a car in which the basic elements and engineering features were familiar to them.' Men do not want to look foolish; they do not want to buy a car with which they are unfamiliar, unsure of how things work, uncertain in front of others.

This was all radical stuff, quite different to anything that had been offered up before to Chrysler, or indeed to any other manufacturer at the time. It was a new way of thinking. It was even more radical given that the whole Chrysler Plymouth campaign up to that point in 1939 had emphasised how different this car was. The advertising copy actually read 'This car is different from any other one you have ever tried.' According to Dichter, this campaign was actually counter-productive – it aggravated the fear of change; it made the whole thing much worse. Dichter suggested that they should base the campaign around reducing the fear, and emphasise the fact that it would only take a few minutes to feel at home in the new car.

This campaign was a major success in commercial terms, and J. Stirling Getchell took him on as a full-time employee. In subsequent years Dichter turned his attention to lipstick (a phallic shape has a massive effect on sales, according to Dichter because it offered a subconscious invitation to fellatio, 'but one has to be careful not to go overboard', he warned, 'and make the parallels too obvious'). Then, perhaps most controversially of all, he turned his attention in the late 1940s to cigarette smoking (Dichter 1947) and here, one could argue, he made the biggest difference of all, and we are all, one way or another, still trying to deal with the consequences.

Why we smoke – a depth psychology approach

His starting assumption was that cigarette advertising up to that point (like so much other advertising) had got it seriously wrong. The ads at that time were all designed to emphasise the flavour of the cigarette, or how mild they were (the Chesterfield ad from the 1940s had Alan Ladd say 'I like Chesterfields – they're my brand because they're MILD'; 'Lucky Strike means Fine Tobacco'). Based on depth interviews with 350 smokers, Dichter concluded that things such as taste, mildness or flavour, were 'minor considerations' when it comes to smoking; the main appeal of cigarettes was the range of psychological pleasures that you get from them. He argued that, from a psychological point of view, cigarettes work in a number of distinct ways. First, they allow you to behave like a child again, able to 'follow your whims.' They offer a 'legitimate excuse for interrupting work and snatching a moment of pleasure.' Like children, we crave rewards – 'a cigarette is a reward that we can give ourselves as often as we wish.' Dichter argued that they should use this insight of self-reward as the basis for a marketing campaign.

However, that was only part of his observations about the nature of smoking as an *activity*. Some of his respondents had also commented that with cigarettes, you never really feel alone. Perhaps, this was tapping into the primitive concept of fire, a warm glow, a conditioned stimulus rooted in our evolutionary past associated with the group assembling around the fire. One of Dichter's respondents said when I 'see the glow in the dark, I am not alone any more …', and Dichter added that the use of cigarettes to combat feelings of loneliness and isolation was critical. He also added that 'the companionable character of cigarettes is also reflected in the fact that they help us make friends.' This insight formed the basis of a number of marketing campaigns.

I have music in my head from my earliest days of childhood, and a tag line that I cannot forget. I can see the black–and–white TV in the corner of the room. The smartly dressed handsome man in the raincoat and trilby walks slowly through the wet and deserted London street. He is walking very slowly as if he has nowhere really to go. Why is he on his own at that time of night? Has he been stood up? He gets out his packet of cigarettes, lights up and smiles briefly. I close my eyes and I can see that contented smile of his. That is the hook. Then the words come over the music: 'You're never alone with a Strand.' That slogan will never leave me. I may forget the most important words that my children have ever said to me (and even shamefully their very *first* words), but I cannot forget those words, carefully selected by the mechanics of the mind. This 'lonely man' ad ran from 1959 onwards. 'Strand … the cigarette of the moment. Strand, the new tipped cigarette, wonderful value at three and tuppence for twenty.' Over the next four or five decades I saw many lonely people reaching for a fag to attempt to alleviate their crushing loneliness, primed by this ad playing at some point in their past. (Although they did need a new generation of ads to evolve this symbolic elicitation of the concept of loneliness and to highlight the positive end results. Strand highlighted loneliness, but perhaps too negatively and too vividly. Embassy, Strand's successor from W.D. & H.O. Wills, part of Imperial Tobacco, depicted how loneliness could be cured by smoking, and was based on the image of the 'lonely' man at a party ignored by everybody, until he pulls out his pack of Embassy and offers them around. Embassy was an enormous commercial success. Loneliness, physical, social or symbolic, was still the key.)

The emphasis in Dichter's approach was on understanding the range of roles and functions that cigarettes can play in people's lives. In other words, he wanted to start with some psychological understanding of what cigarettes *do* in people's lives, following again what he had learned from his reading of Margaret Mead and other cultural anthropologists. His functional analysis built from there. Repeatedly he found that people smoke to relieve tension and as a reward for something that they have done. They smoke to reduce stress in anticipation of an event. They smoke as a symbolic statement about how daring they are. They smoke as a way of bonding with others. They smoke as part of a ritualised performance that requires little planning but it allows for a projection of sophistication. Cigarettes are used before sex because people are nervous, and after sex as a relaxing reward. All of these observations are critical in the marketing process.

Then, of course, there is the oral pleasure that derives from smoking, 'as fundamental as sexuality and hunger.' Here, he was reminded of some great psychoanalytic truths about early stages of psychological development and frustration and how people deal with it. What is smoking in essence? It is a form of behaviour, heavily overladen with symbolic and social connotations, where you put something in your lips to comfort yourself at times of stress or frustration, or as a reward. It is about oral gratification, as infantile in the context of Freudian theory as sucking your thumb. However, it is a socially acceptable way of obtaining this oral gratification by simultaneously sending out a powerful message about virile maturity and potency. It is so powerful because it simultaneously satisfies infantile desires and yet symbolically sends out a very adult signal. Young people smoke to look adult (as my friends did when they were eleven or twelve), old people smoke to look 'potent', according to Packard (1957).

Dichter also highlighted the power of lighting a cigarette (as well, of course, as its more 'social' connotations). It was the power of fire that helped define and shape *Homosapiens* in evolutionary terms. So we carried this fire with us in our evolutionary history and we also did so in our own personal history, and it represented a milestone in development. Indeed, you knew you were leaving childhood behind when you wanted to carry that one object. It was the object that you now most desired, not a toy any more, no more Fort Apaches or missile launchers, no more knights on horseback. It was a lighter, just a normal little tin lighter, but one that could never come in your Christmas stocking. It represented another break of that family bond and the building of that bond with your mates, your alternative family. I don't know which of my childhood gang got the first lighter, but I do remember this Prometheus passing it round and talking us through it, like it was a complex bit of machinery. Pull the little wheel back slowly, slowly now, now let it spark up. Feel the power. Not every time, sometimes it would take four or five strokes of your soft-skinned, boyish thumb until it fired into life. According to Dichter, this was a design feature of lighters, a case of variable ratio reinforcement (like slot machines) to keep you hooked. However, it was worth the wait, it was a genuine reinforcer; you had the power of fire in your hands. This was a primitive power rooted in group dynamics and survival, full of deep emotional significance that any evolutionary biologist might understand. 'Smokes, lads, light up,' and all the fags held lightly in the various damp childish mouths would gravitate towards the tip of the fire, all at more or less same time, as if there was an invisible chord pulling them in close.

I *found* my first lighter, which was very fortunate; in other words, I didn't have to steal or buy one (which was always going to be unlikely given both the cost and the embarrassment). The lighter was plastic and a sort of orangey red, like cheap lipstick. Not one colour or the other, perhaps designed for girls who couldn't make up their mind about the colour of their lipstick. Maybe they wanted a lighter to match. So in the back row of the cinema, the lighter would draw attention to the lips. Only a certain sort of girl would light the fag of the man anyway, my mother always said. The lighter was very temperamental; it was on its own very variable ratio schedule. I carried it with me even though I didn't smoke. 'Anybody got a light?' one of my mates would say. And I would pull it out. 'Are you not having a fag? We can share if you don't have the readies to buy your own.' 'I'm alright,' I said.

Duck called them coffin nails, funny even then. 'Who wants a coffin nail?' And they'd all stick out their hand to the fella in the big picture, with a pack of twenty. Nobody asked where the packet of fags came from. Most of the lads could just afford fags bought individually from the sweet shop ('One Park Drive please, Mrs B.'). And they all sat in the park blowing smoke rings, sometimes straight up with their heads right back, and putting their lit fag through the fading halo, a little stabbing movement with a pencil thin dart. It was all only play, I knew that. The playing of roles they had seen and they somehow aspired to. They blew smoke rings like cowboys from the Westerns, the bad 'uns who needed time to think, and stubbed their cigarettes out like gangsters with a job to pull. It looked business-like, serious, they looked like they were not to be messed with, time to leave. All our parents smoked but they looked different when they smoked. We were recreating smoking for ourselves, the way every generation does, with new role models, and fashions, and all sorts of symbolic signalling of, and for, the moment. Our little gang looked cool smoking, or that's what most of them thought, our parents just looked sad, gasping at theirs.

I sat years later with Duck in a dark bar in Belfast in the middle of the day. He was still smoking, of course. We talked about old times and our boyhood scrapes. Duck was shaking with laughter as he told one story, until his fag ash dropped on the table. He saw me watching the drooping ash fall almost hesitantly to the smeared table top. 'You still not smoke?' he asked. 'You don't know what you're missing. It's one of life's little pleasures that they can't take away from us.' And he lit another one, almost immediately, with a shiny gold lighter. He saw me admiring it; at least that's how he read my look. 'Only the best, these days,' he said. 'Still the fella in the big picture,' I offered. 'Still the fella in the big picture,' he replied, and he drew the smoke deep into his lungs and held it there, as if it might never come out. He was saying to me that I am the man in control. However, I never ever agreed. And then he blew it my way, until I gave a brief and embarrassed cough.

Of course, Duck is dead now. We talk about lifestyle choices and Duck made his, but Ernest Dichter helped direct these choices. In order to promote smoking in Duck, or my mother, or Aunt Agnes, Dr Dichter says that we have to recognise the psychological needs associated with smoking and what smoking provides us with in our everyday lives, be it in uptown Manhattan or in the less salubrious surroundings of a politically divided city in Northern Ireland. At the same time, Dichter argued, we have to deal with the essential psychological conflict that smoking generates. He wrote 'One of the main jobs of the advertiser in this conflict between pleasure and guilt is not so much to sell the product as to give moral permission to have fun without guilt.' There were clearly echoes of selling the Chrysler Plymouth to the wives of the car buyers here. Learning to smoke in childhood or in the teenage years is always going to be associated with a degree of guilt, no matter how defiantly it is initially carried out. The guilt associated with smoking was compounded by the fact that certainly by the 1950s there was growing evidence that smoking was indeed very harmful (although Dichter is cynically dismissive of the accumulating evidence – 'Scientific and medical studies on the physiological effects of smoking provide a confused picture: Some conclude that smoking is harmful; others deny it. This same confusion prevails among smokers themselves'). Cigarette companies were trying to use the message that they would not kill you as part of their pitch. This was often done by having doctors (and dentists interestingly enough) recommend particular brands as being 'healthier'. Dichter thought that this was fundamentally misguided. It was unconsciously associating cigarette smoking with increased mortality, the 'not' was not necessarily the critical element in how such messages were interpreted by the public. Dichter concluded that smoking offers 'a psychological satisfaction sufficient to overcome health fears, to withstand moral censure, ridicule, or even the paradoxical weakness of "enslavement to habit"'. Ads now focussed on powerful men relaxing with a cigarette as a reward for their efforts. Sometimes these busy, powerful men with their feet up were doctors. However, this was not a doctor trying to reassure you that the cigarettes would not kill you; this was 'one of the busiest men in town … on call 24 hours a day', 'a scientist, a diplomat, and a friendly sympathetic human being all in one', taking a hard-earned rest and smoking for pleasure. These ads had everything; they broke the associative connection between smoking and health/ill health/mortality/death highlighted in the previous ads involving doctors, by using the doctor merely as a reassuring role model, and an exemplar of the class of busy, successful men who deserve a break. In addition, the doctor is described as a 'scientist' no less (how many times have you heard a run-of-the-mill GP described as a scientist?). A scientist who was presumably capable of evaluating the accumulating evidence and then making a conscious, reflective choice to smoke Camels ('More Doctors smoke Camels than any other cigarette'). Interestingly, the capital 'M' in 'More' and the capital 'D' in 'Doctors' are in red (thus 'M.D.'), to use a perceptual grouping cue, to pull the letters 'M' and 'D' together, and to make them stand out from their background. In other words, we are talking here about medical doctors – real doctors rather than Ph.D.'s or (even worse) quacks – proper medical doctors. These were powerful and effective ads in terms of their effects, that is to say their sales figures.

However, Dichter did something else in his work on the psychology of smoking and the effective marketing of cigarettes that has rarely been commented on. He laid down a marker for future attempts to defend smoking and the promotion of smoking by suggesting that any evidence for a statistical relationship between smoking and ill health could very well be an artefact of something else. He wrote

> Efforts to reduce the amount of smoking signify a willingness to sacrifice pleasure in order to assuage … feelings of guilt. The mind has a powerful influence on the body, and may produce symptoms of physical illness. Guilt feelings may cause harmful physical effects not at all caused by the cigarettes used, which may be extremely mild. Such guilt feelings alone may be the real cause of the injurious consequences.

(Dichter 1960)

In other words, it is not smoking that gives you the cancer; it is the guilt that you have about smoking (and this guilt originally derives from your parents attempting to censure this form of behaviour in their offspring, even when they themselves smoked). Don't blame cigarettes for your ill health; blame your parents! However, bear in mind that he had also said that the role of the advertiser was 'not so much to sell the product as to give moral permission to have fun without guilt'. He was going to help us have fun without guilt and, therefore, reduce the physical harm of smoking. He must have known this was a load of baloney even then.

The 'conflicted' scientific evidence and the funding for the work

I do find it incredible that in the 1960s and 1970s ordinary people were not more alarmed by smoking. How could many ordinary people not see the dangers it posed? Perhaps it was because they were confused by the scientific evidence. Apparently, not every scientist agreed with the research findings on the link between smoking and lung cancer, or so it seemed. I remember hearing Hans Eysenck, perhaps Britain's best known post-war psychologist, in the mid-1990s, say (even then!) that the apparent statistical link between smoking and lung cancer was really just an artefact of personality. He argued that certain personalities were prone to lung cancer and certain personalities were prone to cancer and it was this underlying personality dimension that was the significant factor here. It was not smoking that gave you lung cancer; it was your genetically determined personality which gave you lung cancer. In other words, he was arguing that the scientific research was confounded; it was, in effect, fatally flawed. Moreover, Eysenck had been doing this work since the 1960s. So what chance did my mother or my Aunt Agnes, who left school at 14, have? Eysenck was publicly disputing the scientific evidence linking smoking and lung cancer, successfully turning the issue into a 'debate' between scientific experts. Smokers could cling onto this 'uncertainty' to rationalise their own behaviour.

In 2011, Pettigrew and Lee carried out an extensive review of recently released tobacco industry documents (released, it has to be said, because of litigation) that reveal a great deal about how the industry fought back against the growing scientific evidence on the relationship between smoking and lung cancer. The tobacco industry wanted to open up a great 'debate' about the effects of smoking on health, to suggest that the medical evidence was far from conclusive, to show that there were differences of opinion amongst experts on this topic. The tobacco industry created the Council for Tobacco Research (CTR) in 1953 to fund research that could be used in this fight. One recipient of this funding was the distinguished scientist Hans Selye, the so-called 'father of stress', who had extremely impressive academic credentials with 1,700 articles and 39 books to his name (and apparently nominated for the Nobel Prize ten times). Pettigrew and Lee discovered that it was Selye who first contacted the tobacco industry (rather than vice versa) as far back as 1958, seeking funding for his research on stress. This first request was not successful. However, the following year a law firm representing the tobacco industry now involved in litigation, wrote to Selye offering him US$1,000 to write a memorandum demonstrating that 'medicine has previously seen striking correlations suggested as representing cause and effect, only later to find that the significance, if any, of the correlation was otherwise' (Pettigrew and Lee 2011: 412). Selye agreed to do this for the money offered, but only on the understanding that any quote used would not be attributed to him; neither did he want to appear as a witness in any court case. This, as they say, was just the start of a very long and rewarding relationship. Given his academic credentials, he was of enormous value to them. He was after all an objective scientist, or at least that's how it would have seemed to the public if they did not know about his financial connection with the industry. Selye advised the tobacco industry that it should defend itself by focussing on the 'prophylactic and curative' aspect of smoking. Smoking was to be marketed as a way of adjusting to a stressful lifestyle. Selye was prepared to argue that it is stress that kills rather than smoking. Smoking, he suggested, can actually help you cope with this stress; it was in fact beneficial. In 1969, Selye, according to Pettigrew and Lee, 'testified before the Canadian House of Commons Health Committee arguing against antismoking legislation, opposing advertising restrictions, health warnings, and restrictions on tar and nicotine' (2011: 413). He was now being funded to the tune of US$100,000 a year, back in the 1960s (about three-quarters of a million dollars in today's money). He appeared on the Canadian Broadcasting Corporation arguing for the benefits of smoking for those under stress. Smoking, he argued, was a 'diversion' to avoid disease-causing stress. Oddly, he failed to mention this conflict of interest in the broadcast; he failed to point out that the tobacco industry was paying him as a spokesperson.

In the UK in the meantime, Hans Eysenck was playing a similar role in this 'debate' about the harmful effects of smoking. He was another very high profile and influential academic (indeed it was one of Eysenck's books that got me interested in psychology in the first place) who publicly disputed the link between smoking and health. Like Selye he was also secretly receiving money from the tobacco industry, from the 1960s onwards. There are those, of course, who argue that this money from the tobacco industry was just research funding, and that scientists like Eysenck have to find funding for their research from wherever they can. They argue that such funding need not necessarily hinder the scientific objectivity of the researcher. If you believe this, then it is perhaps worth taking the time to reread Eysenck's first book on this topic, *Smoking, Health and Personality*, first published in 1965, which was a significant year for tobacco in the UK in many ways. The *Report on Smoking and Health* had been published by the Royal College of Physicians in England in 1962 and this had warned of the close connection between lung cancer and smoking. The findings of this report were widely publicised in the press. These were now clearly critical times for the tobacco industry. Eysenck aimed to show that the results of all of this medical research were 'by no means immune to challenge'. At one level, this is perfectly reasonable. It is the duty of scientists to challenge the established orthodoxy, to present alternative hypotheses, to question and probe. But I cannot read this book and feel that I am just witnessing an inquiring scientific mind in action. There is just something about the tone and the nature of the arguments that he presents that makes me extremely uneasy, and not just with the benefit of hindsight. This book goes way beyond reporting a psychological theory that could have implications for the research on smoking and health, it does much more than that in, what seems to me, a cynical and calculated manner. It is not like any psychology book that I have ever read.

Eysenck's hypothesis was that there are certain types of personality that are prone to cancer and that there are certain types of personality inclined to smoke. He argued that it was personality that was the critical and confounded factor in cancer risk (Dichter, of course, had said that it was 'guilt' that was the confounded factor, Selye said it was 'stress'; clearly money bought a lot of possible unaccounted for factors). Eysenck proposed that certain types of personality, namely extroverts, are drawn to nicotine because it is a stimulant and therefore has introverting effects – in other words, extroverts smoke for good 'genetically-determined' reasons. Of course, extroverts differ in many other ways as well to introverts; for example, they have a

> preference for coffee and alcohol, for spicy foods, for premarital and extramarital intercourse, their impulsive and risk taking behaviour – all these can easily be deduced from this general hypothesis. We may similarly deduce from it that extraverts would be more likely to seek for the stimulation afforded by cigarette smoking, and it is on this basis that the original hypothesis was formulated.

> (Eysenck 1966: 75)

So already, you have the idea that many smokers may differ in a number of significant ways from non-smokers and that any differences in health, like cancer risk, may not be attributable to the act of smoking per se.

Then, Eysenck quotes the conclusions of Doll, who he describes as 'one of the scientists most prominently associated with the promulgation of the theory that smoking causes cancer' as saying

> When the nature of the disease makes it impossible to carry out logically conclusive experiments there is always room for honest difference of opinion. In the case of smoking it is

particularly hard to envisage how a conclusive experiment could be carried out and no such experiments have been made.

(Eysenck 1966: 12)

Eysenck then adds 'Doll goes on to quote a famous saying of Claude Bernard, to the effect that "There are no false theories and true theories, but only fertile theories and sterile theories"' (Eysenck 1966: 12).

Eysenck here does a number of things more or less at the same time. He suggests that in the case of lung cancer, conclusive experiments cannot really be carried out and therefore 'there is always room for honest difference of opinion'. In other words, what he is about to present in the rest of the book is just an 'honest difference of opinion' but, in addition to this, he also rejects the idea that theories can either be true or false, instead he tries to replace this with the distinction between 'fertile' or 'sterile' theories. It is not that some theories are right and some are wrong, he is saying, it is just that some are more 'fertile' than others are, and what he is going to outline is a particularly new and fertile theory. In other words, he is really undermining the reader's confidence in their ability to know whether a theory is right or wrong, by suggesting that this neat distinction does not actually apply to scientific theories. Theories about smoking and cancer are not right or wrong, they are something else altogether!

He then goes on to undermine the connection between lung cancer and smoking by pointing out that in the past, smoking was blamed for a whole series of other ailments as well. He writes

Among the ailments blamed upon smoking were lunacy, cerebral haemorrhage, paralysis, delirium tremens, laryngitis, bronchitis, dyspnoea, tuberculosis, dyspepsia, gastritis, intestinal rupture, heartburn, hepatic lesions, diarrhoea, flatulence, impotence, baldness, typhoid, skin diseases and many others. The children of smokers were supposed to suffer from hypochrondriasis, hysteria and insanity.

(Eysenck 1966: 16)

He adds that these accusations were based 'on no scientific evidence of any kind'. What he is saying here is that smoking has been blamed for a whole series of things, which, with the benefit of time and hindsight, turn out to be quite ridiculous. He is implying that the same thing might be true of lung cancer and smoking. What specific effect might this have on the reader? Well, nobody wants to look ridiculous (at least nobody I have ever met), so perhaps it is better not to jump to any conclusions about the connections between smoking and lung cancer or you might be in the same boat as those that have concluded that there is also a relationship between smoking and flatulence.

Eysenck then reviews the epidemiological evidence of the relationship between the risk of contracting lung cancer as related to the average amount of tobacco smoked and the evidence seems to suggest from research published in 1961 that there is a strong correlation between smoking and Group 1 lung tumours, which are 'made up of epidermoid carcinomas, and small cell anaplastic carcinomas', but no relationship between smoking and Group 2 lung tumours. Group 2 tumours 'are made up of adenocarcinomas and bronchial or alveolar cell types'. Again he deliberately tries to undermine the reader's confidence by saying that 'lung cancer clearly is not just one undifferentiated entity; we are dealing with presumably at least two and possibly more quite different types of disease and each of these different types has different relations to smoking' (Eysenck 1966: 20). But his next attack is even more extraordinary. He says that 'the problem with correlating risk with smoking is that there are many different variables associated with the act of smoking which impact on the precise chemical composition of the smoke'. Thus,

> Some of these variables are the intensity of the suction applied, the length of the pull, the length of intervals between pulls, and the particular part of the cigarette which is being smoked, i.e. whether it is the first inch or the last inch of the cigarette. Thus what we in fact inhale depends very much on the way in which we smoke a cigarette, and it is quite impossible to generalize in any sensible way without knowing more about these different variables we have enumerated.
>
> (Eysenck 1966: 20–21)

Therefore, what he is suggesting is that there are potentially important factors connected to the act of smoking itself, which researchers have not controlled, and that this problem underpins all of the science relating smoking and lung cancer. Thus, he writes

> We can ask people how many cigarettes they smoke and we may even get a fairly truthful answer. However, we cannot ask them just how they smoke these cigarettes because they themselves would be unable to give us a reasonable answer, and we cannot find out by observing them either because the very act of observation would make them change their pattern of behaviour. Under these circumstances all statistics relating to smoking must be regarded with considerable caution.
>
> (Eysenck 1966: 23)

In other words, here, he is saying that any statistical data, which shows a relationship between risk and lung cancer, is faulty because we cannot, with any certainty, isolate what the critical variable is. It is not necessarily the number of cigarettes you smoke, it is the way you smoke them, and this lets every heavy smoker, with their own signature style of smoking, off the hook.

Another chapter is called 'Giving up Smoking?' Eysenck poses the question

> Is it rational for him [the typical smoker] to give up smoking or continue to do so? If he continues smoking heavily then he runs the risk of having at the end of 75 a shorter life than a non-smoker by roughly 1.4 years. He might reasonably reply that there are so many hazards involved in life in any case that this relatively short period of longer life, problematical as it is, would certainly not compensate him for the lack of pleasure that would be involved in giving up smoking. Is this a rational or an irrational attitude? … Certainly many people when questioned give some such answer in explanation of why they don't give up smoking; the immediate loss of pleasure and satisfaction is not compensated for by the problematical

increase of a year or two in their life span at the age of 70 or above.

(Eysenck 1966: 111–112)

He is saying explicitly that it is not irrational to continue smoking even if smoking were found to increase one's mortality.

His final chapter is entitled 'Where There's Smoke There's Fire', where he argues

The evidence also suggests, however, that atmospheric pollution is probably an even more important factor, and that it would be unwise to concentrate all available research efforts and legislative measures on smoking. It is psychologically much easier to cause people to give up those habits which lead to atmospheric pollution than to give up smoking, and if our aim is the lessening of the terrible toll which lung cancer takes of life nowadays this avenue seems to be the more promising to take.

(Eysenck 1966: 116)

Put your efforts elsewhere, he is saying; leave those nice tobacco companies alone.

However, we now know that Eysenck received more than £800,000 through a secret United States tobacco fund called Special Account Number 4 (*Independent*, 31 October 1996). Eysenck was, of course, not alone in secretly taking this money, as we have already seen.

Oreskes and Conway in their excellent 2010 book *Merchants of Doubt* describe how on 15 December 1953, the presidents of four of America's largest tobacco companies – American Tobacco, Benson and Hedges, Philip Morris and U.S. Tobacco – had met with John Hill, CEO of the public relations firm Hill and Knowlton, at the Plaza Hotel in New York. Their aim was to challenge the scientific evidence that smoking could kill you. In the words of the authors:

They would work together to convince the public that there was 'no sound scientific basis for the charges,' and that the recent reports [about cigarette tar and cancer] were simply 'sensational accusations' made by publicity-seeking scientists hoping to attract more funds for their research. They would not sit idly by while their product was vilified; instead, they would create a Tobacco Industry Committee for Public Information to supply a 'positive' and 'entirely pro-cigarette' message to counter the anti-cigarette one. As the U.S. department of Justice would later put it, they decided, 'to deceive the American public about the health effects of smoking'. At first, the companies did not think they needed to fund new scientific research, thinking it would be sufficient to 'disseminate information on hand.' John Hill disagreed, 'emphatically warn[ing] ... that they should ... sponsor additional research,' and that this would be a long-term project. He also suggested including the word 'research' in the title of their new committee, because a pro-cigarette message would need science to back it up. At the end of the day, Hill concluded, 'scientific doubts must remain'.

Eysenck is not mentioned in the book on those who marketed doubt for a living. But his work, along with Selye and many others, contributed greatly to the uncertainty about smoking and cancer, and again in the words of Oreskes and Conway, 'throughout the 1950s and well into the 1960s, newspapers and magazines presented the smoking issue as a great debate rather than as a scientific problem in which evidence was rapidly accumulating'. My Aunt Agnes liked to read about the debate in the papers and perhaps it was all hypothetical anyway for her. The statistics on those who worked in the carding room suggested that starting with the age of 75 and deducting a few years was always going to be unlikely in the first place. 'Did you know?' she said one day, 'scientists used to think that smoking gave you wind. I think that's bloody stupid. It's the opposite if anything. It's always the non-smokers who are the worst in the wind department.'

Then there was all that pleasure and satisfaction from smoking. 'The only pleasure we get around here,' in my mother's words. I can recall old cigarette ads from my childhood with a mixture of nostalgia and revulsion – these are fragments of memories of my childhood. I research some others from that time. I watch cigarettes square dancing, healthy, vigorous and perhaps most importantly, connected. The cigarettes are the people in this American advert and they are all moving as one. 'Are you feeling alone, isolated?' the implicit message in the ad says, 'Have a cigarette and you will connect.'

I'm now sitting on a beach in Santa Barbara in California and watch one good-looking blonde Scandinavian teenager, perhaps eighteen or nineteen, approach two Californian girls of approximately the same age, lying there on the beach in pink bikinis. He asks them for a light and he bends down as they pull a lighter out of their beach bag and light his cigarette, and they make a connection instantly and effortlessly. How else could he have achieved this? What else could he have said or asked for? 'Have you got a map? Do you have a compass? Do you have a water bottle? Do you have a syringe? Have you got some after sun?' None of it would have worked. However, there was always the slick and easy 'have you got a light?'

I have on that beach in front of me a classic Marlboro ad from the 1970s (reproduced and analysed in Bullock 2004). The ad features a cowboy on horseback rounding up some stray horses. There are a number of outlines of horses; some can be clearly seen. However, when you look closely Bullock argues, things are not what they might at first appear. The horse he is trying to round up is very feminine in a human sort of way, with distinctive female features, soft and yielding. However, the horses in the background of the advert are the most significant. I trace their outlines carefully and I realise that they are not horses at all, but wolves, wolves that have been embedded in the scene. You need to look carefully to see them. Psychologists have studied these sorts of ambiguous visual stimuli for years, and this is one such visual illusion, there are really two figures in one. The idea is that these ambiguous figures are open to different interpretations but only one can be in consciousness at any one time. We normally see the figures as horses but really they have the outline of the wolf, and our unconscious mind can pick this up. Nevertheless, these hidden interpretations can impact on the brain. The wolves in the background remind you implicitly and unconsciously of loneliness (the lone wolf) and induce a degree of despair (after all the wolves are bearing down on you), but not enough for you to consciously notice. How do you reconnect with other human beings and how do you cope with the anxiety that is being induced at that point in time? That in a sense is the material essence of the ad and a cigarette is the solution to both problems. A cigarette will allow you to connect with others who signify their identity through smoking and a cigarette will allow you to use a form of infantile behaviour, like sticking something in your mouth, like a teat, or a thumb to calm your nerves, but all in a socially acceptable way to deal with the anxiety.

We all know that smoking is inherently unhealthy; they are coffin nails, Duck was right back then, even if he said it as a joke, so why did he and all the others smoke? Was is partly because they still had a little seed of doubt at the back of their minds about how dangerous cigarettes really are, a seed planted by the tobacco firms working in conjunction with credible scientists, who were on commission and somehow failed to declare this extraordinary conflict of interest to the public. However, there might be more to it than this. Ernest Dichter saw to that. Smoking, it seems, is, as much as anything else, driven by our great fear of being alone, a great fear deliberately induced and manipulated by insightful psychologists from the private psychology labs in the US all those decades ago. Cigarettes were marketed to help us connect ('You're never alone with a Strand'), partly building upon that great unconscious symbolism of the connecting influence of fire and partly on the sharing of fire, pleasure and the relief of tension. Cigarettes may indeed help us connect, but not in a good way.

I think back to my Aunt Agnes, in the mill and their smoke breaks, away from the dust of the carding room and the machines where the factory girls could chat in relative quiet, and reconnect and clean their lungs with menthol cigarettes when they could afford them. They could feel that they would never be alone with a Strand, or even a Park Drive or an Embassy, and they weren't. My Aunt Agnes was in her early sixties when she died and many of the girls from the carding room died at that sort of age. But, at least, they were all together, united, the carding room girls, the big smokers, great friends, my mother always liked to say and that is one way of looking at it. However, it is not my way.

The ad men who had some special insights brought the unconscious mind into focus; and then targeted and manipulated this unconscious mind relentlessly in pursuit of profit. It was a direct attack on the unconscious mind (whilst it was still out of favour in academic psychology), and like any conflict, one side eventually won, and, of course, it was not the side of the ordinary man and woman who emerged unscathed. They fell for it back then, and they still do; and to me that is an awful tragedy.

Chapter summary

- Ernest Dichter applied psychoanalytic methods to the marketing of cigarettes.
- He was not afraid to consider and target the unconscious mind.
- Dichter argued that you need to see below the surface, and *access* the unconscious both to cure neurosis and to *manipulate* the unconscious to sell brands.
- He suggested that if you want to understand how people think and feel about products, you cannot just ask them directly – psychoanalysts would never do that, it would be ludicrous ('please tell me about your neurosis'); you need more indirect and more intense methods.
- You need the psychoanalyst's couch, but on an industrial scale.
- You do not take what they say at face value, you need to understand instead the symbolic importance of products in people's lives, and you need to interpret what they say.
- You need to look out for defence mechanisms and projection.
- Dichter wrote that 'a number of human motivations are irrational, unconscious, unknown to the people themselves. This principle means that most human actions have deeper motivations than those which appear on the surface, motivations which can be uncovered if the right approach is used.'

- He argued that, from a psychological point of view, cigarettes work in a number of distinct ways – they allow you to behave like a child again, able to 'follow your whims'.
- They also offer a 'legitimate excuse for interrupting work and snatching a moment of pleasure'. Like children, we crave rewards – 'a cigarette is a reward that we can give ourselves as often as we wish'.
- Dichter argued that this insight of self-reward should be used as the basis for a marketing campaign.
- However, that was only part of his observations about the nature of smoking. Some of his respondents had also commented that with cigarettes, you never really feel alone.
- This was tapping into the primitive concept of fire, a warm glow, a conditioned stimulus rooted in our evolutionary past associated with the group assembling around the fire. One of Dichter's respondents said when I 'see the glow in the dark, I am not alone any more ...' and Dichter added that the use of cigarettes to combat feelings of loneliness and isolation was critical.
- Dichter wrote that 'the companionable character of cigarettes is also reflected in the fact that they help us make friends'.
- This insight formed the basis of a number of marketing campaigns.
- He also recognised the oral pleasure that derives from smoking, 'as fundamental as sexuality and hunger'.
- Smoking is about oral gratification, as infantile in the context of Freudian theory as sucking your thumb.
- Smoking is a socially acceptable way of obtaining this oral gratification by simultaneously sending out a powerful message about virile maturity and potency.
- Smoking is *so* powerful because it simultaneously satisfies infantile desires and yet symbolically sends out a very adult signal.

- Dichter argued that we have to deal with the essential psychological conflict that smoking generates.
- He wrote 'One of the main jobs of the advertiser in this conflict between pleasure and guilt is not so much to sell the product as to give moral permission to have fun without guilt.'
- He also argued that it is not smoking that gives you cancer; it is the guilt that some people have about smoking that causes cancer. This is clearly false.
- Dichter implied that if you can actually smoke guilt-free ('fun without guilt') then you will be fine.
- This was part of a widespread and systematic effort by the tobacco firms to generate doubt about the relationship between smoking and cancer.
- On 15 December 1953, the presidents of four of America's largest tobacco companies met with the CEO of a public relations firm to plan their challenge to the scientific evidence that smoking could kill you.
- Their goal was to convince the public that there was 'no sound scientific basis for the charges', and that the recent reports [about cigarette tar and cancer] were simply 'sensational accusations' made by publicity-seeking scientists.
- Hans Eysenck, one of Britain's foremost psychologists, suggested that the link between smoking and cancer was really an artefact of personality – certain types of personality are prone to stress and smoking, and also prone to cancer.
- Eysenck received more than £800,000 for this research through a secret United States tobacco industry fund called Special Account Number 4.
- Many people, including members of my family and my friends, bought into the glamour of smoking, and were reassured by those esteemed scientists, these 'merchants of doubt' in Conway and Oreskes' words.
- Many of them died through smoking-related diseases.

4

CONFLICTED COGNITIONS

It was 1993; it was an important year for the man and the boy in the room. The odd couple. They were standing in his parlour in front of a pair of scales. A grey-haired man in his fifties stripped to his underpants and a small, slight Arab boy. On one side of the room was a large bookcase. There were a lot of books on Irish history. Black covers with the green of the shamrock. Serious reading. It could be the parlour of a minor academic or a priest. On the other wall was a large framed photograph of Herol Graham, the Graham of years ago, the Graham of eternal optimism and promise, the most famous boxer from Sheffield who would take on all comers with one hand behind his back, the man who nearly became the champion of the world. Nearly. The grey-haired man got on the scales first. 'Twelve stone dead. Now it's your turn, and don't forget I've been warning ye.' His Irish brogue was as thick as buttermilk. The small Arab boy stepped forward in a mock swagger. 'It'll be all right, Brendan, don't worry.' His was a cocky Sheffield accent. 'I'm young, fit. I *am* the business.'

Brendan Ingle averted his gaze from the scales just for a moment. He felt that he needed to explain. 'The problem with Naz or Prince Naseem Hamed, as he's known in the ring, is that he knows he's good. At that age it's bound to go to your head. He loves himself and why not? I've had the lad since he was seven; he's nineteen now. His father is from the Yemen. I was passing on this bus up the road here, and the bus stops outside a school. It's three o'clock and the school is just getting out. There's this little kid who I thought was a Pakistani pinned up against these railings fighting these three white kids off. All three of them are kicking and punching at him. My first thought was that life doesn't change. I can remember getting into scraps in Dublin when I was a kid. Sure, they always had some reason to pick on you for a fight –"You're not proper Irish – your grandfather's English." "What kind of a name is Ingle, for God's sake?" They could always find something. And if it wasn't that, it would be "You think you're great because your brothers are boxers." I was from a big family – I had ten brothers and four sisters. But I was impressed with this young Pakistani kid. I can spot talent a mile off. I'll go anywhere where there's a fight. I'll get me distance and I'll watch. I won't get involved but I'll watch them. I've always been interested in what goes off in confrontations between people whether they're arguments or fisticuffs. I'm interested in human nature, and that's what you see when people fight and argue. I like to see what starts trouble and how it goes on. I like to watch who's involved, who makes themselves busy, who's the matchmaker, and who's stirring the whole thing up. I watch and I learn. I could see this young Pakistani kid had talent. I ran home and told my wife Alma. I was right, as well. Naz has won seven British titles, and he's boxed for England as an amateur. Now he's a professional but even as a newcomer he's earning good money. But it's still only the start, now it's all about self-discipline.'

Naz climbed onto the scales

'These scales never lie, Naz, remember that … Eight stone nine. What did I tell ye? What did I say? You were boasting about all the crap you'd eaten yesterday. Fish fingers and chips. Well, this is what you get. You're three pounds over the weight. I've said to you time and time again – you're eating all wrong and you're sleeping wrong. You're up far too late playing snooker.'

'But, Brendan, I'm beating everybody. I'm knocking them all out. You know how good I am.'

'You may be the greatest thing since sliced bread, but this is your come-uppance. Three pounds overweight two days before a big fight can be hard for any fighter to shift let alone a bantamweight. You've got less than two days. This will be a test of what you're made of outside the ring.'

'I always knew that young Naz would fail to make the weight someday,' said Brendan, exactly one month later. 'That lad could eat for England. I didn't allow him to eat anything for the remainder of the Monday or on the Tuesday morning. At lunchtime on the Tuesday I weighed myself again – I was twelve stone again. I explained to Naz that by the time we got down to London, with the stress and strain of me driving all the way, I'd have lost two pounds. It wouldn't be so easy for him. We were staying in a flat above the Thomas a Becket gym. I'd brought my scales with me. When we got to London my weight was down to 11 stone 12 pounds, exactly as I'd predicted. Naz had lost a pound, but he still had two extra pounds to shift. Naz's room was cold. I took the blow heater out of my room to give to him. I also switched on the sunbed in the corner of his room. It's my job to see he's as comfortable as possible before a big fight. I explained to him that he'd lose nearly one pound sleeping. We were both starving. I hadn't had anything to eat or drink all that day either. It's no good me trying to motivate or inspire somebody else if they're trying to make the weight and I'm eating.

'It was a rough night. The bed was damp and somebody down below was playing some old Beatles records. By the next morning I was down to nearly 11 stone 11 pounds, I'd lost almost another pound. Now I was counting in ounces. I went to the toilet and I was now only six ounces over the weight I'd set myself – I had to lose three pounds just like Naz. Naz was less than a pound over the weight. So I went to the toilet again. Naz accused me of having something to drink. He said that I must have sneaked a drink. I kept going to the toilet and my weight kept dropping. Naz couldn't believe that I was going all this time without having something to drink. But the proof was in the scales. He could see the ounces coming off. He knew I wasn't cheating, and that he and I were going through this thing together. But every time I went to the toilet I had to reassure him by stepping on the scales again to show that the weight was coming off, and that I wasn't sneaking a drink. We were watching each other like frigging hawks. I took him for a walk and by the time we got to the weigh-in he was half a pound under the weight. He hadn't had anything to eat or drink since the Monday, that's thirty-six hours without anything. I took him to a restaurant after the weigh-in, but he couldn't finish his soup or his spaghetti. His stomach had shrunk. But he felt good. I told him that day that he'd grown in my estimation. Naz has this little routine when he gets into the ring. He jumps over the ropes, just like Chris Eubank, but then he does a flip holding on to the ropes and then three flips across the ring. He's a bit of a showman. But I told him that night that I just wanted one flip from him, then he was going straight to work. I told him that he was going to mentally and physically destroy his opponent. Incidentally, his opponent was unbeaten before that night. Naz had him down three times in the first round. He knocked him out in the second. I told him afterwards that there is nothing to stop him becoming world champion. "Who's going to stop you now?" says I. "Nobody," says he. "Right," says I.'

Talk the talk; walk the walk

Brendan's got a certain way with the boys. He must have. They come from all over Yorkshire to train and spar in his gym in Wincobank, although most, it must be said, come from the streets round about. This small gym had by then produced four British or European champions, and almost a world champion in Herol Graham. Now Johnny Nelson had gone the whole way (or part of the way depending upon who you listened to, because most fight fans seemed to regard his recent acquisition as a bit of a Mickey Mouse title), and taken the WBF world cruiserweight title from Dave Russell in Melbourne. The title was not recognised by the British Boxing Board of Control. It's the Irish blarney, they were all saying. 'The blarney did all that?' I asked incredulously.

Matthew was twelve, with a round, open face. Brendan was perched on some wooden steps by the side of the ring. He called Matthew over. 'How long have you been coming to the gym?' 'Three years,' said Matthew. 'Tell Geoffrey what it was like before you came to the gym.' 'It was terrible, I had no friends and I was being bullied all the time at school.' 'Tell him what it's like now,' said Brendan. 'It's great. I've got lots of friends, and I'm not bullied now.' Brendan squeezed his arm tighter. 'This lad here can't fight. He'll never be able to fight. I'll teach him to dodge a bit in the ring. I'll teach him to mess his opponent around, to make the other feller look bad. I'll build up his confidence. I taught him that if anybody comes up to him on the street and starts to bully him, that he should just shout "Piss off," and run away. I'm teaching him personal and social skills for life. My job is to get these lads through life as safely as possible, both inside and outside the ring.

'It can be rough around here. I was the one to bring the first blacks into this area to my gym. So the National Front put posters all over my house and scrawled their name on the walls of the garages outside the gym. You can still see their graffiti to this day. But they've gone and I've survived, and that's what it's all about. I knew this guy who was big in the National Front, and he ended up marrying a black girl. So it was all a load of bloody bollocks anyway.'

In the ring above us there were five boxers. Two were black. One was a powerfully built novice boxer, the other was Johnny Nelson. Two were small white boys, probably no more than ten, the fifth was a serious-looking Asian youth, dressed in a black polo and black tracksuit bottoms, who stalked his opponent before unleashing incredibly ineffectual-looking punches. They took turns at the sparring with each other, with one always left out. Johnny Nelson with the muscled black novice, then Johnny with one of the boys. 'Only body shots up there. I won't stand for any boxer in this type of sparring giving his opponent one accidentally on purpose like to the head,' said Brendan. '*Time!*' he shouted, and all five boxers walked slowly around the ring in an anti-clockwise direction. 'In my gym the professionals train with the novices. They can all learn something from each other. Bomber Graham used to stand in the middle of this ring and the lads would try to land a punch on him. They never could. *Change over!*' The boxers touched gloves gently, as if they were in some barn dance, and started again with a different partner.

A sixteen-year-old stood by the ring bandaging his hands. Brendan called him over. 'How old were you, Ryan, when you came to the gym for the first time?'

'Six.'

'What did I say to you?'

'Do you know any swear words?'

'So I got him to tell me every swear word he knew: "fuck", "bastard", "wanker", the lot. So says I to him, "From now on you don't swear when you're in this gym and you do as you're told." It took him by surprise, you see. Then says I to him, "What do they say about the Irish where you come from?" And he says, "They're all tick bastards." But this tick bastard says that this lad will be winning a gold at the Olympics in three years. When the English shout "Fuck off, you tick Irish Mick," at me, I just remind them that they were riding around on dirt tracks before the Irish came over.'

He pulled out a book that he has been carrying around in the pocket of his anorak to show me. It has pages of nineteenth-century political cartoons on the Irish problem. 'This shows you what the English thought of the Irish. The Irishman was always portrayed as a wee monkey. Here's the Irish Guy Fawkes, a wee ugly monkey in a hat, sitting on top of a keg of gunpowder before setting light to it. The tick wee monkey bastard. But the Irish are too cunning for the English. I've had the British super-middleweight champion. When I was starting him off I called him Slugger O'Toole. The Irish are great boxing fans, so I reckoned that they'd turn out in force to see an Irish boxer with the name O'Toole. Slugger would come into the arena dressed in green, and it wasn't until he'd taken his dressing gown off that they would see that he was black. So they'd all be shouting, "He's not Irish!" and I'd say "What's the matter with you? Haven't you ever seen a black Irishman before?" And then when they asked me his real name, I'd reply, quite truthfully as it turns out, "Fidel Castro Smith." They'd not believe me anyway.'

Brendan pulled Ryan close to him.

'Who's the only person who's ever going to lick you?'

'Me, myself.'

'Who's responsible for you?'

'Me, myself.'

'Correct.'

This was the routine they had rehearsed many times. Ryan knew when to come in, and he knew all the unvarying responses. It was like the litany from a church service.

'Some people think it's easy to be a boxing trainer and manager. You just cream off your twenty-five per cent and the lads do all the work. But that's not how it is. I take these lads in when they're kids and I have to work on them. I have to build up their confidence. I have to teach them about life and replace all the crap they've learned. They come here and their heads are full of it.' He called over a somewhat shy-looking boy with a thin moustache and dull greyish shorts. His girlfriend had been sitting in the corner of the gym biting her nails all afternoon.

'What school did you come from, Matt?'

'Arbourthorne.'

'What kind of school is it?'

'Special needs.'

'What were you there for?'

'Because I was a thick bastard.'

'What are you now?'

'A clever bastard.'

The responses were instantaneous, starting almost before the question finished. He pulled Matt closer until their faces were almost touching.

'Who didn't you like when you first came here?'

'Pakis.'

'Pakis and blacks?' asked Brendan.

'No, just Pakis. I always thought that the blacks were all right.'

'Who don't you like now?'

'Nobody.'

'When that lad came here he had nothing going for him,' said Brendan. 'Now he's part of a team in here. There are a lot of Pakistanis in the team. He trains with champions. He'll be sparring with Johnny Nelson in a couple of minutes. I can identify with these lads. When I was a boy I had what you would call now "learning difficulties". Over in Ireland I was just a "tick bastard". I struggled with my spelling, my reading and everything else. I struggled with Latin and Gaelic. I can still say in Gaelic "What is your name?" "My name is Brendan Ingle." "Where do you live?" "Dublin City." "Do you have any money?" "No, I haven't." I can recite all these verses in Latin, but I've no idea what any of them mean. These verses were beaten into me. One of the nuns was a right bastard with her leather strap. I was beaten because I was tick. But this taught me a valuable lesson: you can't change people's attitude by mentally or physically abusing them. The only way that you can change people is by engaging in dialogue with them. Only dialogue.'

He shouted over to Matt. 'Who is the only person who can beat you?'

'Myself,' replied Matt across the crowded gym.

'My lads come to me with all their problems. I always say to them that if you haven't killed anybody, then you haven't got a real problem. I can sort everything else out.'

He turned to the boxers in the ring. 'Now lads, before you get down out of the ring, I want to see you one by one jump over the ropes.' Johnny Nelson did it with some flair, the rest struggled to get over. 'I let them jump off the second rope, if they can't manage it,' said Brendan. 'I do it to build their confidence in all aspects of life. Boxing isn't just about punching and how to slip a punch. It's about building confidence and learning to survive.' He shouted up to Matt, now sparring with Johnny Nelson. 'Matt, what do you say if some dirty pervert comes up to you in the street?'

'I shout "Fuck off!"'

'What do you do then?'

'I run like fuck.'

'I'm teaching them how to survive inside and outside the ring,' said Brendan, 'which isn't that bad for a tick Mick.'

Brendan Ingle used to call himself a professor of kidology, it wasn't just for my benefit, but he really was a maker of champions. Naz won the world title from Steve Robinson on the 30th of September 1995 at Cardiff Arms Park. According to John Ingle, Brendan's son and Naz's trainer, Naz won the fight at the weigh-in.

'It was like Muhammad Ali predicting that he was going to knock the bear, Sonny Liston, out in five rounds. Everybody used to laugh except the guy he was talking about. Naz got to Steve Robinson at the weigh-in. He was looking straight into his face and saying, "Steve, you're going to get beaten." It wasn't done in a nasty sort of way; it was just done in a matter of fact way. The cold stare of Naz can be quite intimidating. I could feel Steve Robinson crumbling inside as Naz was saying it. I said to Johnny Nelson, "Look at that, he's gone already."'

Naz was then twenty-one years old, and the champion of the world. Brendan Ingle had been training him in his run-down gym in St Thomas' Boys Club in Wincobank in Sheffield since he was seven. Of course, Naz had exceptional talent, but there was something else – there was that special bond between them, like father and son, and this intensive boxing training, and psychological training, over all of those years by the professor of kidology, someone who used his intuitive skills, shaped by years of experience, to mould the body and the mind of a champion, but with demonstrable world-class results. I witnessed significant sections of those years of preparation, as I hung about the gym, observing the comings and goings, sparring to fit in better (with Brendan concerned with my safety; 'Don't let Mick Mills use you as a punch bag,' he chided me). I watched Brendan planning it all, the road to the world championship, getting Naz to practice his entrance to the ring and that iconic and arrogant somersault over the ropes. The flip over the ropes was part of the routine that Brendan made all of his boxers practise in the ring (even those who would never have a professional fight). It was part of his confidence-building exercises. And it worked; I saw it happening before my very eyes over the months and years I spent in that dusty gym. All the boys knew that the fighter's entrance to the ring was a critical psychological moment.

I always recall David Remnick's description in his classic book *King of the World*, of how Floyd Patterson entered the ring in 1962 to defend his world heavyweight title against the challenger Sonny Liston:

He bent through the ropes and into the ring, but he did it stealthily, nervously, with quick glances all around, like a thief climbing in a window on the night he knows he will be arrested at last. He was in a terrible state. His eyes flicked around the ring. Rarely had fear been so visible on a fighter's face.

Liston won, of course; Floyd Patterson was knocked out in the first round.

Brendan always knew that the way a boxer entered the ring could leak a lot of information about his internal emotional state. The flip over the ropes was the greatest mask of them all. The fighter could be churning up inside and his opponent would never see it. As long as you got it right, and Brendan saw to that. It required concentration and hours of practice to carry it off. The practising of the entrance to the ring was as routine down in St Thomas' as sparring itself. Importantly, perhaps critically, the flip over the ropes distracted the fighter himself from what was going on inside.

I remember one afternoon in the gym watching Naz being taught a new, more eye-catching somersault. 'Get your arms straighter,' said Brendan, 'get a bit more spring into it.' Brendan had a great idea at the time that the Arab Prince should make an entrance on a flying carpet, courtesy of Paul Eyre's carpets, a firm which was big in South Yorkshire. Ali Baba comes to boxing. It was all being mapped out on a little scrap of paper on the dusty steps at the side of the ring. In the drawing, Naz was sitting cross-legged on the Paul Eyre carpet. Naz pointed at the drawing. 'Where's the fans, Brendan?' he asked.

'Oh, that's them down there,' said Brendan, shading the bottom of the page with the thick lead of the pencil. It was just a great black smudge. 'There's hundreds of them just waiting for "The Prince" to arrive.'

'Draw us a few more, Brendan,' said Naz.

And Brendan shaded a bit more of the paper: 'Is that enough for you? Or do you want a few more, you greedy beggar?' And they both laughed.

'How do I get down off the carpet?' enquired Naz nervously.

'Oh, we'll worry about that a bit closer to the time,' said Brendan. He folded up the bit of paper and put it in his pocket, and left Naz and me to talk some more.

Naz always recognised its importance. He said to me, 'Well, if somebody did it to me, I'd think, "Well, that is a confident man. I just hope he can back it up."'

But it was the verbal routines he used on all the lads that really stuck out. We heard him with Matt earlier:

'What kind of school is it?'

'Special needs.'

'What were you there for?'

'Because I was a thick bastard.'

'What are you now?'

'A clever bastard.'

Over and over, it went. Matt's responses built into a conversational routine, until it was his automatic response. 'What are you now?'… 'What are you now?'… The other boys would be told to gather around to listen to Matt's responses, Naz included. Then it would be the turn of another member of the group, then Naz's turn. These were the sounds of that gym with the high ceilings and the sharp acrid smells of sweat and testosterone, gloves slapping on hard bodies, the squeak of the wooden floorboards with fast, shuffling feet, boys standing upright, reciting liturgies about themselves, liturgies about their beliefs and their aspirations, as the others stood in a reverential silence. 'I am a clever bastard.' 'I won't let anybody bully me.' 'I will be the champion of the world.'

Brendan Ingle, with no formal education, and from the slums of Dublin, soaked in Roman Catholicism, understood the power of the word, and of the group, and the nature of group influence. He also understood the power of getting these lads to articulate these things – things that they did not actually believe about themselves ('clever', 'non-prejudiced', 'clever enough to survive on the street'), or their upcoming opponents ('nothing compared to me', 'a muppet', 'a nobody'), or their destinies ('world champion in the making', 'the new Naz', 'a millionaire with all the trimmings'), but they needed to say them, over and over again, so that one day they might actually believe them. Did Matt really believe that he was 'a clever bastard' at that time? Of course not. But, I watched him say it so many times, in front of his friends and training partners, that I sometimes wondered whether he may have started believing that he was, at least, 'a cleverer bastard', and certainly no longer 'the thick bastard' that had turned up lost and alone at that gym. But that's not quite the same thing, far from it.

Where did Brendan pick this up from? Perhaps, partly from his Roman Catholic upbringing. 'Forgive me, Father, for I have sinned', at the start of every confession, saying that you had sinned because that is what is required, even when you couldn't think of one. But if you say it enough times of your own free will (and who's actually forcing you) then you must have sinned. You start believing it, so you begin that search for your less apparent sins, sins of the heart, sins of omission, sins of impure thought. Brendan's Catholic background certainly found its way into the tone and automaticity of these verbal routines. But, of course, it was also partly from Cassius Clay, 'the Louisville Lip', ever since he had gone bear hunting in 1964 with his bus with the slogan 'CASSIUS CLAY ENTERPRISES. WORLD'S MOST COLORFUL FIGHTER' and 'SONNY LISTON WILL GO IN EIGHT'. He called his opponent Sonny Liston, the man who had knocked out Floyd Patterson in the first round, the 'big ugly bear'. He wrote poems about what would happen in the fight.

> Clay comes out to meet Liston
> And Liston starts to retreat
> If Liston goes back any further
> He'll end up in a ringside seat.
> Clay swings with a left,
> Clay swings with a right,
> Look at young Cassius carry the fight.

He predicted how long the fight would last. As Norman Mailer commented before the fight (see Kempton 1964), if Clay were to win the heavyweight crown, then 'every loudmouth on a street corner could swagger and be believed'. Being a loudmouth was no longer a good indication that you couldn't fight as well. Clay understood the power of language, in this case playing the fool in front of Sonny Liston. He said 'Liston thinks I'm a nut. He is scared of no man, but he is scared of a nut.' Ergo, Clay is saying, he is scared of me. Later, Clay admitted that he had only ever been truly afraid only once in his career, and that was in this first fight with Liston. 'That's the only time I was ever scared in the ring. Sonny Liston. First time. First round. Said he was gonna kill me.' Cassius Clay had found a way of dealing with his fear. Floyd Patterson, who talked freely about his fear, indeed more freely perhaps than any other boxer in the history of the sport, perhaps did not. Patterson articulated that fear:

> A prize-fighter who gets knocked out or is badly outclassed suffers in a way that he will never forget. He is beaten under the bright lights in front of thousands of witnesses who curse him and spit at him … The losing fighter loses more than just his pride and the fight; he loses part of his future. He is one step closer to the slum he came from.

When Cassius Clay became Muhammad Ali he told the world and himself enough times that 'I am the greatest!' so that both we and he came to believe it. His shining charisma derived in large part from his self-belief. He seemed invincible, and for years he was. This was the power of language for changing history, and for determining the belief structure of the individual to make that possible. This was not lost on the twenty-four-year-old Ingle. His own boxing record was mixed, with seventeen wins and four losses. He didn't try these techniques on himself, but he could train others to use them. The seven-year-old Naseem Hamed in the corner of the gym, telling everyone that he would one day be the world champion, until everyone was bored with it. Later, in the build up to the world championship fight, Brendan would say 'The greatest thing since sliced bread. They used to call Muhammad Ali the greatest. Wait until they see what Naz is going to be doing over the next few months.' The tabloids called him 'Megamouth' or 'Motormouth'. They were saying that he had a level of ambition and plans for world domination only seen before in a Bond villain. Some called Naz confident, most called him arrogant. He belittled his opponents with his showboating. He told them to their face that they didn't have a chance. He became champion of the world, but at a cost.

The footnote to all this is not nearly so positive. Naseem Hamed, with all that confidence, went too far. The father and son relationship broke down in the late 1990s (see Beattie 2002) and they haven't spoken since. According to the author Nick Pitt (1998), the whole thing finished after an argument brought on by Naz teasing Brendan once too often. Naz is reported to have taunted Brendan with 'What did you win, Brendan? Nothing. You never even won an area title.' Brendan apparently reacted to this, and then Naz administered the coup de grace with,

> You know your trouble, Brendan? You never stood up to anybody. You never stood up to anybody in your life. You always let people bully you. Like the time with Mickey Duff [a boxing promoter] when he slagged you off and you just stood for it.

According to Pitt, 'Brendan became obsessed by what Naseem had said, as if Naseem had stained his whole life.' Pitt says that the comments stung so much because there was an element of truth in them,

> But the person he had failed to stand up to was not Mickey Duff, or indeed any of the others who had given him trouble over the years. It was Naseem. Brendan had allowed himself to be bullied by the bully he had, in part created.

Naz called Brendan 'Judas' for discussing their finances and these other issues with Pitt. Even as a practising Muslim, Naz would have known how much that would have hurt the Roman Catholic Ingle.

In 2015, Naz, about to be inducted into the International Boxing Hall of Fame in Canastota, New York State, said that he hoped for a reconciliation. Hamed said that Ingle too should be in the Hall of Fame with him. 'He's produced so many world champions. The time I had with Brendan was an amazing time. It was priceless,' he said at the time (*The Star*, 16 June 2015). But there was to be no reconciliation.

Leon Festinger and cognitive dissonance

But there is a valuable psychological lesson here, perhaps, a lesson about what you say and what you end up believing, and in the case of Naseem Hamed, perhaps a cautionary tale about how this can work too well in some cases, and where this might take you. Brendan Ingle has never heard of Leon Festinger but they seem to have similar views on this subject. Festinger working in the 1950s developed his classic theory of cognitive dissonance. A theory of what happens when *cognitions* ('opinions, beliefs, knowledge … and knowledge of one's own actions and feelings', Festinger et al. 1956: 25) conflict with each other. Conflict here means that 'they do not fit together – that is, if they are inconsistent, or if, considering only the particular two items, one does not follow from the other'. They use the example of a cigarette smoker who believes that smoking is bad for their health but continues to smoke. They point out that the smoker may have 'other opinions, beliefs, or items of knowledge that are consonant with continuing to smoke but the dissonance nevertheless exists too' (Festinger et al. 1956: 26).

The essence of the theory is very simple. They say that

> Dissonance produces discomfort and, correspondingly, there will arise pressures to reduce or eliminate the dissonance. Attempts to reduce dissonance represent the observable manifestations that dissonance exists. Such attempts may take any or all of three forms. The person may try to change one or more of the beliefs, opinions, or behaviors involved in the dissonance; to acquire new information or beliefs that will increase the existing consonance and thus cause the total dissonance to be reduced; or to forget or reduce the importance of those cognitions that are in a dissonant relationship.
>
> (Festinger et al. 1956: 26)

There are a number of things to note about how Festinger and his colleagues formulated this hypothesis. The first is the lack of specification in the original hypothesis, specifically in terms of what you might call implicit quantification. Do *all* 'opinions', 'beliefs', 'knowledge of the environment', and 'knowledge of one's own actions and feelings' that conflict produce dissonance? How important do these have to be? Are some categories (for example, 'beliefs' compared with 'opinions') more important than others in producing dissonance when they conflict with 'knowledge of one's own actions'? Do all conflicting cognitions (broadly defined) produce 'discomfort'? What is discomfort in this context? Does it have a physiological component, or is it purely psychological? Is it continuous or can it be intermittent? Is this temporal dimension important? Can dissonance be observed by any other means other than the one specified? Festinger, after all, does say that 'Attempts to reduce dissonance represent the observable manifestations that dissonance exists'. So, if there are no attempts to reduce dissonance does that mean that dissonance does not exist? Or that it does exist, but (in times of acute behaviourism) that we are unable to speculate about its existence? A change in one set of cognitions to draw them out of conflict with another set may be observed, but can we be confident that these cognitions (be they opinions, beliefs or knowledge of one's own actions) have actually changed or is there the possibility of social desirability effects operating here (after all, most of us do not wish to appear too inconsistent with ourselves)? Alternatively, according to Festinger and his colleagues, individuals may 'acquire new information or beliefs that will increase the existing consonance and thus cause the total dissonance to be reduced', but such acquisition may take time, so do we backdate evidence of any such acquisition to identify extant dissonance in the past? How do we distinguish this from other processes of acquisition? Are we in danger of using tautological reasoning to identify and label any processes of development and change in our belief statements? And finally, Festinger et al. say that the third coping mechanism is that individuals can 'forget or reduce the importance of those cognitions that are in a dissonant relationship'. In other words, if individuals can forget the original conflicting thought, opinion or belief, how do we know that it existed in the first place? How do we know that there is (or was) an originally conflicting cognition?

Nevertheless, this was how the original cognitive dissonance theory was formulated in 1956, and you might say that in its first articulation, at least, it left a lot to be desired. But what was eye-catching from the beginning was the associated empirical work, and in particular their early detailed ethnographic study of a cult in Chicago that had formed around a housewife named Dorothy Martin (called 'Marian Keech' in the book to preserve her anonymity). This cult was observed and described in some detail by Festinger's research assistants covertly as they waited for the end of the world in a great flood scheduled, according to the extra-terrestrial messengers, 'The Guardians', for the 21st of December 1954. Festinger described how this cult reacted when the prophecy failed. Festinger and his colleagues wanted to show how his hypothesis about cognitive dissonance could help us understand the behaviour of the cult when none of their expectations were met and there arose an obvious (and very public) conflict between their expressed beliefs ('the world is going to end with a great flood tonight but our small group of believers are going to be transported to a distant planet by a spacecraft') and the observable real world events (they were left sitting looking at each other in the front room of their house in Chicago, checking, at the last minute, if the clocks were right).

Festinger and his colleagues say (and it is worth quoting them in detail here because their logic is so interesting):

> The dissonance [the cult experienced] would be largely eliminated if they discarded the belief that had been disconfirmed, ceased the behavior which had been initiated in preparation for the fulfilment of the prediction, and returned to a more usual existence … But frequently the behavioral commitment to the belief system is so strong that almost any other course of action is preferable. It may even be less painful to tolerate the dissonance than to discard the belief and admit one had been wrong. When that is the case, the dissonance cannot be eliminated by giving up the belief.
>
> Alternatively, the dissonance would be reduced or eliminated if the members of a movement effectively blind themselves to the fact that the prediction has not been fulfilled. But most people, including members of such movements, are in touch with reality and cannot simply blot out of their

cognition such an unequivocal and undeniable fact. They can try to ignore it, however, and they usually do try. They may convince themselves that the date was wrong but that the prediction will, after all, be shortly confirmed; or they may even set another date.

... Rationalisation can reduce dissonance somewhat. For rationalisation to be fully effective, support from others is needed to make the explanation or the revision seem correct. Fortunately, the disappointed believer can usually turn to the others in the same movement, who have the same dissonance and the same pressures to reduce it. Support for the new explanation is, hence, forthcoming and the members of the movement can recover somewhat from the shock of the disconfirmation.

But whatever explanation is made it is still by itself not sufficient. The dissonance is too important and though they may try to hide it, even from themselves, the believers still know that the prediction was false and all their preparations were in vain. The dissonance cannot be eliminated completely by denying or rationalising the disconfirmation. But there is a way in which the remaining dissonance can be reduced. If more and more people can be persuaded that the system of belief is correct, then clearly it must, after all, be correct. Consider the extreme case: if everyone in the whole world believed something there would be no question at all as to the validity of this belief. It is for this reason that we observe the increase in proselyting following disconfirmation. If the proselyting proves successful, then by gathering more adherents and effectively surrounding himself with supporters, the believer reduces dissonance to the point where he can live with it.

(Festinger et al. 1956: 27–28)

This is an interesting argument for a number of reasons. Perhaps, mainly because one of the principal ways of reducing dissonance now introduced seems to be proselytising about the belief system itself – 'If more and more people can be persuaded that the system of belief is correct, then clearly it must, after all, be correct.' And if you read reviews of the social psychological literature that outline the importance of the theory of cognitive dissonance, this is the point that is picked up and endlessly repeated, that proselytising increases when our expectations are not met as a way of dealing with the cognitive dissonance. But, of course, this was not part of the original hypothesis. It was introduced to help explain behaviour specifically when prophecies fail, as in the case of this cult in Chicago (although it might seem a little bit like the prediction about behaviour was added after the facts rather than before, despite the narrative flow of the book). The theoretical justification for this addition is drawn (somewhat controversially) by Festinger and his colleagues from the early days of Christianity and the behaviour of the Apostles after the crucifixion of Christ the Messiah at Calvary, which can be taken as a disconfirmation of the belief system (at least in terms of how many would have understood what would become of the promised Messiah, leaving Christ's own teachings to the side for the moment). In the words of Graetz, speculating on the mindset of the Apostles and cited by Festinger:

> The only stumbling-block to their belief lay in the fact that the Messiah who came to deliver Israel and bring to light the glory of the kingdom of heaven, endured a shameful death. How could the Messiah be subject to pain? A suffering Messiah staggered them considerably, and this stumbling-block had to be overcome before a perfect and joyful belief could be reposed in him.
>
> (Cited in Festinger et al. 1956: 24–25)

Festinger was, in effect, suggesting that the preaching of the Apostles, and the spread of Christianity, was really down to an attempt to reduce their cognitive dissonance. They had given up their jobs and homes (and become fishers of men) to follow Christ and here he was crucified like a common criminal, crying out on the cross, then buried in a sepulchre. But, of course, the great theological question is whether Christ had to die to redeem our sins, and Festinger, despite drawing heavily on this example ('the *best* instance of such a movement', my italics), does recognise that Christianity might be too 'inconclusive' as a test of his theory because of these fundamental theological disputes. Hence the detailed observations of a 'cult' in progress. Some would describe Festinger's attempt to explain the behaviour of the Apostles in terms of cognitive dissonance as naive in the extreme.

Festinger and his colleagues' description of the Chicago cult is considered as a classic piece of research in social psychology in that golden era of research in the 1950s before the 'experimental revolution' that did so much to curtail its imagination and flair (see Sears 1986). Festinger says that he and his colleagues 'were alerted by the story in their local newspaper with the headline 'Prophecy from planet. Clarion call to city: flee that flood. It'll swamp us on Dec. 21, outer space tells suburbanite.' The first thing to note is that the cult and their beliefs were already being made public, and indeed ridiculed, when Festinger decided to intervene with his detailed study. This could be significantly important. Marian Keech was the source of the messages from the Guardians in outer space through her automatic writing. The messages came from 'spiritual beings' from the planets Clarion and Cerus. Her most important source was Sananda, who later revealed himself to be Jesus Christ himself and she was shocked by these messages coming through to her at first. Her first attempts to connect with fellow believers was met with very mixed success. She discussed her experiences with people from other planets with her husband, but he was 'quite unreceptive' (according to Festinger). He did not believe a word of it, but left her to it. But she did eventually find like-minded souls in the form of Dr and Mrs Armstrong, who had served as medical missionaries in Egypt. Mrs Armstrong had had a nervous breakdown on her travels, and subsequently suffered from acute anxiety. They could not understand why all of this psychological distress had happened to them, despite their good works as missionaries. In their words, 'We finally decided there must be a reason and we started searching.' The Armstrongs contacted Mrs Keech after hearing of her work from a local expert on flying saucers. Sananda (or Jesus) told Mrs Keech about life on the planet Clarion (the weather was apparently just like earth but you didn't need warmer clothes when it got colder because your body adjusts to the temperature). He promised landings from outer space, and contact with space people, and warned of the approaching apocalypse. But some would be saved. 'We are planning to take some people for a trip to our plane – that is, planet. We are trying to make arrangements for a party of six from Westinghouse to visit our territory' (Festinger et al. 1956: 46). The first visit by spacemen was scheduled for the 23rd of July. Mrs Keech was told to be at Lyons field, a military air base, at noon to witness the landing. Mrs Keech, the Armstrongs and some other friends got there in good time with a good view of the runways so that they could watch the flying saucers land. They brought a packed lunch, and waited. And waited. They eventually saw a man walking along the road. Mrs Keech offered him some food but he declined and continued walking. They spent two hours looking up into the sky for the flying saucers. None came. They were all very disappointed, but not for long. Ten days later, Mrs Keech got another telepathic message from Sananda informing her that he himself was the stranger who had turned down the gift of a sandwich and a glass of fruit juice. Mrs Keech felt 'an exultation that far outweighed the disappointment over the disconfirmed prediction. For, although no saucers had landed at Lyons, a greater gift had been bestowed upon her. She had looked upon Jesus (in another body, of course, and in disguise), had talked with him, and had performed the simple Christian act of offering hospitality to the casual, undistinguished stranger' (Festinger et al. 1956: 51). According to Festinger, 'the conviction overcame her that she was especially selected, that the voices she heard and the presences she felt were real, were valid, were the very stuff of transcendent life – and she their humble early vehicle' (Festinger et al. 1956: 51). Mrs Keech's confidence in her abilities grew. She would spend up to fourteen hours a day receiving messages from outer space. News of the apocalypse soon followed. There would be a great flood covering much of the US, with France, England and Russia all submerged like Atlantis. Dr Armstrong understood his responsibility to 'tell the world' and he sent fifty copies of an open letter to various American editors and publishers, warning them of what was to happen without mentioning the specific date. The response to this was 'remarkably small', with about a dozen people becoming interested, although it did prompt a visit from two of the authors of the Festinger et al. book. They then arranged for clandestine observers, two pairs of psychology or sociology students, to join the group. The first male observer was able to join the group by telling a made-up story about his personal experience of a ghostly passenger in his car; the female observer gained acceptance by reporting a 'psychic experience' that came to her in a dream, a 'completely fictitious dream' (as noted by Festinger), to the Armstrongs, constructed with enough detail to reinforce the delusional beliefs of these emotionally unstable and highly vulnerable individuals (Mr Armstrong had, after all, identified Mrs Keech as Mary, the mother of Jesus; Mrs Armstrong had not recovered from her nervous breakdown). The female observer said that she had dreamt that 'she was standing near the foot of a hill on which stood a man, surrounded by an aura of light; there were torrents of water raging all about, and the man reached down and pulled her up to safety' (Festinger et al. 1956: 70). The Armstrongs concluded that she had been 'sent' by higher powers.

So now we have effectively two deceptive researchers infiltrated into this small group of only eight 'heavily committed individuals' (Festinger et al. 1956: 75, 82), the observers evidently quite prepared to make stories up that fitted the delusional fantasies of the group to facilitate their role as participant observers in this febrile situation. In terms of numbers alone, one cannot underestimate the impact of these observers on the dynamics of the group. But when you consider aspects of the behaviour of some of the core members their influence becomes significantly greater. As participants in the group they were expected to play important roles. For example, one evening one of the observers (undercover, of course) was asked to lead the group. He asked them to meditate for twenty minutes of 'tense silence' according to Festinger. Suddenly, one of the legitimate members of the group, Bertha Blatsky, who had trained as a beautician, started panting, and gasped 'I got the words, I got the words' repeatedly. Mrs Keech had now got a competitor in terms of extra-terrestrial transmission. Sananda was now going to come through Bertha as well, but in speech rather than in automatic writing. Mrs Keech, it should be noted, had always longed for the power of speech in her communication with the men from space; now she had been outdone. The messages from Sananda came pouring out, although Dr Armstrong didn't think that they amounted to much, except perhaps for Sananda, through the voice of Bertha, the Polish beautician from Iowa of course, telling the group that she was now the de facto leader of the group. Now that was significant. She soon upped the stakes when she explained that it was actually the Creator himself speaking through her rather than Sananda, thus trumping Mrs Keech. Now that they had the Creator himself on the line, indeed all through the night and into the next morning, they wanted to check the date of the apocalypse (just to be on the safe side). The Creator was a little bit vague on the date, but he was clear on one thing – 'tonight you are in the presence of the Creator who has chosen the greatest prophet, Bertha, whoever was or will be (Festinger et al. 1956: 99). Bertha was now top dog: the Creator, after all, said so. Fortunately, Dr Armstrong soon found out from another medium that he had his own unique gifts:

> He will give power and be a beam of power. He will create an aura. He will be charged with electro-magnetic force that will fill all the cells of his body and make him immune to any death or disease. And that will be done on a space craft.
>
> (Festinger et al. 1956: 104)

In terms of how the research was conducted, you can easily imagine how important the four observers (two embedded in each of the two groups of seekers) were for the dynamics of this cult. After all, each had presented with their own 'interesting' and highly relevant, and yet completely fictitious, personal experiences of psychic and paranormal phenomena. Meanwhile, the rest of this group were all jockeying for position within it, using any means possible, including channelling the voices of God himself, or various informed extra-terrestrials, to bolster their claims. The observers must surely have presented as much more stable than the other group members (how could they not have?). Bertha was voicing the words of the Creator, who constantly reminded the group how important she was as leader, and changed aspects of the underlying ideology at a whim (God through Bertha suggested that this vegetarian group should henceforth eat meat). She told them to quit their jobs on the basis that they could manage because 'there was so little time before the end'. Often, she made no sense at all. The observers would have been effectively the rocks of the group (and not necessarily in the St Peter sense, but perhaps that as well). Bertha, meanwhile, who had always been desperate for a child (in real life), was instructed by the Creator that she was to give birth to the new Christ and that if her husband continued to threaten her with the visit of a psychiatrist to certify her insane then he, the Creator, would strike him down. At some meetings there were ten genuine group members and four observers, all pretending to be something they weren't, all apparently subscribing to the unfolding set of delusional beliefs, all involved in continual deception and noting everything down in this pioneering psychological case study (Festinger et al. 1956: 126). Mrs Keech had apparently 'a growing conviction that her home was under surveillance by unfriendly people' (Festinger et al. 1956: 108). This might have seemed like another paranoid fantasy, but how right she was, on this point at least.

Even Festinger et al. note that

> In spite of the relatively ordinary, non-exotic stories that the Lake City observers told Mrs. Keech she subsequently made much the same use of their appearance on her doorstep as the Armstrongs had with the Collegeville observers. Her imagination embroidered the circumstances somewhat and, within a week of the first observer's call, Mrs. Keech was explaining to other members of the group that a girl had come to her door, upset, excited, wringing her hands, and so terrified that she could not speak; the girl had not known why she had come, and obviously she had been 'sent' by the Guardians. Then, Mrs. Keech added, a man had also called, again not knowing why he was there, confused, upset, and unsure of his errand. She elaborated not only the bewilderment and emotionality of the observers but also her own warmth of response and comforting actions toward them. Her account was retold in Collegeville by the Armstrongs, just as their

> versions of our observers' visits to them were retold in Lake
> City. In both cases the visits were given as illustrations that
> 'strange things are happening'.
>
> (Festinger et al. 1956: 242)

But it is not just that the stories of their arrivals were embellished (after all, what students wouldn't have arrived at the house of the seekers appearing somewhat 'confused' and 'unsure of their errand'?). It was how they made sense of this that was the problem. Jesus Christ himself had been on the road to meet them one dark night, that at least was believable, but a set of psychology and sociology students, so polite and so plausible, living with them as part of their group, sharing their personal psychic experiences, true believers waiting with them for the end of days, but secretly every so often nipping off to the bathroom to write it all down. Now that would be beyond belief.

The end of the world was approaching fast. Then at about ten o'clock on the morning of the 20th of December, Mrs Keech received the message that they had all been waiting for. It read:

> At the hour of midnight you shall be put into parked cars and
> taken to a place where ye shall be put aboard a porch [flying
> saucer] and ye shall be purposed by the time you are there. At
> that time, you shall have the fortuned ones forget the few
> who have not come – and at no time are they to be called for,
> they are but enacting a scene and not a person who should be
> there will fail to be there and at the time you are to say 'What
> is your question?' ... and at no time are you to ask what is
> what and not a plan shall go astray and for the time being be
> glad and be fortuned to be among the favored. And be ye
> ready for further instructions.
>
> (Festinger et al. 1956: 159)

The end was coming: in just fourteen hours they would, after all that waiting and preparation, be picked up by flying saucers and whisked away. Festinger et al. comment: 'This message brought a great release of tension to the believers. This was it. Now they knew what was to happen and when. Now they could wait easily and comfortably for midnight. They relaxed, and spent the day in peaceful idleness' (Festinger et al. 1956: 159). Festinger then notes sardonically,

> When Arthur Bergen [a fifteen-year-old college student] arrived late in the afternoon and told the group his mother had threatened to call the police if he were not home by two o'clock the following morning, the believers smilingly assured him that he need not worry – by that time they would all be aboard a saucer.

In the final hours there was a burst of activity from Sananda coming through Mrs Keech and from the Creator himself speaking through Bertha. Sananda and the Creator were giving different directions and Marian and Bertha were doing their best to see if both agreed to what was being written down as instructions for the group. Mrs Keech would write out her messages from Sananda and read them back to the Creator for checking or the Creator would speak and they would request verification in writing from Jesus. It must have been very confusing as the two great prophets of the group vied for attention and dominance. Reporters kept ringing, but were dismissed with 'no comment'. In the meantime, the group were removing all metal from their clothes and shoes – this was something that Sananda and the Creator himself had both apparently agreed on. But there was a last minute panic.

> When Arthur Bergen suddenly remembered that his shoes had metal toecaps, it was too late to cut them out. From the ensuing excitement emerged the suggestion that he should simply loosen the laces and step out of his shoes before entering the saucer. At about 11:35, one of the authors let it be known that he had not removed the zipper from his trousers. This knowledge produced a near panic reaction. He was rushed into the bedroom where Dr. Armstrong, his hands trembling and his eyes darting to the clock every few seconds, slashed out the zipper with a razor blade and wrenched its clasps free with wire-cutters. By the time the operation was

complete it was 11:50, too late to do more than sew up the
rent with a few rough stitches. Midnight was almost at hand
and everyone must be ready on the dot.

(Festinger et al. 1956: 162)

Note again that the researchers were not mere passive observers
here, with no influence on what is unfolding, or on the underlying
set of (clearly delusional) beliefs. By announcing that his zipper was
intact, at that last minute, he is contributing to the near hysteria of
the group. He is helping build this group to its emotional climax.

For the last ten minutes they sat with their coats on their laps, just
waiting. There were now five researchers actually present. There
were two clocks in the room, one was fast. When the slower one
struck midnight, Mrs Keech exclaimed 'And not a plan has gone
astray!' Nobody else said anything. At five past the Creator, as
voiced by Bertha, announced that there was to be a slight delay. At
half past twelve the Creator promised something – a miracle, that
the unbelieving Mr Keech, asleep in another room, having retired
at 9 p.m., would die and then be resurrected. The group repeatedly
checked to see if he had died, but he was breathing normally. The
Creator (through Bertha) was at least very resourceful. He now
explained that the death and the resurrection of Mr Keech had
already actually occurred but in *spiritual* terms only. He was now
spiritually alive, whereas before he wasn't. Finally, at about half past
two in the morning, Jesus or Sananda coming through Mrs Keech
urged the group to have a coffee break.

There was now some time to reflect, and what happened next is
at the core of psychological theory on cognitive dissonance. But
again the observers are instrumental in terms of what occurred next.
Festinger notes that

In response to some of the observers' prodding about that
message [the one about the space craft landing] during the
coffee break, the Creator stated that anyone who wished
might look up that message … He found it and read it aloud
to the group. The first attempt at reinterpretation came
quickly. Daisy Armstrong pointed out that the message must,

of course, be symbolic, because it said we were to be put into parked cars; but parked cars do not move and hence could not take the group anywhere.

(Festinger et al. 1956: 167)

The 'parked cars', they concluded, were their physical bodies (there at midnight, of course), the 'flying saucer' was 'the inner light which each member of the group had' (except perhaps for the five researchers). What is important is that one of the researchers had actually initiated this search for reinterpretations of the prophecy through his actions. He was actively working to maintain the delusional belief system in the group. Mrs Keech broke down and sobbed at the disappointment of it all, but again one of the observers, having stepped outside for a chat with Dr Armstrong, reported that talking to the doctor had significantly lifted the spirits of Dr Armstrong, whose 'return cheered the group and brought visible relief to Mrs. Keech', who now felt sufficiently buoyed up, to relay another message from Jesus that the cataclysm had been called off because 'The little group, sitting all night long, had spread so much light that God had saved the world from destruction' (Festinger et al. 1956: 169), and even went so far as to ring the newspapers with this Christmas message. This was the first time that she had spoken directly to the press.

When she got the next message from Jesus that on Christmas Eve they were to gather outside her house and sing carols, and there they were to be visited by spacemen, she informed the press and invited members of the public, presumably partly as a function of her recent experience in talking to the press. No spacemen arrived on Christmas Eve either (of course), although in one newspaper interview Dr Armstrong said that they might actually have been there 'in disguise'. Of the eleven members of the group there that night, waiting for the spacecraft to arrive to whisk them away before the flood, six maintained their beliefs or these beliefs got stronger, and five either gave up their beliefs or harboured extreme doubts. This latter group included Bertha Blatsky, who had been the mouthpiece of the Creator himself, but perhaps there's no mileage in being the top dog in a discredited group.

In terms of the psychological reaction to the disconfirmation of their expectations about the spacemen, the flood and the apocalypse, Festinger emphasises the *active* steps that the members of the cult took to maintain their beliefs. Foremost amongst them was public and personal proselytising, the public proselytising signalled through publicity seeking and 'the precipitous change in attitudes towards the press' (temporarily forgetting that Dr Armstrong had contacted the press directly also much earlier and before any disconfirmation), and the 'explosive immediacy within minutes after the group had developed the rationalization for the major disconfirmation on December 21' (Festinger et al. 1956: 209–210). The rationalisation being that these true believers had saved the world through their actions. Festinger's basic hypothesis was that:

> If more and more people can be persuaded that the system of belief is correct, then clearly it must, after all, be correct. Consider the extreme case: if everyone in the whole world believed something there would be no question at all as to the validity of this belief. It is for this reason that we observe the increase in proselyting following disconfirmation. If the proselyting proves successful, then by gathering more adherents and effectively surrounding himself with supporters, the believer reduces dissonance to the point where he can live with it.
>
> (Festinger et al. 1956: 27–28)

But there are a number of points to be made here. First, the press had become more and more insistent, more and more intrusive. Was it not best to talk to them directly? After all, many individuals hounded by the press do succumb eventually and agree to talk, even when they don't have a message to sell. They eventually pick up the phone. What was different about this set of circumstances? Second, would this proselytising through the press ever have occurred, if one of the researchers had not lifted Mrs Keech's spirits (no pun intended) at a critical point in the disconfirmation on that fateful night in those critical minutes after midnight? What would have happened if she had been left there at that time, broken down in floods of tears, visibly shaken by the non-occurrences that night? Would she have had the strength of character to ring the press in tears and talk them through the events? Did the researcher not urge them to try to reinterpret the events of the night through his actions? In other words, were the actions of the researchers not critical to the outcome of the whole thing? Were they not influencing the results of the field experiment, given that this whole proselytising idea is presented as an *a priori* hypothesis? Third, as I have already suggested, the four (or sometimes five) researchers who have made up stories to be part of this small group (thus violating most ethical principles of research, including ethnographic research), who have indeed become important and 'stable' members of the group (compared to many of the others), were outsiders who had heard about the group from further afield. Was this not a lesson to the group that some form of proselytising was essential to attract the 'right' kinds of people? Festinger at one point seems to admit a number of facts relevant to this without necessarily recognising what would seem to me to logically follow from this. Thus,

> There is little doubt that the addition of four new people to a fairly small group within ten days had an effect on the state of conviction among the existing members, especially since the four seem to have appeared when public apathy to the belief system was great and there were very few inquiries or new faces in either Collegeville or Lake City. Most important of all, perhaps, is that the four observers could not be traced through any mutual friends or acquaintances to existing group members and thus the most common and expected channel of recruitment was evidently not responsible for their appearance.
>
> (Festinger et al. 1956: 243)

The Armstrongs, of course, thought that the researchers had been 'sent by the Guardians' and that was taken as further proof that the Guardians were looking after us on earth. But again we see how these outsiders were critical to the development and maintenance of the delusional belief system. Even their arrival contributed to it. The researchers also secretly sharing notes about what was going on meant that they ended up with information that they couldn't possibly have known from conventional channels. Mrs Keech assumed that this omniscience derived from their direct contact with the Guardians, rather than being a by-product of communication in a network of duplicitous researchers who had infiltrated the group. Again, were the researchers, and their conduct and back stories, not important influences on the outcome of the whole thing? And, if so, where does that leave the concept of cognitive dissonance and the active and immediate steps that individuals in a group with sufficient social support take to deal with it?

Festinger completes the book by saying that:

> we had to conduct the entire enquiry covertly, without revealing our research purpose, pretending to be merely interested individuals who had been persuaded of the correctness of the belief system and yet taking a passive and uninfluential role in the group ... the effects of disconfirmation were striking enough to provide for firm conclusions.
>
> (Festinger et al. 1956: 252)

I don't believe that the researchers did play a passive and uninfluential role in the group. Indeed, I think that at certain significant moments, their behaviour was critical to what happened next. I therefore think that the conclusions drawn from the effects of disconfirmation on behaviour are a lot less firm than Festinger might have us to believe, even in this group of highly vulnerable, extremely gullible, and very atypical individuals.

The book *When Prophecy Fails*, the detailed field study, so redolent of the golden era of social psychology in many academics' eyes, is considered a classic in the field. The theoretical ideas on cognitive dissonance were then developed and published in a second book in 1957. This new book represents something of a volte face, in my opinion. In this second book published a year after the first, Festinger attempts to map out a broader 'theory' of cognitive dissonance, based on this same basic idea. 'The existence of dissonance, being psychologically uncomfortable, will motivate the person to try to reduce the dissonance and achieve consonance' (Festinger 1957: 3). Dissonance, according to Festinger 'is a motivating factor in its own right' (Festinger 1957: 3). When the dissonance arises, the changing of one's behaviour 'as a method of reducing or eliminating dissonance is a very frequent occurrence' (Festinger 1957: 19). Or, of course, attitudes, opinions and beliefs may change. Festinger, as before, defines cognitive dissonance as 'nonfitting relations among cognitions' (Festinger 1957: 3) so he has to assume (and does) that 'if the behavior of the organism changes, the cognitive element or elements corresponding to this behavior will likewise change' (Festinger 1957: 19). But surely one can imagine situations where behaviour and beliefs may be at odds, but there is no dissonance. For example, say someone reports strong pro-environmental beliefs, even strong pro-low carbon beliefs (apparent explicit cognitions after all) but unconsciously within the first few seconds of looking at everyday supermarket products pays little attention to their carbon labels (Beattie 2010; Beattie et al. 2011) and makes few low carbon choices as a consequence (Beattie and McGuire 2015; 2016). Will they suffer from dissonance, this 'motivating' factor, that will lead them to behaviour change? Are we meant to be consciously aware of all aspects of our behaviour, including our very quick, automatic behaviours that guide visual attention and the selection of products when shopping? Indeed, the selection of the very same products that may well be at odds with our deeply held convictions about anthropogenic climate change and the role of consumerism in this? Will this actually be 'psychologically uncomfortable', as Festinger has hypothesised? One problem with Festinger's theory is that it assumes a close connection between behaviour and cognitions/knowledge of behaviour. Indeed, this is central to the theory, but there would seem to be many aspects of our behaviour of which we have minimal awareness (see Kahneman 2011). If this is the case, then why would we predict that cognitive dissonance should arise between behaviours that conflict with expressed attitudes, and if there is no dissonance why would we predict any behaviour change?

'Communism is the way of the future'

The most well-known studies reported in Festinger's 1957 book are the studies of forced compliance, where 'forced compliance' is an interesting term used as 'shorthand for public compliance without private acceptance' (Festinger 1957: 87). The term is perhaps even more interesting when one considers the geopolitical context in which the work was being carried out. Festinger's research was begun in 1951 during the time of the Korean War (1950–1953). The research was funded by the Ford Foundation. Festinger says that he was approached directly by Bernard Berelson, director of the Behavioral Sciences Division, and asked whether he would produce a substantive summary of research on 'communication and social influence'. This was a serious and pressing contemporary topic because of the concern being expressed in the US about American prisoners of war captured by the Chinese in Korea. There was grave concern about the lack of escape attempts by the prisoners, there was apparently little by way of camp organisation and resistance, and there was even more concern that some prisoners of war had started broadcasting propaganda for the enemy, as 'guests of the Chinese People's Volunteer Army'. There was extreme anxiety that the Chinese had found, and were beginning to exploit, weaknesses in the American character which they were now using to control them. A very informative example of the moral panic that was setting in can be seen in the film *The Ultimate Weapon*, narrated by Ronald Reagan, the future American president, where the ultimate weapon in the title is not the nuclear bomb but the human mind itself. The Chinese were supposed to have perfected a new sort of brainwashing of these prisoners of war; effective brainwashing without apparent brutality, hypnosis, drugs or even coercion. Prisoners were asked to write down a few pro-communist statements ('Communism is wonderful'; 'Communism is the way of the future'). According to Wiseman (2012), many of the prisoners were happy to oblige 'because the request seemed trivial' in and of itself in the endless months of captivity. Later they were asked to read the statements aloud to the group, and to discuss these with the group. To encourage them, they were reinforced with small rewards – small portions of extra rice, sweets, subtle praise. Rewards, not great enough to be obvious determinants of behaviour, rewards not great enough to blame. This was a more dangerous type of brainwashing, according to the film, based on discussion amongst prisoners, public criticism of fellow prisoners, and then public self-criticism. It was thought to be a type of brainwashing where prisoners would inform the guards of the bad attitudes of other prisoners, thus breaking down the ties between the men, and where the men ended up no longer trusting one another and becoming isolated and vulnerable. The death rate amongst the American prisoners of war in Korea was very high, 30 per cent by some estimates, but according to Reagan's narration this was principally down to 'giveupitis', where the prisoners just gave up the will to live rather than endure the brutal and inhumane conditions (although William Shadish's book *When Hell Froze Over: The Memoir of a Korean War Combat Physician Who Spent 1010 Days in a Communist Prison Camp* might persuade you otherwise. See also Lee et al. 2013, for an analysis of the causes of death of prisoners of war who fought for the Communist side, where tuberculosis and dysentery were the main causes of death). The film maintains that the cause of this high mortality rate was psychological rather than physical, and the US government wanted something to remedy this, to make the American prisoner stronger, to halt this moral decline in the American character. Washington also needed to understand the implications of these methods for the future security of the US. After all, significant numbers of prisoners of war would be returning to the US after their periods of captivity. How would this 'forced compliance' of these prisoners by their Chinese guards, with only minimal reward and encouragement, impact on their underlying attitudes, opinions and beliefs? Would these ex-prisoners of war turn out to be Communist sympathisers because of their experiences in the camps of North Korea, as many clearly feared?

This is the geopolitical background to Festinger's experimental research, although interestingly and tellingly the Korean War, and the experiences of the prisoners, is not mentioned in the book, even though the book was completed in March 1956 when these concerns were being widely voiced in the media.

Festinger's experiments are very simple both in terms of theory and execution. If you are offered a large reward (say a million dollars), or a large punishment ('I will shoot you') to say something that you do not believe ('I like comic books'), then little cognitive dissonance will be produced. But what psychological effects will this actually have? Well, first you are very likely to go ahead with the offer, or the threat, that's for sure. But there will be no effect on your underlying attitude about comic books. Festinger writes,

> There is some slight dissonance, to be sure. You said you liked comic books and you really do not. But there are some very important elements that are consonant with having uttered this public statement, namely, the knowledge of the money now in your pocket. Relative to this, the dissonance is negligible.
>
> (Festinger 1957: 91)

Similarly, with the threat of the bullet to the head. Festinger reasons that

> As the promised reward, or threatened punishment, becomes smaller in importance, the dissonance resulting from compliance increases. The maximum possible dissonance would be created if the reward, or punishment, was just barely enough to elicit the desired overt behaviour or expression.
>
> (Festinger 1957: 91)

It is clear why this is so redolent of the experience of the prisoners of war in Korea. This was what alarmed the American public. It was the very small rewards that were instrumental in getting the prisoners to behave in particular ways, and, of course, these experiments by Festinger and his colleagues seemed to demonstrate that they were indeed effective in producing an apparent change in underlying opinion. A number of experiments attempted to determine exactly what minimum level of incentive should be offered to get behavioural compliance (i.e. to say or write a counter-attitudinal statement) and thereby produce maximum dissonance and hence the greatest effect on underlying opinions and attitudes.

This theory of cognitive dissonance is considered by some to be one of the greatest achievements of social psychology. But there are a number of points worth making. The first is that in contrast to the

Seekers waiting for the Great Flood who, Festinger claims, did everything possible to hold on to their beliefs when the predicted events did not occur, the forced compliance studies suggest that we can change underlying opinions, attitudes and beliefs quite easily. Indeed, in the case of the Seekers they were prepared to engage in *more* dissonance (through clear psychological discomfort and public ridicule) to maintain their beliefs, but suddenly in this new research, beliefs can be changed just by offering small rewards to get people to say counter-attitudinal statements. Second, in the case of the Seekers, a number of them, including Mrs Keech herself, the very epicentre of the group, said things that were clearly counter-attitudinal to her underlying beliefs, for example, when the spacemen didn't turn up and she expressed her disappointment and sorrow for letting the group down (only to be subsequently lifted by one of the covert researchers), in a sort of mea culpa. This was not forced on her by any great reward or punishment but driven by the small demands of everyday social interaction, where we have individual responsibilities for our actions. She did express her disappointment that the prophecy, relayed through her, had not taken place. She said it, but according to Festinger, her underlying attitudes and beliefs remained intact. Indeed, he doesn't even attempt to tie the two things together. And, of course, this is just one example, of what happens in everyday life where we say many things in public (usually in conversation), for myriad (small and subtle) social reasons – to be provocative, to appear different, to fit in, to agree, to disagree, to stand out, to get a conversation going, to close it. We may say many things but our opinions are surely resistant to change to fit these ('forced compliance') verbalisations. Does Festinger really predict that when we say something in conversation (let's say) to be provocative, just guided by the social demands of talk, that our opinion would change under these circumstances? Has anyone gone to the trouble of checking this in everyday conversation?

Of course, the interpretation of Festinger's theoretical conclusions have been questioned by a number of researchers. Bem (1967) suggested that cognitive dissonance was primarily an issue of self-perception, Tedeschi et al. (1971) suggested that impression management on the part of the participant is key. Greenwald and

Ronis (1978) suggested that it is about maintaining self-esteem by being consistent with oneself. But one of the most important caveats that is rarely mentioned is who might, or might not, suffer from the sort of dissonance that has to be resolved when encouraged to say something at odds with their underlying beliefs. Festinger raises this issue in the final chapter of his book, when he writes 'For some people dissonance is an extremely painful and intolerable thing, while there are others who seem to be able to tolerate a large amount of dissonance' (Festinger 1957: 266–267). In other words, he is saying that for some individuals (or perhaps even for many), that they may say things that they don't actually believe and there is no painful dissonance to deal with, and therefore no behaviour change (although it is interesting that he wants to still say that 'dissonance' will still be present here, even though he has previously defined dissonance as 'psychologically uncomfortable', which, of course, might not be the case in these instances).

And then there is another issue. Does it matter *how* you deliver your counter-attitudinal statement? I am momentarily transported back to that gym in Sheffield and I see the boys lined up to give their confessions to Brendan Ingle, to tell the group that they are now 'winners', that their upcoming opponent is a 'nobody', and that they were going to go all the way, and I could see in their eyes that they didn't believe a word of it. It was simply Brendan's gentle cajoling that made them do it (perfect for attitude change, according to Festinger). It wasn't just the lack of confidence in the delivery, it was something else. It sounded routine, there was no variation in the eye gaze with the group (so redolent of talk itself, see Beattie 1979; 1983). It was all or none. With Naseem Hamed, it was always different. He said those things, and he came to believe them, and after he was defeated as World Champion and humiliated, he still tried to cling on to the belief that he was special. But this, of course, is so much more complex that Festinger's theory of cognitive dissonance would have us believe.

Of course, the theory satisfied one audience – the American public in the 1950s. The prisoners of war *had been brainwashed* by subtly being persuaded to make pro-Communist statements. You can see why individual differences in reactions to 'dissonance' might not have been at the forefront of Festinger's research. The prisoners of war were all subject to the same brainwashing techniques and they all succumbed, or would have, when it was done properly. They were all tortured heroes. That was an idea that the American public could live with. That, and the idea that of course there was no merit in the communist philosophy, and that the philosophy itself was not the real reason for the change in attitudes. Why, forced compliance even works when it's applied to people making statements about comic books. Isn't that what Festinger's research had demonstrated? Communism, comic books, it's all the same really. Surely?

Chapter summary

- Festinger wrote that when we have a conflict between what we say and what we do, cognitive dissonance arises and produces 'discomfort'.
- Festinger says that there will then arise pressures to reduce or eliminate the dissonance.
- In Festinger's words, 'The person may try to change one or more of the beliefs, opinions, or behaviors involved in the dissonance; to acquire new information or beliefs that will increase the existing consonance and thus cause the total dissonance to be reduced; or to forget or reduce the importance of those cognitions that are in a dissonant relationship.'
- Festinger carried out a detailed observation of a cult in Chicago waiting for a great flood and safe passage by spaceship to another planet. The research was conducted by a set of covert researchers who joined the cult.
- The spacemen never came (neither did the great flood).
- The 'cognitive dissonance' of the members of the cult was dealt with by an increase in proselytising after the prophecy failed, according to Festinger.
- The behaviour of the observers might have been critical to how the cult behaved at certain times, and the conclusions may therefore be in jeopardy.

- Festinger also studied cognitive dissonance experimentally.
- If you make public statements on behalf of something that you do not agree with (counter-attitudinal statements), and you do this without any significant incentive or threat, then your attitude changes to reduce the dissonance.
- This can apply to those who make pro-communist statements.
- Festinger's forced compliance experiments may not be as generally applicable as some have assumed.
- The geopolitical context of Festinger's research was the Korean War, and in particular the 'brainwashing' techniques of the Chinese used on American prisoners of war.
- The theory did satisfy one audience – the American public in the 1950s.
- From the theory's point of view the prisoners of war *had been brainwashed* by subtly being persuaded to make pro-communist statements.
- Individual differences in reactions to 'dissonance' were not at the forefront of Festinger's research.
- The prisoners of war were all subject to the same brainwashing techniques and they all succumbed, or would succumb (it was assumed) when the brainwashing was done properly.
- They were all tortured heroes, from this theory's point of view, but a potential threat when they returned home according to the theory (and the various *assumptions* about what was done to them to force them to comply).
- These assumptions (and Ronald Reagan's diagnosis of 'giveupitis') might have been very wide of the mark in this most brutal of wars.

5

CONFLICTED TALK

I miss her terribly; she told me that I would. I can't say that she didn't warn me. 'Your mother should be number one. You'll regret not taking me out more,' she used to say. Then the emotion and the tears would come. 'I'm way down the list; I think that you care more about Louis than you do me.'

Louis was my boxer dog and the object of great envious resentment. 'I cannot believe that you let that dog kiss you, you let it slobber all over you,' my mother would say, and I always thought that this complaint was occasioned more by jealousy than by concerns over personal hygiene. Sometimes I felt that Louis could also sense her resentment.

I would ring her every afternoon. I would be sitting in my bright, airy office in a university over in England, the laughter and the chatter of the students in the corridor outside filtering through, in this busy and self-important world. She would be sitting in front of the television in her front room, in the middle of the day, retired from the mill now, alone. She missed the work and the company; never wanting to retire in the first place. The laughter filtering into my office made it sound like I was at a party. 'I'm not living anymore, I'm just surviving,' she would say. 'I'm lonely all day; you're having the time of your life.'

I would feel those sharp pangs of guilt that you can anticipate but can't avoid. They cannot be dulled even with full expectation, and mental preparation. I had my life, my family, my children, my career and my busy, busy schedule but she never understood how universities worked or how you build a career. 'What time do you have to be in at?' she would ask. 'No time really unless I've got lectures or tutorials, but I have to get stuff done. It's extremely competitive.'

'So you can go into work whenever you like but you only come over here to see me once in a blue moon. I'd be ashamed of myself, if I was you.' I tried to get back home as often as I could and she would visit at Christmas, Easter and the July fortnight, but it would never be enough. When I did visit, I would often bring a computer with me and that would be the basis for the first argument, as I hoisted the bulking computer in through the front door. 'You're here to see me, not work. Put that bloody thing away, or I'm not even going to go out with you.'

She knew that I would try to mix visits home with work-related activities and occasionally it worked better. I would take her with me. We went together to a literary awards evening sometime in the 1990s. One of my books had been shortlisted for a literary prize. My mother had a few drinks at the posh reception and talked to Brian Keenan, the former hostage, who talked in a whisper after all those years locked in a Beirut cellar. 'Speak up, Brian,' she kept saying to him. 'I can hardly hear you; speak up, Brian, for God's sake.' Brian kissed her when they announced his name for the prize for his book *An Evil Cradling*. 'He deserved it,' she said to me, 'for all those years sitting in the dark in that bloody cellar. He told me all about it. I told him that I knew what it was like. I said that I never get out either.'

We saw Andrew Motion across the room. He later became the poet laureate. He had published my first non-academic book and I'd had a drink with him in some pub in London near his publishers. I told my mother that I knew him. He nodded almost grudgingly as he passed. She noticed it too, and then she glanced at me to see my reaction. 'He's not a very good friend of yours then, is he?' said my mother. 'I notice that you haven't got many good friends, not like when you were a wee boy and all your friends would hang about our hall laughing and joking.'

We walked across town afterwards to a piano bar and she told the man playing the piano that it was her birthday to get a free bottle of champagne, even though it was not strictly true (or even approximately true). He played 'Please Release Me' for her as a special request. Some girls at the next table on a hen night were getting a little rowdy, one wanted to kiss me because she was getting married. 'Leave him alone,' said my mother. 'The young hussies these days have no shame.'

A few years later, we both went to another awards ceremony held in the City Hall. My novel *The Corner Boys* had been shortlisted for the same prize. I had been told that Chris Patten would be there to hand out the award, and that the republican politician Gerry Adams would be attending the function. 'I'll have one or two things to say to old Gerry,' my mother had warned me, 'after what he's put us through. There's no two ways about that. I'll have a wee word in his ear alright.' She was looking forward to the event, but I was worried about what she might say; all that day she had been getting excited talking about prize-givings of the past. 'When you and your brother were young,' she said, 'you won all the prizes in St Mark's from the JTC and the CLB. My neighbours used to tell me that it wasn't worth going because the Beattie boys won everything that was going.' I had to get out of the house so I went shopping and then I realised that I was going to be late so I rang her from town and told her to make her own way there. I would go straight from town.

I stood at the back door of the City Hall waiting for her, and saw the Call-a-Cab car drive in past security. The driver nodded at me, as if he recognised me, and got my mother's wheelchair out of the boot. She was still chatting away to him. 'Do you remember playing "foot in the bucket" when you were young?' she asked him after he had opened the door to let her out. 'That's the problem with young people nowadays; they don't know how to keep themselves amused.' I pushed her into the City Hall slowly and carefully. The other guests all stood around in the centre of the room, holding their wine glasses delicately. I noticed that the men all seemed to be wearing grey suits, and all the women elegant black dresses with silver brooches. Then there was me in my puffa jacket and my mother in her pink anorak, with Top Shop bags, from that day's shopping, balancing on her wheelchair. She was wearing the wig that the dog liked to chase around the house. 'I'm starving,' she said, after we had pushed through the crowd. 'I haven't had any dinner. Go and get us some of them whatever they are.'

I went in search of food and got my mother a large glass of white wine. 'I'm thirsty,' she said. 'I haven't had a drink all day.' The speeches were starting, there were television cameras dotted around the room and every now and then, some small circular area would suddenly light up in intense, white light. Chris Patten's report on the future of the RUC was just about to be released and the cameras were there partly to capture a few comments from him. The other contestants and their coteries of friends stood in a group in the middle of the floor. The women in their expensive dresses adorned with silver bracelets in intricate Celtic patterns looked appreciatively up at him; my mother was concentrating on the food in front of her.

The waitress with the nibbles had found us on our own, stranded from everybody else. 'I'm starving,' said my mother to her, 'these little things don't fill you up.' 'Here you are love,' said the waitress, handing her a larger plate, as Patten started to speak. 'This is my son,' said my mother. 'He's up for the prize tonight, you know, but he won't win it. You have to be in the know to win prizes, and he doesn't know anybody.'

'Yes, but it's nice to be invited,' said the woman with the nibbles.

'Of course,' said my mother 'that's what I tell him. You should be proud just to be invited to the City Hall.'

'Exactly,' said the waitress.

'Have you met Gerry Adams?' said my mother.

'Oh yes,' said the waitress, 'he's a regular. Him and Martin McGuinness, they're never out of here, that is when they're not up in Stormont running around as if they own the place.'

My mother was sitting in her wheelchair making blowing noises. 'Who would have believed it?' she said. 'They're running the country and there's no two ways about that. They got everything they wanted. The Protestants got nothing.'

I stood there against the wall. I noticed that there were black stains up the outside of the arms of my jacket. I spent some time just staring at them and trying to rub them off with spit. The waitress had gone to get her some more wine.

'You're too backward,' my mother said to me. 'Go and talk to those men over there. Tell them that you're a professor.'

The waitress had returned with more wine and more food and overheard this.

'Is he a professor?' asked the waitress.

'He is indeed. But you couldn't tell to look at him,' said my mother.

'Are those his bags?' said the waitress. 'In the old days you wouldn't have been allowed in here with bags like that.'

'Does Gerry ever try to bring big bags in with him?' asked my mother and they both started laughing. 'Is Gerry not coming then?' asked my mother, whom I think was disappointed in some strange way.

Chris Patten looked in our direction. It was probably the laughter that attracted his attention. He said something about my novel. I couldn't hear what it was.

'What's in those mushroom pates?' asked my mother.

'Mushrooms,' I said.

'What else?' she asked irritated. 'Do you know; you can't get a sensible answer out of you sometimes.'

The waitress went off to fetch some more drinks. We were still standing in the same spot. I made some pretence and then pushed my mother's chair so that she was now facing the wall, with her back to Chris Patten. 'I can't see,' she said. 'There's nothing to see,' I said. The waitress had returned. 'Are you not watching what's going on?' she asked. Chris Patten was just about to announce the winner. 'And the winner is …' he said.

I didn't hear the name but I knew that it wasn't mine. 'Never mind,' said my mother. 'Never mind,' said the waitress, 'Have some more of these lovely mushroom pates.' We could hear the chatter from across the room. 'What time does the bar close?' asked my mother. 'It's open as long as you like,' said the waitress. 'Within reason,' she added. 'Let's have a few more wee drinks then,' said my mother. 'And for God's sake go and speak to some of those people. You're never going to win a prize like that if you don't speak to people,' she said. 'That's his problem he never speaks, except to bloody women. But then he's had a lot of practice at that.'

I wandered off to find a toilet and I tried smiling at one or two people unsuccessfully. My mother had decided that it was time to go. 'By the way, is there a wee phone around here for us to call Call-a-Cab when all this drink finishes?' she asked the waitress. 'We don't want to be stranded here all bloody night with nothing to eat.' I went to ring Call-a-Cab but they were engaged, so I just hung about by the public telephone at the back door and then I bumped into a female TV producer from Dublin who just smiled at me and asked me if I had enjoyed the proceedings. It turned out that she was there to make some arts-based programme about the evening for RTE, but that all the interviews she needed were now in the can. I blurted out that my book was on the shortlist. It was too late to be relevant to anything; it was a moment for chitchat, nothing more. 'Really?' she said, and I looked at her expression and I regretted saying it even more. 'It's a pity that we didn't get to talk earlier. Oh here's my car, I'm just off.' I smiled at her and walked off before doubling back to ring Call-a-Cab once more. Luckily, I got through this time.

I pushed my mother out into the back courtyard of the City Hall to wait for the taxi. She smiled over at the security man and he smiled back at her. 'I think that your man thinks that he's scored,' she said. I wasn't sure whether she was joking or not, so I pretended that I hadn't heard. We hung about outside in the cold, night air, a woman in a wheelchair and a man in a grubby coat. It was the professor and his proud mother going back home to the turn-of-the-road from the literary prize giving, the professor who had departed from his working-class roots, but had not quite arrived anywhere else yet.

These are the moments I remember; I cling onto them because that is all there is. They are even sadder at the time of year I started writing this, with Mother's Day approaching. I would send her flowers every Mother's Day and ring her to make sure that they had arrived. 'They are lovely,' she would say. 'I've shown them to all my neighbours, they're all very jealous,' and, at that moment, I would feel ecstatic. Then, she would add 'It would have been much nicer if you'd brought them in person.'

Of course, I would love to pick up the phone today, and just order the flowers and then ring that old number of hers in Belfast just to hear her say … anything. She was right a lot of the time, and sometimes I wished that I'd listened more in that busy, busy life of mine.

I wrote about my mother and our relationship for the *Belfast Telegraph*. One elderly lady from Belfast wrote to me to say that 'despite the kinds of things that were said between the two of you, it was obvious that you loved each other', as if this could ever have been in doubt. 'That's just how mothers sometimes talk to their sons,' she wrote 'and vice versa. You were just as bad as each other, but the love shines through. I wept when I read your wee article.'

But why is this? Why do we say these sorts of things to one another? Why do we feel constrained to deal with each other in these sorts of ways? How does this pattern mutate and evolve over time?

If ever the mind is conflicted, it would seem to be conflicted most when we talk to those we love. We say things that we know are going to be hurtful and wait for those missives to land. My father died when I was a 13-year-old boy, but when I said hurtful things to her, especially during my adolescence, driven no doubt by an unarticulated anger over his death, she knew the most hurtful thing to say back. It was always the same. 'If your father was alive today, he'd be ashamed of you.' I can picture her saying it now: I can hear the tone in her voice and see her face, contorted in that blend of sadness and defiance, but still somehow looking up for the effect on me, the coup de grace.

These sorts of conversation were like an arms race, escalating turn by turn, and this, we both knew, was the nuclear option.

Of course, I remember how it felt and what my response was: sadness, despair, anger, frustration, guilt, usually contained, but sometimes I would lash out verbally. However, I never contested it. I felt unable to comment on the truth or validity of the statement, on my father's perceptions and interpretations of me as a developing adolescent. I could not bear to talk about my father because it was just too painful, let alone talk about how he might feel, if he was alive, which he clearly wasn't. There was none of 'How would he feel about you?' or 'Perhaps we wouldn't be arguing like this if we were not both consumed with grief that we are unable to deal with.'

Sometimes I was more composed. I would go to hug her and put my arm around her, and she would stiffen (it wasn't over just yet), so I would take my arm away, and she would say 'I know you don't love me, you always loved your father more than me. You can see it in all our wee photos by the seaside, you're always sitting next to him, not me.'

And I would stand there, staring straight ahead, unable to move, hardly able to breathe, as she sobbed right in front of me, within arm's reach. However, my arm could not reach forward of its own volition. I could not walk away or move forward. I just stood there watching a woman getting older through grief, and knowing that if I was not the ultimate cause of that grief (my father's untimely death surely was), that I was also not, in any way, part of the solution. Even when I went off to read psychology at university over in England, across the water, they say in Belfast, to emphasise the great distance of a few miles of water, I knew there was no escape.

I came back home at Christmas at the end of my first term, talking excitedly about psycho-genetics and learning theory, Pavlov's dogs, Skinner's rats and Konrad Lorenz's ducks. Maybe, it was the mention of the ducks that did it, maybe she was expecting me to have learned something about human emotions, or human sadness and loss, or maybe it was my description of the way that the ducks had imprinted on Lorenz himself. Maybe that was the final straw. 'They just never left him,' I said enthusiastically, with awe and naivety. 'They just followed him everywhere like he was their mother.'

And she cried. Not at the wonders of science, or what we can learn from imprinting experiments, or even how ducks and children can vary, but how 'carried away' I was with my new life, how all I cared about was 'number one', and how psychology doesn't necessarily give you any insights into anything that matters.

Gregory Bateson and the 'double bind'

A year or so later, I read Gregory Bateson's classic book *Steps to an Ecology of Mind*. I wanted to understand some of the intellectual background to the new thinking about madness in the works of R. D. Laing and others. This was all the rage; schizophrenia was now to be regarded as a breakthrough rather than as a breakdown, in the universities at least. She wasn't impressed.

'Have you ever been to Purdysburn?' she asked. 'Or do you know anybody who's had to be put in there and shocked until their head sizzles? Well, I have and that's no bloody breakthrough. You could have fried a bloody egg on old Mary's forehead.'

I was pointed towards Bateson at university; Bateson as the intellectual giant. 'The vision of Blake,' my earnest, heavily bearded philosophy lecturer said one afternoon. One could see all of life in a grain of sand, the other could understand all of human experience in the most basic atom of conflict in communication. Bateson discovered the 'double bind', that simple little twist of communication that changes everything. 'That was the starting point for Laing. Schizophrenia is only partly in the genes, it's mainly in the environment, and particularly in those close interactions between family members. It is the family that's really dangerous. Bateson knew that.'

And he leaned back in a heavily worn brown leather armchair, a chair which no doubt violated every university rule of standard office furniture, drew heavily on his Gauloise, and then expertly expelled the smoke into the vacant gap in front of him, where three of his second year tutees sat, desperately trying to avoid eye contact, either with one another or with him. He closed his eyes briefly and almost whispered as if confiding to us, 'To see a world in a grain of sand/And a heaven in a wild flower/Hold infinity in the palm of your hand/And eternity in an hour.'

The tutorial felt like an eternity. He opened his eyes again, as if coming out of a long sleep, and took one more long drag on his cigarette. 'So what are your families like?' he asked. There was silence. I looked down at my boots, and noticed that there was some grass at the end of the left boot. It was sticking out at an odd angle, stuck in that gap between the upper and the sole. It had probably been there for some time. 'Do any of you have a schizophrenogenic mother? There was still silence, so I pulled the grass out slowly and flicked it onto his beige, coffee-stained carpet.

'A castrating mother who is going to fuck you up. You might not know just yet. You might not *know*, after all what is knowledge, but you might be starting to sense it.' I started choking on his cigarette smoke, louder and louder, so loud that he couldn't continue.

He looked straight at me. 'Some might see your *disruption* here, as highly significant,' he said directly to me. 'Ask your psychology tutors about defence mechanisms. Ask your psychology tutors whether rats have them?' And he laughed loudly at his own joke. 'Perhaps, that's why they only study rats over there. They're afraid of what real psychology might reveal to them.' The tutorial finished early.

Despite this, or maybe because of it, I borrowed Bateson's book from the library and read it carefully, in private. In reality, it was not a disappointment. It seemed to explain everything; its scope was magnificent. It was indeed the world in a grain of sand, as William Blake would have said. It explained how madness is a rational response to an irrational situation, how irrationality is constructed in talk, how certain family members propagate this irrationality through their behaviour. And all of this boiled down to one simple behaviour, the double bind, an utterance or a series of utterances that put the recipient in an 'impossible' situation, because of an inherent contradiction in the communication. Any possible response was wrong. What jumped off the page for me was the description of the behaviour in question. I knew that I had seen it before somewhere:

> A young man who had fairly well recovered … was visited in the hospital by his mother. He was glad to see her and impulsively put his arm around her shoulders, whereupon she stiffened. He withdrew his arm and she asked, 'Don't you love me anymore?' He then blushed, and she said, 'Dear, you must not be so easily embarrassed and afraid of your feelings.' The patient was able to stay with her only a few minutes more and following her departure he assaulted an orderly and was put in the tubs.

(Bateson 1973: 188)

The fact that the young man in question had been suffering from acute schizophrenia made this all the more poignant. He had been driven mad because of this conflicting communication, literally mad.

Bateson goes on to write that

> Obviously, this result could have been avoided if the young man had been able to say, 'Mother, it is obvious that you become uncomfortable when I put my arm around you, and that you have difficulty in accepting a gesture of affection from me.' However, the schizophrenic patient doesn't have this possibility open to him. His intense dependency and training prevents him from communicating upon his mother's communicative behaviour, though she comments on his and forces him to accept and to attempt to deal with the complicated sequence.
>
> (Bateson 1973: 189)

I could almost feel a chill when I first read these descriptions of a double bind. But, like every undergraduate, I saw examples of every psychological topic that we studied, from manic depression to delusional thinking, in my own life. My life at that time was full of chills. Our psychology lecturers had warned us to be careful about this extrapolation process; you need to examine the evidence more carefully, they explained. My heavily bearded philosophy lecturer, however, told me to be bolder. 'Recognise your experiences. Fight your intense dependency. Liberate yourself from the shackles of the family. Don't become a victim.'

I went home and listed the double binds in my own life. Some were easily recorded, as I talked to my mother on the telephone, or on one of my visits home, and I found myself surreptitiously reaching for my notebook:

> I want you to work hard for your exams. You never make time for me.
>
> Why don't you come home in the summer? Remember, there's nothing over here for you to do.

> You were such an affectionate boy. Now you just pretend to be affectionate – when you want something.
>
> What are you writing down in that notebook? Why don't you pay any attention to me?

Some, however, were not solely verbal, but were harder to record, they were highly subjective. They were embodied in the conflict between the language and the nonverbal behaviour, but they were very reminiscent of what Bateson himself had described.

I wrote slowly and carefully for my philosophy lecturer:

> I go to hug her, she stiffens, then sighs. I take my arm away, and she looks mildly disgusted at my withdrawal. The look of disgust was a very brief expression, a micro-expression at best, that only I could have detected. The sigh, however, was quite audible.

But when I studied my list as a whole, I realised that although many of the utterances might be slightly contrary, they were hardly the stuff of pathogenesis. Or were they? Some were somewhat 'contradictory'. But was that enough? I dreaded showing my double bind diary to my philosophy lecturer. How would I defend the presence of the micro-expression? How could I prove its existence? Existential issues reared up in front of me, making me approach the book again, then avoid it, then eventually I picked up the book.

Bateson wrote 'The mother's reaction of not accepting her son's affectionate gesture is masterfully covered up by her condemnation of him for withdrawing, and the patient denies his perception of the situation by accepting her condemnation' (Bateson 1973: 189).

So it is clear that the double bind is not just about two mutually contradictory communications, stiffening and sighing and then a micro-expression of disgust, for example, it is also about the son accepting the condemnation of his mother, agreeing to her version of reality. In other words, Bateson maintains that double binds are about control – not just of the course of the interaction, and not just about the interpretation and meaning of the acts that constitute the interaction, but about the very nature of the situation itself. They control the 'reality' of the situation. This puts the young schizophrenic patient, the recipient of the double bind, the 'victim', in his own existential dilemma, which Bateson explains as follows – 'If I am to keep my tie to mother, I must not show her that I love her, but if I do not show her that I love her, then I will lose her' (Bateson 1973: 190).

But this is clearly not how it felt for me. I just thought that she was being 'awkward' or 'difficult'. I felt no underlying existential dilemma. But I was being urged by my lecturer in no uncertain terms to persevere. 'Philosophy takes the commonplace and makes it difficult. If it seems clear, then you're not thinking hard enough. If it seems incomprehensible, then you're thinking more clearly.' I blinked back at him. 'I see,' I said.

I went back to search for moments of simplistic clarity in Bateson, which might turn out, on further study, to be bordering on the incomprehensible. I only half succeeded.

Bateson attempted to specify in detail what features constitute these 'double binds'. He said that 'the necessary ingredients' are as follows: it must involve two or more people, usually (and controversially) the mother. I say 'controversially' because there did not seem to be any a priori theoretical reason why this should be the case. Bateson added a qualification of sorts: 'We do not assume that the double bind is inflicted by the mother alone, but that it may be done either by mother alone or by some combination of mother, father and/or siblings' (Bateson 1973: 178). In other words, the role of the mother either acting on her own or in combination with other members of the family seems clear and unambiguous in his thinking. And interestingly, all of the clinical examples he cited in support of his theory involved the mother.

Second, it must be recurrent rather than a one-off: 'Our hypothesis does not invoke a single traumatic experience, but such repeated experience that the double bind structure comes to be an habitual expectation' (p. 178). Third, it must have a primary negative injunction issued by one member of an intense relationship to another. This may have the form of 'Do not do so and so, or I will punish you', or 'If you do not do so and so, I will punish you'. Bateson and his colleagues assumed that punishment 'may be either the withdrawal of love or the expression of hate or anger, or most devastating the kind of abandonment that results from the parent's expression of extreme helplessness'. Fourth, there must be a secondary injunction, a more 'abstract' communication that conflicts with the first and again 'enforced by punishments or signal which threaten survival'. He wrote that 'This secondary injunction is commonly communicated to the child by nonverbal means. Posture, gesture, tone of voice, meaningful action and the implications concealed in verbal comment may all be used to convey this more abstract message' (p. 178).

He also made the point that 'the secondary injunction may impinge upon any element of the primary prohibition'. If one were to translate the secondary injunction into words, then it would translate as 'Do not see this as punishment', 'Do not see me as the punishing agent', 'Do not submit to my prohibitions', 'Do not think of what you must not do', 'Do not question my love of which the primary prohibition is (or is not) an example'. He also wrote that the secondary injunction may involve others acting in tandem with the mother such that 'one parent may negate at a more abstract level the injunctions of the other' (p. 179). The fifth feature is that there must be 'A tertiary negative injunction prohibiting the victim from escaping the field' (p. 179). Bateson added, 'if the double binds are imposed during infancy, escape is naturally impossible'.

Therefore, this set of features specify a double bind in this classic paper grandly called 'Towards a Theory of Schizophrenia'. However, not all of the features need to be present and this is one of the most curious features in their account when the description of a recurrent pattern of communication is turned towards a focus on the perceptions of one of the two individuals involved (the 'victim'). Bateson writes that the complete set of ingredients is no longer necessary when the victim has learned to perceive his universe in double bind patterns. Almost any part of a double bind sequence may then be sufficient to precipitate panic or rage. 'The pattern of conflicting injunctions may even be taken over by hallucinatory voices' (Bateson 1973: 179).

This makes the formal identification of double binds and their possible instrumental role in psychopathology that much more problematic because their characteristic defining features do not actually have to be present.

So was this the incomprehensible element that my lecturer had urged me to pursue. A double bind is a mutually contradictory communication that doesn't actually have to contradict, except in the head of the mad person. The double bind was now being framed as an issue to do with perception where critical aspects like the conflicting injunctions can be imagined through hallucinations. I thought that my double bind diary might not be as useful as I had originally thought.

However, the ambition of Bateson was not to be halted. He boiled it down later in the same paper to a simple recipe (to continue with his own metaphor of 'ingredients'). He said that the general characteristics of a double bind are:

> (1) When the individual is involved in an intense relationship; that is, a relationship in which he feels it is vitally important that he discriminate accurately what sort of message is being communicated so that he may respond appropriately. (2) And, the individual is caught in a situation in which the other person is expressing two orders of message and one of these denies the other. (3) And, the individual is unable to comment on the messages being expressed to correct his discrimination of what order to respond to, i.e., he cannot make a metacommunicative statement.
>
> (Bateson 1973: 180)

Bateson accepts that this can occur in 'normal' relations and that in such situations the victim will also behave defensively, but that with pre-schizophrenics (his word, but without the hyphen), they feel 'so terribly on the spot at all times' that they end up confused about messages and their intentions. They are, according to Bateson, particularly confused about the meta-communicative system – the system of communication about the communication.

> If a person said to him, 'What would you like to do today?' he would be unable to judge accurately by the context or by the

tone of voice or gesture whether he was being condemned for
what he did yesterday, or being offered a sexual invitation, or
just what was meant.

(Bateson 1973: 182)

Bateson says that in response some become concerned about
hidden meanings behind every utterance (and he says we call this
'paranoid'). Some accept literally what is said regardless of whether
it is contradicted by 'tone or gesture or context' and laugh off these
meta-communicative signs (and we call this 'hebephrenic'). Some
choose to ignore all utterances and 'detach his interest from the
external world and concentrate on his own internal processes' (and
we call this 'catatonic').

'Do not see this as punishment'

It need hardly be pointed out that the criteria for the double bind
here (from Bateson et al. 1956, listed on page 180 in the 1973
volume) had shifted somewhat from those specified earlier in the
same paper (page 178 in the 1973 volume), as Schuham (1967) and
others have noted. The second set of criteria includes a statement
about the *intensity* of the relationship and the victim's *motivational
state* ('he feels it is vitally important that he discriminate accurately
what sort of *message* is being communicated'). There would appear
to be very significant differences between these two sets of criteria
which raise important conceptual and methodological issues about
how we go about making judgements about the intensity of
relationships and the motivational state of the victim, and therefore
very serious issues about the formal identification of double binds.
But as Schuham also notes, 'It is not clear in this paper whether the
authors thought these two sets of criteria to be equivalent or to
apply to two independent situations' (1967: 411). In other words, it
is not clear in the original paper whether or not Bateson and his
co-authors foresaw these issues or not.

Of course, there is another major difference between the two sets
of criteria, which has given rise to even more confusion in the
published literature. In the first set, Bateson and his colleagues focus

on the concept of 'level' of communication in the double bind. One criterion specifies 'A secondary injunction conflicting with the first at a more abstract level, and like the first enforced by punishments or signals which threaten survival'. They also say that

> The secondary injunction is more difficult to describe than the primary for two reasons. First, the secondary injunction is commonly communicated to the child by non-verbal means. Posture, gesture, tone of voice, meaningful action and the implications concealed in verbal comment may all be used to convey this more abstract message. Second, the secondary injunction may impinge upon any element of the primary prohibition. Verbalization of the secondary injunction may, therefore, include a wide variety of forms; for example, 'Do not see this as punishment'; 'Do not see me as the punishing agent': 'Do not submit to my prohibitions'; 'Do not think of what you must not do'; 'Do not question my love of which the primary prohibition is (or is not) an example'; and so on.
>
> (Bateson et al. 1973: 178–179)

In the second set of criteria, Bateson et al. focus on the concept of 'orders of message', as in 'the individual is caught in a situation in which the other person is expressing two orders of message and one of these denies the other' (1973: 180).

Schuham (1967) has pointed out that the concept of levels associated with double binds are associated with a number of quite different dimensions. Bateson et al. (in the first set of criteria) put most emphasis on the abstract–concrete dimension but the other levels, which have also been discussed in this same context, are the verbal–nonverbal dimension, the communicative–meta-communicative dimension, the literal–metaphorical dimension, the particular–contextual dimension and the content–relationship dimension.

Verbal and nonverbal communication

Of course, what is even more confusing is that Bateson seems to assume that nonverbal communication necessarily represents a more 'abstract' form of communication than verbal language. But this can be seriously disputed. Some of the communicative effects of nonverbal communication may be more direct than verbal language (e.g. facial expression) especially in terms of commonality of production and interpretation (see Ekman 1975). Kahneman (2011) argues that the interpretation of emotional facial expression is an example of automatic System 1 type thinking – automatic, fast and effortless ('As surely and quickly as you saw that the young woman's hair is dark, you knew that she is angry', Kahneman 2011: 19). Some forms of nonverbal communication are specifically iconic (McNeill 1992; Beattie 2003; 2016), where the nonverbal gesture (the signifier) bears a similarity in form to the concept, object or action that is being communicated about (the signified). This would clearly make them less 'abstract' and much more 'concrete'. David McNeill (1992) has argued this consistently in the case of hand gestures. But he also argued that the mode of communication of gesture differs in other ways to speech, and not just in terms of iconicity, but again in ways that do the opposite of making them more 'abstract'. McNeill says that the method by which nonverbal gestures convey meaning is fundamentally different to the way language does this. Language acts by segmenting meaning so that an instantaneous thought is divided up into its component parts and strung out through time, as in:

> *the table can be [raised up towards the ceiling]*
> Iconic: hands are resting on knee; hands move upwards, palms pointing down, forming a large gesture, hands continue moving until the hands reach the area just above shoulder level.

The single event here is being described both by language and by the accompanying iconic gesture. The square brackets indicate the start point and end point of the gesture. The speech does this in a linear and segmented fashion, first identifying what is being raised ('the table') and then describing the action ('can be raised up') and then describing the direction of the action ('towards the ceiling'). The linguist de Saussure (1916) argued that this linear-segmented character of language arises because language is essentially one-dimensional whereas meaning is essentially multidimensional. Language can only vary along the single dimension of time with regard to the units out of which it is comprised. As the psychologist Susan Goldin-Meadow and her colleagues note in 1996: 'This restriction forces language to break meaning complexes into segments and to reconstruct multidimensional meanings by combining the segments in time.'

But the gestures that accompany language don't convey meaning in this linear and segmented manner; rather they convey a number of aspects of meaning at the same time in a single multidimensional gesture. The gesture on page 144, for example, depicts the table (and its size), and the movement (and its speed), and the direction of the movement, all simultaneously. The important point is that, as Goldin-Meadow notes, the iconic gestures which accompany speech 'are themselves free to vary on dimensions of space, time, form, trajectory, and so forth and can present meaning complexes without undergoing segmentation or linearization'. So does this make nonverbal communication more abstract? Or less abstract because gestures are not necessarily divided into linguistic units with a syntax necessary for the interpretation of meaning? It is almost certainly the latter.

Speech also relies on 'bottom-up' processing, in that the meanings of the words are combined to create the meaning of the sentence. To understand a sentence, you have to start with the lower level words (hence 'bottom-up'), whereas in gestures we start with the overall concept portrayed by the gesture. It is this concept which gives rise to the meaning of the individual parts (hence 'top-down'). McNeill provides the following example:

> The gesture is a symbol in that it represents something other than itself – the hand is not a hand but a character, the movement is not a hand in motion but the character in motion, the space is not the physical space of the narrator but a narrative space, the wiggling fingers are not fingers but running feet. The gesture is thus a symbol, but the symbol is of a fundamentally different type from the symbols of speech. This gesture–symbol is global in that the whole is not composed out of separately meaningful parts. Rather, the

> parts gain meaning because of the meaning of the whole. The
> wiggling fingers mean running only because we know that
> the gesture, as a whole, depicts someone running.
>
> (McNeill 1992: 20)

The important point to remember here is that when produced by
this same speaker, this wiggling finger gesture may well have a
different meaning (McNeill points out, for example, that it was also
used for 'indecision between two alternatives'). In order to argue that
gestures are processed like language in a bottom-up fashion, you
would need to be able to demonstrate that the three components
which comprise the running gesture – the V hand shape, the wiggling
motion and the forward movement – have relatively stable meanings
in the person's communicational repertoire, which can be recognised
and interpreted wherever they are used. But this is not the case.

Another important difference between speech and gesture is that
different gestures do not combine together to form more complex
gestures:

> With gestures, each symbol is a complete expression of meaning
> unto itself. Most of the time gestures are one to a clause but
> occasionally more than one gesture occurs within a single
> clause. Even then the several gestures don't combine into a
> more complex gesture. Each gesture depicts the content from a
> different angle, bringing out a different aspect or temporal
> phase, and each is a complete expression of meaning by itself.
>
> (McNeill 1992: 21)

Gestures also convey meaning in a different way because there
are no standards of form with gestures. Standards of form are a
defining feature of all languages. All linguistic systems have standards
of well-formedness to which all utterances that fall within it must
conform, or be dismissed as not proper or not grammatical. Gestures
have no such standards of form. Thus, different speakers display the
same meaning in idiosyncratic but nevertheless recognisable ways.
As McNeill (1992: 41) says: 'Lacking standards of form, individuals
create their own gesture symbols for the same event, each

incorporating a core meaning but adding details that seem salient, and these are different from speaker to speaker.' This non-standardisation of form is very important for theoretical reasons:

> Precisely because gestures are not obliged to meet standards of form, they are free to present just those aspects of meaning that are relevant and salient to the speaker and leave out aspects that language may require but are not relevant to the situation.
>
> (McNeill 1992: 22)

In the example on page 148 (Table 5.1), each of the three speakers creates the spinning movement of the table, but they do this differently. One uses one finger, two use both arms, two use clockwise movements, one makes an anti-clockwise movement, two make two movements, one makes three movements (Beattie and Shovelton 2002a). The point of this particular picture in the cartoon story is to show the chaos caused when Billy gets on a chair that now spins, causing a table to spin. One of the gestures seems to focus specifically on the rapid speed of the spinning; one specifically on the extent of the spinning; and the third depicts both aspects simultaneously.

Therefore, iconic gestures and speech convey meaning in radically different ways, with speech relying on a lexicon for breaking meaning down into its component parts and a syntax for combining these various elements into meaningful sentences, whereas iconic gestures represent multidimensional meanings simultaneously in one complex image. Each speaker creates the iconic gestures spontaneously without relying on a lexicon with defined standards of form, and even consecutive iconic gestures do not combine into higher order units. Each gesture is complete in itself, and the overall meaning of what is being portrayed represented in iconic form gives the meaning to the individual components.

These gestures work in this multidimensional and iconic manner not just when physical events are being described, but also when they are being used 'metaphorically' in much of everyday interaction, for example, when the hands move close together to indicate the

TABLE 5.1 Iconic representation in gesture

The signifier: the actual speech and gestures produced by three different narrators	The signified: the event referred to
[It like spins round] *Iconic*: Left index finger makes three rapid, small clockwise movements.	Billy Whizz causes a table to spin around.
The table went [spinning] *Iconic*: Right arm moves in two large clockwise circles, while the left hand moves away from and then towards the right arm.	
Wrecks everything [spinning round and round and round and round and round] *Iconic*: Both arms make two large rapid anti-clockwise movements.	

'intimacy' of a relationship, the hand or hands move upwards to indicate 'higher moral standards', the hands move apart to indicate different positions on a burning political issue, etc. Whether this combination of attributes makes the nonverbal gestures more 'abstract' than speech remains to be seen. You could clearly argue the opposite, that the iconicity of gesture, and therefore the inherent relationship with the thing being described, allows communication to progress in a more concrete way than is the case with verbal language where words do not have these iconic properties. The gesture also represents meaning in one whole, without an abstract syntax for combining the meaning from the various sequential gestures. Again, you could consider this as more 'concrete' than what occurs with speech. The meanings of these gestures are processed 'effortlessly' alongside the speech itself (Beattie and Shovelton 1999a; 1999b; Holler and Beattie 2003a; 2003b). When the gesture does not match the speech, and this does happen in certain situations where, for example, people are asked to intentionally deceive (Cohen et al. 2010), or when a speaker's underlying, implicit attitude to something like the environment and their self-reported attitude do not match, and where they report that they are 'greener' than they actually are, then this can affect both the message received (in that the messages from both channels are integrated) and the perception of the person speaking (Beattie and Sale 2012). Those with mismatching speech and gesture are liked less, and listeners are less confident that what they are saying is true. None of these sorts of considerations were ever considered, by Bateson, even though some early work on gesture (see Beattie 2003, ch. 4) significantly predates Bateson's own theorising about the 'concrete' and 'abstract' nature of speech and nonverbal behaviour.

One might well be tempted to conclude that nonverbal behaviours like gesture are significantly 'more concrete' than verbal language because of their non-arbitrary and iconic nature. Critically, gestural movements seem to be rooted in sensory–motor schemas, which are clearly very concrete indeed, and gestures do not rely on combinatorial rules, or syntax, to communicate their meaning.

Nonverbal communication could, however, be considered more 'abstract' in one particular way, and that is because if it is not itself encoded in verbal language then its subsequent encoding into language (by way of description) does require a degree of abstraction from the primary mode of its representation. But that, of course, is more a point about analytic description rather than its mode of operation in everyday interaction.

Of course, another of the examples used by Bateson ('the implications concealed in verbal comment') can be more abstract than the straightforward interpretation of simple utterances, especially if the implications are relevant to the interpretation of the content of the language ('Do not see this as punishment') or relevant to the signalling and interpretation of the nature of the relationship ('Do not see me as the punishing agent'). What is implied by any utterance within the context of family interaction can be very abstract indeed as it may require knowledge of previous conversations, previous interactions and previous experiences to work out the implications of what is being communicated (see Garfinkel 1967). Thus, it might be very difficult for researchers (even researchers in their role as therapists with more detailed knowledge of the nature of the relationship) to ascertain exactly what is going on, and to determine exactly what is being implied at any point in time. Of course, that is not to deny that what is being implied by any utterance in a conversation is not critical to the action, it is just to flag up the difficulty in identifying these either from an emic or etic perspective.

Bateson et al. do not help matters here by quickly moving on (in the same paper) to the concept of 'orders of message' that deny one another. Are 'orders of message' meant to be synonymous with 'levels'? And is the specified criterion 'the other person in a relationship is expressing two orders of message and one of these denies the other' (1973: 180) meant to be synonymous with 'a secondary injunction conflicting with the first at a more abstract level' (1973: 178)? One criterion specifies *denial* as a core feature, the other specifies *conflict*. Of course, the connotations of conflict and denial would seem to many to be quite different. Denial, as a process, would seem to be a more active process and perhaps even more deliberative. Conflicting messages, on the other hand, surely are the stuff of everyday life. Teasing, joking, flirting, sarcasm, humour all involve conflicting communications. Whether they also involve the more active processes of actual *denial* is more open to question, although they may on occasion ('I wasn't really asking you out; you misinterpreted what I was saying' after a very flirty discussion of a good place for lunch) might be one explicit verbal denial following something altogether more ambiguous.

One other important issue about the double bind, as specified by Bateson and his colleagues, is whether or not the victim actually needs to be (consciously) aware that he or she is indeed a target of a double bind communication. As Schuham himself observes 'If not, does this negate the pathogenicity of what the observer would describe as a double bind situation?' (1967: 411). Schuham goes on to examine Watzlawick et al.'s (1967) further elaboration of the essential criteria in this context. They argued that double binds are not simply contradictions or examples of conflicting communication where there are responses open to individuals, they said that double binds are about paradox, where 'choice itself is impossible'.

Schuham points out that this confuses the concept even more because it now establishes that it is the nature of the relationship itself that is necessary for inferring the existence of double binds rather than the communication patterns per se. Indeed, Watzlawick

(1963) asserted that 'Indeed, it would be impossible to imagine any emotional involvement, such as for instance courtship, in which double bind does not constitute a core element' (1963: 145). This changes the focus from communicational patterns per se to a focus on the nature of the relationship – many relationships generate conflicting communications, only some generate genuine paradoxes. This makes certain types of research on the double bind (which just focus on the identification of conflicting communication) even more problematic.

How problematic in the first decade after its formulation is clearly spelt out in the Schuham paper. He points out that 'The great bulk of the literature ... consist[s] of the presentation of case histories, transcripts of family psychotherapist sessions, clinical descriptions and anecdotes' (1967: 413). Schuham rejects this work on the basis that it cannot be accepted as scientific evidence to validate the theory in question. He found only five studies using a more scientific approach in that first decade after the theory was proposed, and the most important feature of these studies (quite simply) is that they did *not* involve analysis of actual real-life face-to-face interaction, which is what the theory was all about. They involved testing 'memory' for double binds, or behaviour in simulated games, tone discriminations, the resolution of metaphors, the analysis of letters, but no analysis of multichannel face-to-face communication. For example, Berger (1965) asked schizophrenics to estimate how frequently double bind communications had been made by their mothers and found that the schizophrenic group scored significantly higher than any other group. But, of course, this difference in frequency of identification could be attributable to different levels of sensitivity to these kinds of communications, or symptomatic of more general negative attitudes to the mother as part of a process of blame ('she should have protected me more, then I wouldn't be in this state'). Potash (1965) tried to elicit double binds in a game situation but found that withdrawal 'was neither exclusive nor differential to schizophrenics'. Ciotola (1961) tried to generate double binds in an experimental situation in which the discrimination of two auditory tones was impossible. The results of the study did not, however, support the hypothesis that schizophrenics would react worse to the double bind situation. Loeff (1966) presented emotional metaphors to schizophrenics and controls, but found that the schizophrenics were more influenced by the metacommunicative elements, contrary to Bateson's apparent prediction that they would have problems at this level. Ringuette and Kennedy (1966) asked five groups of judges to identify double bind communications in letters written by parents to their hospitalised schizophrenic and non-schizophrenic offspring. One group of judges consisted of three of those researchers actually involved in the formulation of the double bind hypothesis. The inter-rater reliability of the identification of the double binds was extremely low (inter-observer reliability for the experts was 0.19), and only one group (the experts) could differentiate the letters received from the schizophrenics from the letters received from the non-schizophrenics.

Schuham's conclusions on the basis of this ten-year review of evidence were extremely pessimistic. He said that there was little agreement about what communicative phenomena are unique to double bind communication and concluded that 'there is no evidence that double bind communication is exclusive to, or differentially associated with pathological communication processes and not associated with normal communication processes'. He went on to say that 'There is no evidence that the double bind phenomena has an etiological connection with the development of the schizophrenic thought disorder' (1967: 415).

Double binds are now everywhere and nowhere

One might imagine that this might have been the end of this particular intellectual journey and that the concept of the double bind might have fallen away. But in many ways it was quite the opposite. It became part of our everyday thinking and, in addition, Bateson's view of the mother and her potential to produce psychological damage in her offspring through the use of double bind communications seeped into other areas of pathology beyond schizophrenia. Bugental and her colleagues applied a form of 'double bind analysis' to interaction in families with 'disturbed' children. At least this time it was actual face-to-face interaction that was the object of study. The disturbed children had been referred by their school to a university psychology department with a variety of 'serious and chronic behaviour and emotional problems'. They were matched with 'controls' on various measures and their patterns of interaction were analysed as they waited for five minutes for the study to begin and then when they discussed what they would like changed in their family. Double binds were operationalised as 'conflicting' communications, if the evaluative tone of the verbal content, facial expression or tone of voice differed on certain scales (the evaluation of each channel defined by a consensus of 4/5 judges).

The conclusion drawn from this study was that 'A much higher proportion of the mothers of disturbed children was observed to produce conflicting messages than of the mothers of normal control children. No equivalent difference was found between the fathers' (1971: 9). The conclusions are couched specifically in the language of the double bind. The authors say that they have studied 'contradictory messages' that 'effectively constrain' the child from responding. The double bind, they seem to assume can be operationalised in terms of conflicting channels and that this provides 'a fruitful avenue to an issue which has previously defied empirical analysis'.

The study, at first sight, appears to be a controlled investigation that yields statistically significant data. Although, even then it is hard to justify the language used throughout the paper. Mothers of the disturbed children somehow become 'disturbed mothers' (a neat but not so subtle shift of usage) as in 'The conflicting messages produced by *disturbed mothers* included conflict between verbal content and facial expression, and between verbal content and tone of voice' (1971: 9). To illustrate this observation, the authors write 'one mother typically cooed all here [sic] criticisms, for example, "That's not n-i-ce", in a "syrupy" voice' (1971: 9). Why cooed? Why do they not say that the single mothers (45 per cent of the 'disturbed' families were one-parent, compared to 0 per cent of the control group), trying to control their sons (85 per cent of the 'disturbed' sample were boys) with behavioural problems sitting in a waiting room, attempted to exert a degree of control over their sons by commenting on their behaviour. But these single mothers knew they were being observed throughout, so they tried to soften their various comments and directives with a more positive tone. Why is this not a better description than one of disturbed mothers sending out contradictory signals, with Bugental et al.'s conclusion that 'This is consistent with the double-bind hypothesis, but suggests that conflicting communication is not limited to schizophrenogenic mothers' (1971: 9).

When it comes to control groups, the researchers did not seem to realise that the meaning of this observational situation in a university psychology department would be very different for the experimental and control groups (one set knew that they were essentially on trial). Neither did the researchers seem to realise that a sample size of eighteen in the experimental group and nine in the control group (you have to exclude participants who did not produce 'agreed upon evaluative communications') led to violations of the assumptions of the chi square test, with corrections for small numbers necessary, and that any small statistically unreliable differences that were observed could best be explained by single mothers at their wits' end, in a university psychology department with all of these judges judging their every move (for that is indeed what judges do).

'I said "Sit still you little shit. Behave yourself for once in your life."' I would have liked this shouted so loudly and with such force and anger by the mothers in that experimental situation that the microphones themselves would have shaken. At least, that way the mothers wouldn't be seen as somehow causing their child's 'disturbed' behaviour through anomalous patterns of communication.

And isn't it interesting that the reality (and inescapable existence) of schizophrenogenic mothers is assumed despite the fact that the researchers note that the theory up to that point 'rests heavily on anecdotal evidence' (1971: 6). But presumably no longer in the light of this research (they vainly hoped). Now it was on the basis of *sound* empirical evidence.

This was an experiment which seems to be in search of a conclusion. It was all about generating yet more blame for 'disturbed' mothers, with little understanding, analysis or insight into human communication under the microscope. To equate channels of communication showing a degree of divergence in 'evaluative content' with the concept of the double bind is clearly just wrong, but clearly right enough in some people's minds to allow for the blaming of schizophrenogenic mothers not just to continue but to be broadened in scope. They're not just responsible for schizophrenia, they're responsible for so much else besides.

At this point you may start wondering what exactly is going on. In order to understand this, it is necessary to consider Bateson's work in a much broader context (as Hartwell 1996 so successfully does). This particular Batesonian view of the schizophrenogenic mother (identified through specific recurrent 'conflicting' communicational features) had its roots in much earlier research. Harry Stack Sullivan (1927) described schizophrenia as 'an unhealthy adjustment strategy' (see Hartwell 1996: 276). As Hartwell points out, once you conceptualise schizophrenia in this way you are, in effect, 'providing theoretical justification for psychoanalytically trained psychiatrists like himself to treat schizophrenia' (Hartwell 1996: 276). Sullivan's view, deriving from his therapy sessions with a small number of male schizophrenics, was that schizophrenia was the result of certain types of early childhood experiences, particularly connected to early mother–child relationships. The concept of the schizophrenia-inducing mother was born in his work. Levy (1931) brought to the table the concept of the overprotective mother, a mother who because she apparently resents her prescribed female role, and has significant unfulfilled ambitions, stops her child becoming independent. According to Levy (1931) 'the wife is competent, takes responsibility readily, and is often derogatory of her husband' (1931: 888).

Kasanin et al. (1934) then combined this focus on the importance of early mother–child relationships for schizophrenia from Sullivan's work with this concept of the overprotective mother, and concluded on the basis of observation that the majority of schizophrenic patients had been overprotected and/or rejected by their mothers. Of course, you will notice that 'overprotection' and 'rejection' appear to be two opposite ends of the spectrum, but what apparently linked them in some mysterious way was the absence of true love. Instead the concept of 'pseudolove' was developed (Reichard and Tillman 1950: 256). Fromm-Reichman (1948) introduced the concept of the schizophrenic mother, stating that the position of authority in the family, held by American mothers, was 'the main family problem' and that their domineering influence could be disastrous to the psychological well-being of their offspring.

A fascinating (and horrifying) narrative was now rapidly developing in this time of social flux after the Second World War, in this period characterised, in part, by the breakdown of the traditional gender roles of men and women, where men had gone off to war and women had stepped into the workplace. As Hartwell (1996) notes

> What is interesting is not … unfulfilled female ambition but the attribution of meaning given the maternal quality by therapists; it was pathogenic. Moreover, if a mother of a schizophrenic had begun to actualize her ambitions by rejecting the homemaking role or working outside the home this would also be 'schizophrenogenic'.
>
> (Hartwell 1996: 280)

Hartwell reports one case where a therapist (in the Karon and Rosberg 1958 study), who lived with a family in order to carry out clinical observations, reports that a request by the patient's mother to help with the housework was seen as evidence of the mother's schizophrenogenic tendencies through her 'emasculation of men' (Hartwell 1996: 281). 'Hostile rejection of the homemaking role' was one dimension in parental attitude tests to differentiate schizophrenogenic mothers from normal mothers (Shepherd and Guthrie 1959: 213–214). Lidz et al. (1957) described mothers of schizophrenics as failing to fill 'their wifely functions' – 'They were openly deviant in major areas of interaction and rather habitually disregarded or circumvented their husband's demands.' One 'paradigm case', according to Lidz and his colleagues (from their very biased upper-class New Haven sample), was a former career woman from a wealthy family who hated housework, thus interfering with the child's understanding of masculine and feminine roles and thwarting the attainment of a secure identity (Lidz et al. 1965/1985: 76–77).

This is a major part of the background of Bateson's double bind theory. As Hartwell says, the double bind was

> a theory of schizophrenia that tied together divergent versions of the schizophrenogenic mother … Incongruent findings, a hostile, domineering mother, and overtly weak mother, and a rigid, controlled mother would now be united under one theoretical umbrella. The Palo Alto team salvaged the disintegrating schizophrenogenic mother construct. They set the mother's pathological effect at the metacommunicative level.
>
> (Hartwell 1996: 286)

She also notes that 'The Bateson (1956) article became the most common citation of reports involving the schizophrenogenic mother. Maternal speech was now the focus of attention' (Hartwell 1996: 287). You can perhaps understand now why all of Bateson's examples involved just mothers, even though a theory of communication like this has no a priori requirement to so do. You can perhaps see now why some of its slippery terms had to be exactly so, to tie together such a set of contradictory findings.

Bateson's theory is all about approach and avoidance, as indeed is life itself. It is a fantastical theory that hinges on this single idea. Imagine living in a world where you could not understand the very nature of communication itself. The way that Bateson attempts to tie in all of the various manifestations of schizophrenia to this one idea, and the recurrent embodied communicational features that seem to be at the heart of it, is both brilliant and preposterous. Brilliant in the sense that it explains so much with the simplest of assumptions. Perhaps the clearest instantiation of Occam's Razor that I had ever come across as an undergraduate (or I have seen since). Preposterous because the anecdotal evidence marshalled could not hope to support anything like a 'theory of schizophrenia'. But some ideas take hold, and they take hold for particular reasons, and sometimes we need to look outside psychology to understand these.

Conflict between verbal and nonverbal communication

Of course, central to the whole theory is the relationship between verbal and nonverbal behaviour. So many of Bateson's examples hinged on these types of 'contradictory' communications. We have considered this already in a limited way in the case of gesture but there are other important domains of nonverbal behaviour that Bateson did specifically address. If we want to understand possible 'conflict' in communication, we need to focus on the relationship between these modes or channels of communication. Critical to this thinking was that language and nonverbal behaviour are designed to do different things. The focus on nonverbal behaviour (which is often taken to include both bodily communication and some vocal aspects of speech) as the significant domain through which human emotion is expressed, relationships are built and interpersonal attitudes are negotiated and expressed, has a significant history in psychology and in related disciplines. The argument has always been that language, the verbal channel of communication, is used primarily to convey factual or semantic information about the world, whereas the nonverbal channels have primarily social functions – 'to manage the immediate social relationships – as in animals', according to Oxford psychologist Michael Argyle, writing in 1972. Bateson himself wrote:

> It seems that the discourse of nonverbal communication is precisely concerned with matters of relationship ... From an adaptive point of view, it is therefore important that this discourse be carried on by techniques which are relatively unconscious and only imperfectly subject to voluntary control.
> (Bateson 1968: 614–615)

We can all say 'I love you', some of us rather too easily. It is quite a different matter to fake love nonverbally, or so Gregory Bateson seems to think. So the argument goes that we express relationships nonverbally because these types of communication are less subject to voluntary control, and therefore presumably more honest, and yet at the same time are more nebulous. We send out signals and yet remain unaccountable for their expression.

Bateson also states that 'nonverbal communication serves functions totally different from those of language and performs functions that verbal language is unsuited to perform.' He continues that 'nonverbal communication is precisely concerned with matters of relationship – love, hate, respect, fear, dependency, etc. – between self and vis-à-vis or between self and environment.' The argument therefore within psychology and other disciplines has been that nonverbal communication performs functions that language is unsuitable to perform and that verbal language, on the other hand, that peculiarly human attribute, is concerned with the world of thinking and abstract ideas and the communication of complex information about the world. This functional separation of language and nonverbal behaviour became something of an established orthodoxy in psychology. Michael Argyle, writing with Peter Trower in 1979 stated that 'Humans use two quite separate languages [language and nonverbal communication], each with its own function.' This is perhaps the most basic and therefore the clearest statement of how psychologists view language and nonverbal communication and their relationship. In a similar vein, Peter Trower, Bridget Bryant and Michael Argyle in their book *Social Skills and Mental Health* (1978) write: 'In human social behaviour it looks as if the nonverbal channel is used for negotiating interpersonal attitudes while the verbal channel is used primarily for conveying information.'

This is the broad structure on which the double bind was premised. Bateson saw the connection of the two channels as being critical to the double bind. The double bind involves 'A secondary injunction conflicting with the first at a more abstract level, and like the first enforced by punishments or signals, which threaten survival' (Bateson 2000: 207). Bateson makes the point that this secondary injunction is commonly communicated through nonverbal means – 'Posture, gesture, tone of voice … may all be used to convey the more abstract message' (p. 207). Again, he makes the point that despite the obvious iconicity of many of these nonverbal messages, they are more 'abstract'. One way to understand this is that when he considers elsewhere the use of various communicational modes in human communication, he writes

Examples are play, non–play, fantasy, sacrament, metaphor, etc. Even among the lower mammals there appears to be an exchange of signals which identify certain meaningful behaviour as 'play' etc. These signals are evidently of higher Logical Type than the messages they classify. Among human beings this framing and labelling of messages and meaningful actions reaches considerable complexity, with the peculiarity that our vocabulary for such discrimination is still very poorly developed, and we rely preponderantly upon nonverbal media of posture, gesture, facial expression, intonation, and the context for the communication of these highly abstract, but vitally important, labels.

(Bateson 2000: 203)

So in this sense, Bateson could argue that they are more abstract. They tell you what kind of utterance an utterance is. I say 'I love you', and the nonverbal behaviour tells you that this utterance is

(a) A genuine declaration of my feelings
(b) A joke
(c) An unkind joke
(d) A provocation
(e) An attempt to get someone into bed
(f) An attempt to elicit the same words back, the first part of an 'adjacency pair' in the terminology of Schegloff and Sacks (1973)
(g) An apology.

It could potentially be any of these and the nonverbal behaviour is critical in 'this framing and labelling of messages'. This would suggest that nonverbal signals are especially powerful in the signalling of relationships between people. After all, 'I love you' as a genuine declaration of love and 'I love you' as an unkind joke would have very different effects on the nature of a relationship.

I have described before (Beattie 2003) how there are two sets of critical experiments that are seen to be critical in demonstrating the relative power of nonverbal behaviour over verbal communication in this interpersonal domain. The first set was carried out by Albert Mehrabian at the University of California in Los Angeles and published in the late 1960s (Mehrabian and Ferris 1967; Mehrabian and Wiener 1967). Mehrabian investigated the effects of consistencies and inconsistencies in communication between the various channels of communication, including the actual meaning of the words and the tone of voice in which they are spoken and the facial expressions and the tone of voice, on the communication of interpersonal attitudes, and in particular on judgements of degrees of liking. In the first study he selected three words judged to convey liking – 'honey', 'thanks' and 'dear'; three words judged to be neutral in this regard – 'maybe', 'really' and 'oh'; and three words that conveyed dislike – 'don't', 'brute' and 'terrible'. Two female speakers read each of the nine selected words using positive, neutral and negative vocal expressions and these communications were then played to sets of judges. In a second study, one neutral word was selected, the word 'maybe'. This time the facial expression was varied: it was positive, neutral or negative. Judges in this second study were presented with an audio recording of the message and a photograph of the person delivering the message. The judges had to rate the overall communication to determine how positive or negative it came across.

From these studies Mehrabian concluded that in the communication of interpersonal attitudes the facial and the vocal channels greatly outweigh the verbal channel and he estimated the relative contributions of the three channels as 55 per cent for the facial channel, 38 per cent for the vocal channel and 7 per cent for the verbal channel. Mehrabian's conclusion was 'when there is inconsistency between verbally and implicitly expressed attitude, the implicit proportion [the nonverbal component] will dominate in determining the total message'.

This is the first study that attempted to say exactly how much the verbal and nonverbal channels each contribute to the communication of interpersonal attitudes and it produced a set of figures that have been picked up and adopted within popular culture. Most of us have heard things such as nonverbal behaviour is thirteen times more powerful than language in the expression of interpersonal attitudes, and that facial expression is eight times more powerful than language.

So at first sight we might conclude that nonverbal behaviour is very powerful here, and try to use it to support Bateson's theorising. But that is not how Mehrabian himself saw it. Mehrabian's conclusions about this research vis-à-vis the double bind were that

> Double bind theorists' basic assumption about the relationship between psychological disturbance and inconsistent messages was that the latter were ambiguous and difficult to interpret. However, we now know that this is not true. People do quite readily understand the true meaning when the verbal and implicit parts of a message are inconsistent – they rely on the implicit part and make their judgment accordingly.
>
> (Mehrabian 1971: 86)

In other words, the 'abstract' nonverbal channel might be critical in determining how an utterance like 'I love you' is perceived, but it does not generate any confusion on the part of the recipient.

But, of course, the problem with Mehrabian's basic paradigm is that it does not really consider *language* in the expression of interpersonal attitudes; at least not language as we normally understand it, with meaningful sentences used to express how we feel. Only individual words, like 'honey', 'brute' and 'maybe' were used. Nobody talks in individual words in the real world for prolonged periods of time, when they can help it. 'Honey' as an expression on its own only gets you so far. Then when Mehrabian considered the effects of facial versus vocal cues, these different cues were not presented together on videotape but merely as a photograph accompanying a single word. In other words, the participants in this study were simply presented with a photograph of a particular facial expression and they heard the single word being said and then they had to integrate these two things in their mind and make their judgement. So this experiment made no real attempt to simulate anything approaching normal social behaviour or normal social judgement. Hence, we have to be a little wary about the conclusions that have been drawn from it.

However, two experiments carried out at Oxford in the early 1970s by Michael Argyle and his colleagues seem at first sight to address many of these issues. The experiments were published as two important studies, indeed 'citation classics', by Argyle et al. (1970) and by Argyle et al. (1971). The basic methodology of these experiments is quite straightforward. Three verbal messages, paragraphs this time rather than individual words (hostile, neutral or friendly in one experiment; superior, neutral or inferior in another), were delivered in each of three different nonverbal styles (the friendly style being 'warm, soft tone of voice, open posture, smiling face', the hostile style being 'harsh voice, closed posture, frown with teeth showing'). Care was taken at the outset to ensure that the verbal message and the nonverbal style had approximately the same effects on listener evaluation on certain specific dimensions. Here is an example of the types of message used in this experiment. This is the hostile message: 'I don't much enjoy meeting the subjects who take part in these experiments. I often find them rather boring and difficult to deal with. Please don't hang around too long afterwards and talk about the experiment. Some people who come as subjects are really rather disagreeable.'

The combined communications, with the three verbal messages delivered in each of the three verbal styles, were then rated by judges to see how friendly or hostile the resultant messages were perceived as being. The results again apparently demonstrate quite clearly that the nonverbal channel greatly outweighs the verbal channel in the communication of interpersonal attitudes. For example, on a seven-point scale, where '7' means extremely friendly and '1' means extremely hostile, the hostile verbal message delivered in a friendly nonverbal style was rated as 5.17; in other words, it was perceived as being towards the friendly end of the scale and higher than the mid-point of 4. When the nonverbal style was friendly it didn't really seem to matter what was actually said; the overall communication was perceived as friendly. Similarly, when the nonverbal style was hostile, again it didn't really seem to matter what was said. The difference in perception of the friendly and hostile verbal messages delivered in the hostile nonverbal style was trivial, the scores being 1.60 and 1.80 respectively. Indeed, the hostile verbal message delivered in the hostile style was perceived as slightly friendlier than the friendly message in the hostile style. This latter form of communication is, of course, taken as a conflicting communication of the type Bateson termed a 'double bind'.

These results led Michael Argyle to the conclusion that nonverbal communication is twelve and a half times more powerful than language in the communication of interpersonal attitudes, specifically on the friendliness–hostility dimension, and over ten times more powerful in the communication of a different interpersonal attitude, namely superiority–inferiority.

These figures are very similar to those of Mehrabian. This series of studies obviously struck a chord with the public and gave those who wished to discuss the importance of nonverbal communication precise figures to work with. The studies demonstrate that nonverbal communication is not just highly significant, but also that we can virtually dismiss verbal language if we want to understand how interpersonal attitudes are signalled, and interpersonal relations are built, in everyday life. It also means that we can ignore the connections between language and nonverbal communication because the judges in this experiment seem to do just that. But although they seem to demonstrate the power of nonverbal communication, again Argyle found no evidence of any confusion on the part of the recipient – 'there was no evidence of double-bind effects – where verbal and non-verbal cues conflicted subjects simply disregarded the verbal signals' (Argyle et al. 1971: 401).

Much is built on these two sets of studies. But in my view these pioneering and very influential studies have fundamental weaknesses that really do limit the conclusions that can be drawn. Let's consider what these might be.

The Oxford studies involve judges having to watch a set of nine successive communications on videotape, all from the same person, tapes in which the language and nonverbal communication are systematically varied. The encoders were delivering scripts. Therefore, the whole point of the experiment would be immediately obvious to anyone who took part. Participants could quickly work out what the experimenter was getting at and therefore might decide to play along with him or her. This sometimes happens in psychological research and is called the 'demand characteristics' of the experiment. (Sometimes the opposite occurs: the participants work out what the experimenter wants and deliberately do not go along with it. This is known rather more colloquially as the 'f... you' effect.) This is always a problem for psychological research when the point of the experiment is as obvious as it was here.

Second, in order to try to measure the relative importance of language and nonverbal communication, the strength of the two channels had to be both measured and equated at the outset. They had to be equal in strength when measured independently. These studies therefore, at best, tell us about people's perceptions of a certain class of communication with the range of the strength of the components artificially set. The studies do not tell us anything about the range of effects produced by language and nonverbal communication in the world at large. Perhaps in the real world people do not use such explicitly friendly or unfriendly messages. Consider that hostile verbal statement again: 'I don't much enjoy meeting the subjects who take part in these experiments. I often find them rather boring and difficult to deal with.' Is that ever likely to be said directly to someone apart from as a joke? And when it is accompanied by a friendly verbal style ('warm, soft tone of voice, smile, open posture') how else is this supposed to be understood apart from as some sort of joke with the verbal statement to be dismissed? Don't forget that this is exactly what was found to happen in this experiment.

What would happen if we did not make the message quite as explicit as this? What would happen if we made the verbal message slightly more real and then used the same basic pattern of delivery? How would it then be perceived? Would the nonverbal component still make the verbal component seem completely unimportant? Let's do a quick mind experiment. Let's start with something pretty explicit but (in my experience) quite plausible: 'Would you mind leaving?'

This is delivered in the:

(1)   friendly nonverbal style 'warm, soft tone of voice, open posture, smiling face', or in the:
(2)   hostile nonverbal style 'harsh voice, closed posture, frown with teeth showing'.

You have to imagine both. Perhaps you could try delivering both messages in front of a mirror, or better still try delivering them to a friend. I am afraid that in both cases I think that I would get the message and go. The first message I imagine being delivered by 'the hostess with the mostest', you know the kind of person I mean. She is asking me to leave a posh party. The second I imagine being delivered by a nightclub bouncer. Both are clearly hostile but 'the hostess with the mostest', whilst hostile, is keeping it under control mainly for the benefit of the other guests (hence the friendly nonverbal style). The verbal message is, however, significantly more important in communicating her basic unfriendly attitude here than any accompanying behaviours. It may be explicit but it is a real request, heard many times, I would imagine, at many dinner parties (or is this just me?).

Or what about something that is a statement rather than a request or a command, something as basic as: 'You used to be such a nice person'?

Again this is delivered in the:

(3) friendly nonverbal style 'warm, soft tone of voice, open posture, smiling face', or in the:
(4) hostile nonverbal style 'harsh voice, closed posture, frown with teeth showing'.

My guess is that the nonverbal behaviour in message 3 will neither transform nor soften the basic message. It is not a friendly statement and the fact that it is being delivered in this style could make it even less friendly because it is as if the speaker is still trying to be understanding and yet, despite being understanding, she can still make the basic statement. In message 4 the person has started to lose control.

The point to be made here is that psychologists have never really been able to quantify the relative importance of language and nonverbal communication in interpersonal communication. It would be an extremely difficult and time-consuming experiment to do. I have made it seem easy with a few examples, but think of the generality of the conclusions that people are trying to draw from such an experiment. We would need a representative sample of an enormous variety of utterances, sampling all of the kinds of things that language can do and sampling different contexts as well. I have sketched in a few contexts above, but I am sure you can imagine some different contexts that might affect the basic interpretation of the utterances. Utterances, after all, only make sense in context.

If you don't believe me let's return to the first utterance, this time imagining slightly different contexts for the utterance: 'Would you mind leaving?' Imagine this being delivered at the very end of the evening by a bouncer in a nightclub and delivered in that friendly style 'warm, soft tone of voice, open posture, smiling face'. Suddenly it's quite friendly. Everyone has to leave, it's just that time of night. The bouncer is, after all, asking in a very friendly manner. I tried this experiment, believe it or not. I asked a doorman I knew to ask people to leave using this style of nonverbal behaviour. I then asked the poor innocent punter how he perceived the message. At the end of the night the punter said: 'Everything was fine, the bouncer was polite and friendly. Are you doing some research into customer satisfaction?' I also asked the doorman to say exactly the same thing in the same friendly manner early in the evening to a different punter. This second punter looked confused. He thought that it was a case of mistaken identity; bouncers don't just ask you to leave for no good reason. But how did the new punter perceive the overall message – the 'hostile' message in the 'friendly' style (at this point I really do need to rely on inverted commas)? Actually, he perceived it as very threatening. 'It was the understated way that he asked me,' the second punter explained. 'He was really hostile, as if he was looking forward to giving me a good thump if I didn't go immediately. But I hadn't done anything,' he added, 'That was really the annoying thing.' He smiled when he was told that this was just a little test.

The picture is, as you can see, becoming a little more complicated. The conclusions, which are that interpersonal attitudes are signalled almost exclusively by nonverbal behaviour, are looking a little shakier. The general conclusion that 'humans use two quite separate languages, each with its own function' is looking somewhat less secure.

But to return to the studies of Michael Argyle, how could we make them more convincing? As a starting point we would want to make sure that the behaviours studied in the laboratory mirrored the kinds of behaviours shown in the real world. We can all be hostile using language without being quite as explicit as the speaker was in these experiments. When verbal statements become less explicit and more plausible, and more like the things that are said in everyday life, do they then become more powerful and significant as a consequence, and not so readily dismissed as some sort of joke in an experiment of this kind? The important point is that we do not know because unfortunately this experiment has never been carried out.

At this point you might be wondering how verbal language would function to signal friendliness in subtle and less direct ways in everyday life. (I came up with a couple of quite hostile utterances off the top of my head, again I wonder what this tells you about me.) Here are a few suggestions. You can perhaps add your own here because the range of ways verbal language might do this is potentially quite large. But I would suggest that opening up a conversation in the first place, the use of first names, compliments, disclosure, reciprocated disclosure, the asking of personal questions, verbal engagement, shared perspectives, sharing of childhood memories, offers of help, offers of support, all play some role in the communication of certain interpersonal attitudes by language itself.

How important are each of these verbal strategies compared with the appropriate forms of nonverbal communication like facial expressions, postures, smiles and frowns in the overall communication of interpersonal attitudes? We simply do not know, but my guess is that the verbal statements would not be dismissed quite so readily as they were in those pioneering but somewhat transparent experiments of the early 1970s. Again, this is not to argue against the incredible significance of nonverbal communication, but merely represents an attempt to reinstate ordinary language and the connections between ordinary language and nonverbal communication in the heart of social relationships and the study of human communication.

Let me also add that there are other rather more specific criticisms of these studies that are necessary given the incredible cultural weight which has come to rest on their conclusions. Only one person was used in these Oxford experiments to deliver the nine messages in the first place and she was described as 'an attractive female student'. In other words, we know nothing about the generality of the results. How do we know that the results were not specific to this one individual? Would the results have generalised to male students, to less 'attractive' students, or to the population at large? We do not know. But a number of years ago I tried to replicate the original study using a male speaker, and the results were altogether a good deal less clear-cut. For example, the friendly verbal message in a hostile nonverbal style was rated as 3.90, essentially perceived as neutral rather than as very hostile, as in the original study (see Beattie 1983: 9).

In addition, in the original study the judges were watching the combinations of verbal and nonverbal communication on a video screen and were specifically requested to attend to the video clips. In real life, however, when we are engaged in social interaction we sometimes look at the other person, sometimes we do not. This shifting pattern of eye gaze depends upon interpersonal distance, relative status, seating or standing position, the content of what we are saying, the structure of what we are saying and emotions like shame, embarrassment, guilt, etc. In real life we may miss a number of critical nonverbal signals for a variety of reasons. In the classic experiments by Michael Argyle there was never this possibility. Again, these experiments failed to simulate the complexities and patterns of everyday social life. For this and for the other reasons outlined we need to be extremely careful about how we interpret the results of these classic experiments.

But Argyle and his colleagues also thought that this experimental investigation of manipulated verbal–nonverbal messages could have implications for the double bind theory. In the study on the communication of inferior–superior attitudes, they found 'no evidence of double-bind effects' (Argyle et al. 1971: 401). They found that participants simply ignored the verbal messages when there was an apparent conflict. But in the study on friendly–hostile attitudes they claimed to find some in that when there were inconsistent verbal–nonverbal signals of positive or negative affect the performer was 'judged unstable, insincere and confused'

(p. 400). But of course, that is not really in line with the major prediction from the theory. If the individuals studied by Bateson had concluded that their ('schizophrenogenic') mothers were 'unstable, insincere and confused', there presumably would be no major clinical problem with their children. These after all are dispositional, attributions, presumably more than healthy in this situation. Presumably, it is much worse when you start to internalise these sorts of attributions, or blame the communicational system itself.

But there is another very important point to be made here about the nature of the various channels of communication and how they are built into the double bind theory. Bateson himself had said explicitly (as we have already seen) that

> It seems that the discourse of nonverbal communication is precisely concerned with matters of relationship ... From an adaptive point of view, it is therefore important that this discourse be carried on by techniques which are relatively unconscious and only imperfectly subject to voluntary control.

But at the same time he is saying that the 'framing and labelling of messages and meaningful actions reaches considerable complexity ... and we rely preponderantly upon nonverbal media of posture, gesture, facial expression, intonation, and the context for the communication of these highly abstract, but vitally important, labels'. The obvious conclusion then is that *if* there are recurrent conflicting communications in the family dynamics with a schizophrenic offspring then the double binds are not being deliberately generated (at least not) through the mechanism of sending out the more powerful and 'abstract' nonverbal signals, which frame and label messages, because these are 'relatively unconscious' and 'only imperfectly subject to voluntary control'. This may make one very uncomfortable about labelling any individuals who might generate inconsistent communication as 'binders', with all the connotations of deliberative action. So is it still possible the other way round? Again, consider the classic example: the child hugs his mother, she stiffens, he withdraws his arm, she says 'Don't you love me anymore?' Is the verbal utterance the deliberative action, the 'abstract' and powerful metacommunicative message that confuses the child to such a degree that madness is the only mechanism of adaptation? Possibly, but this flies in the face of everything that Bateson said about the operation of the two channels. The mother is not so much a 'binder' but a 'leaker'.

The logic of the double bind was, in my opinion, fatally flawed. It identified one possible moment in an interactional sequence and drew dramatic and damning conclusions from that moment in time. But consider the following. Assume for one second that the mother did stiffen when her schizophrenic son hugged her. How was the hug itself? Was it not loving enough? Is that why she reacted the way she did? Or what happens if we consider certain types of nonverbal behaviour as System 1 responses in Kahneman's terminology, more automatic, quicker and more unconscious than verbal behaviour? Was the mother leaking her true feelings through this behaviour and trying to compensate with her comment? Well, not necessarily. Nonverbal behaviour can be affected by situation as well as by interpersonal feelings. Perhaps her stiffening was occasioned by being observed by the psychiatrist or Bateson himself. Perhaps, she didn't feel comfortable acting normally in his presence? But liked things even less when her son withdrew his affectionate hug (that's assuming that it was indeed affectionate; many hugs do not have this quality). Hugs are often part of a sequence of interaction that unfolds, but Bateson disregarded all of this in his analysis of the moment. And why would being on the receiving end of the mother's behaviour lead one to fail to understand metacommunication generally? Are human beings not natural dispositional theorists, keen to explain behaviour in terms of the personalities of the actors? Why wouldn't the son step back and think, my mother has a problem with intimacy? A problem with showing her affections in front of strangers? And why didn't Bateson, as the observer, gravitate naturally towards that type of explanation? Why would the son naturally assume that the communicational system was itself wrong rather than something to do with the mother (if indeed anything was wrong in the first place! It's really impossible to judge out of context). And what happens if the mother wanted a different sort of hug, a more affectionate hug, a full body hug, a hug with a kiss? What happens if that hug was not enough for her? She may have been signalling something, but not necessarily what Bateson assumes.

So what are we left with? Isolated observations of behaviour, extracted from their natural context, their sequential organisations disrupted, with gross interpretations of behaviour and intention. System 1 responses recoded in System 2 terms and a generation of mothers blamed, explicitly then implicitly, for every failing in their offspring. I caught my mother using double binds against me, or I thought I did as an undergraduate encouraged and goaded by my philosophy lecturer. Later, I was not so sure, in fact I was not sure at all. I think she wanted more love from me than I had time to give her, and a little more understanding. No more, no less.

'Always acting the bloody fool'

That's where I would have liked to leave it, but sometimes it's not that easy. I was in my spare room recently thinking about her, and what all that psychology had taught me, and perhaps how I had used it against her. I found a bottle top, just where she had left it but I'd never noticed it before. It was in the top drawer in her bedroom. I say her bedroom but it was twelve years since she'd gone, and yet the room still smelt of her, after all that time. It's odd the way that smells linger like that, like old memories that you can't quite shake off. I picked the bottle top up and sniffed it to see if the fragrance of the whisky was still there, but it just smelt of old metal, a rusty sort of smell, hardly anything really, just like old metal railings.

Of course, I remember the drinking, a few glasses in the evening, maybe more, convivial, that's what they say. 'I'm just being sociable,' she said, 'I never get out. When you live on your own you look forward to a wee drink with company.' And she would ask me what whisky I'd bought for her that night and then criticise my choice. Too cheap, too dear, too common, too unusual. Never right, never ever right. 'I'll have a drink with you, you go and get what you bought,' and she always drank it anyway, after her initial ritualistic protestation, and she would start to cheer up by the second glass or so, once the glow had set in.

'I hope you didn't just get the one bottle. I worked in an off-license once and we used to laugh at men with a bit of money about them coming in for their one wee lonely bottle. Sad, we called them, men with no friends, nobody to socialise with, auld bokes. Me and the other girls always said that those sort of men would be in bed at eleven, on their own. When you've got a couple of bottles in the house, at least you've got something to look forward to. The night is young; there's always possibilities.'

And you could see her glancing off into the distance, dreaming of those days of possibilities, when she was still young and on the town, when things might just happen, without willing them.

I assured her that I wasn't that sad.

'You drink awful fast,' she would say. 'I'm struggling to keep up with you.' But she always finished first and that was the cue for me to go downstairs for a refill. I poured her a large glass full of possibilities. 'I'm awful lonely,' she would say, 'ever since your father died. Awful lonely. Sitting on my own every night with my bad ankles, waiting for you to ring me. Then I get over to England to see you and you're always out, enjoying yourself, no time for me, just looking after number one. Is that what I worked all those years in the mill for? To get you an education so that you could just go out and gallivant around the place.'

The tears were starting to form; I couldn't bear to witness it.

'Let's have a good night,' I'd say, and I would drain my glass.

'So you're acting the big fella now, the money man, the fella in the big picture.'

'I drank that one a bit quick; it's made me feel a bit sick,' and I would pretend to boke all over her. And in those moments I would become a child again, back in the old mill house with the damp wallpaper coming off the walls before I left to get an education and come back 'a wee snob', her words, a wee frigging snob ashamed of his background, distracted by all that education, and all those new possibilities. I made more retching noises. She laughed for a moment or two, on that fine balance beam between up and down, good and bad, optimism and despair, before finally settling in that other place.

'All that education and you still talk bloody rubbish. You're only happy when you're acting the fool, at my expense, of course, poking fun at me. Don't think that I can't see it. That drink couldn't make you sick. You're acting all daft about nothing. Does that kind of wee show impress them up in the university? Because it certainly doesn't impress me. You'll regret this one day.'

It was, of course, just my little routine to distract her, to stop her thinking about Belfast and the Troubles and what might be happening back in her hometown while she was visiting me over in England, across the water, she called it, 'way across the water'. It sometimes worked, that was the thing; my fooling around sometimes did the trick, that's why I had to persevere to cheer her up and overcome the guilt. I'd a lot to feel guilty about. I didn't just talk about Lorenz and learning theory and cognition in those vacations as a student, I brought back Eysenck's theory of racial differences in intelligence and why the blacks and the Irish are not as intelligent as the rest (always a good one for livening things up in Belfast), and how mothers use double binds to drive their sons insane. I sat there, with my philosophy lecturer whispering in my ear, commenting on what she had said to me and her nonverbal behaviour; sometimes I used notes from the past, mentally encoded. I explained what a schizophrenogenic mother was, in this new undergraduate language of mine, and slightly amended Belfast accent, and she sat looking back at me, with tears welling slowly in her eyes. 'Why do you hate me?' she said in her heavy Belfast accent.

'It's not you I hate; it's what mothers can do to you. They don't mean to; they just do it.'

Of course, I grew up eventually and regretted it all so very, very much. I was using an unexamined and unsubstantiated theory in my attacks to deal with some deep longing inside for my father that neither of us could do anything about. Later I avoided saying anything significant in our conversations, that was just me, I just tried to be funny (no doubt Bateson would have explained that as well). I was funny as fuck.

And back on that fateful night she said that she'd had enough. 'I'm away to bed. I thought that you might have something sensible to say to me, you with all that education and me living on my own. But no, you just like playing the bloody fool at my bloody expense.'

She left the next morning, to go back home, and I only saw her once again. She died in her sleep a few weeks later, the way she always said that she wanted to go. Her next door neighbour found her. I went back home to arrange the funeral. Her neighbour sat on a floral cushion in her front room that smelt heavily of lavender spray. 'Your mother had a peaceful death the way she wanted it.'

I picked up the bottle top again. She always said that I always bought the wrong type. She said that it was deliberate. I sniffed the metal again, to try to remind myself about those nights sharing a bottle, that's what they say isn't it, *sharing* a bottle. But they weren't there. How would they know about sharing? What did we ever share except an unresolved sorrow that should have bound us together but didn't. And all that psychology not only didn't help us – it made things worse, much, much worse.

Chapter summary

- Double binds are meant to be a form of conflicting communication sometimes found in family communication.
- To be harmful, according to Gregory Bateson, they must be recurring and involve some form of threat.
- According to Bateson, they can be very psychologically damaging for the recipient of the message when they occur within the context of an intense relationship.
- He suggested they leave the recipient with no 'rational' response to the message, and may be linked to the development of schizophrenic thought disorder.
- Bateson said 'We do not assume that the double bind is inflicted by the mother alone, but that it may be done either by mother alone or by some combination of mother, father and/or siblings.'
- The role of the mother either acting on her own or in combination with other members of the family seems clear and unambiguous in his thinking.

- All of the clinical evidence he cites in his work seems to involve mothers.
- This was part of the accumulating evidence for the 'schizophrenogenic mother'.
- According to Bateson, the conflict in the communication involves a 'secondary injunction', a more 'abstract' communication that conflicts with the first and again 'enforced by punishments' or signals which threaten psychological 'survival'.
- Bateson wrote that 'This secondary injunction is commonly communicated to the child by nonverbal means. Posture, gesture, tone of voice, meaningful action and the implications concealed in verbal comment may all be used to convey this more abstract message.'
- A review of the evidence for the first decade of work on the double bind by Schuham was damning, but did not really impact on the spread of the concept.
- Schuham said that 'there is no evidence that double bind communication is exclusive to, or differentially associated with pathological communication processes and not associated with normal communication processes'.
- Schuham also concluded 'There is no evidence that the double bind phenomenon has an etiological connection with the development of the schizophrenic thought disorder.'
- Nevertheless, the idea of the 'schizophrenogenic mother' took hold in our culture.
- This was part of something bigger.
- A fascinating (and horrifying) narrative was now rapidly developing in this time of social flux after the Second World War characterised by the breakdown of the traditional gender roles of men and women, where men had gone off to war and women had stepped into the workplace.
- As Hartwell (1996) notes, 'What is interesting is not … unfulfilled female ambition but the attribution of meaning given the maternal quality by therapists; it was pathogenic'.

- Hartwell also wrote 'if a mother of a schizophrenic had begun to actualize her ambitions by rejecting the homemaking role or working outside the home this would also be "schizophrenogenic"'.
- Bateson's theory was based upon isolated observations of behaviour, extracted from their natural context, their sequential organisations disrupted, with gross interpretations of behaviour and intention and a generation of mothers blamed, explicitly then implicitly, for every failing in their offspring.
- Bateson's double bind theory makes major unsubstantiated assumptions about how verbal and nonverbal behaviour act together.
- The theory is inconsistent in terms of its specification.
- Empirical evidence for the role of the double bind is anecdotal at best.
- Many people used this theory to blame mothers.
- I caught my mother using double binds against me, or I thought I did as an undergraduate student encouraged and goaded by my philosophy lecturer.
- Later, I was not so sure, in fact, not sure at all.

6

CONFLICTED MEMORIES

I was sitting in Tracey Emin's bright, airy studio just off Brick Lane in east London, the winter sun streaming through the windows. She is the artist who, perhaps more than any other, has laid bare her turmoil through her autobiographical art and writing, sometimes disguised in metaphorical and allegorical layers, sometimes barely disguised at all. She seemed to be intrigued by what I, as a psychologist, might make of her and her work. I was waiting for her to arrive, flicking through one of her catalogues, *When I Think About Sex …* The first piece, *Super Drunk Bitch*, is an appliqué and embroidered blanket with short, sharp, dysfunctional messages in big capital letters, as if they had been written or carved on an arm by a disturbed teenager. 'STUPID DRUNK BITCH' (with the 'stupid' crossed out), 'SO WHAT'S YOUR NAME LITTLE GIRL', 'MY NAME IS WALKING HELL'.

'Here,' said her assistant, interrupting me for a moment, pointing at a green couch positioned in front of a photograph of Tracey, sitting in a desert, perhaps Arizona, with clean white trainers and a serious expression, looking at her first book, *Explorations of the Soul*, which chronicles her sexual history. 'You do want her on the couch, don't you?' asked the assistant. I smiled weakly. 'Anywhere will do,' I said. Tracey had been to Elton John's party the night before and was running fashionably late.

'Will she be very hung over?' I asked. 'I couldn't really say,' her assistant replied. She offered to make me some coffee, giving me the chance to look around the studio in a nosier and more prying sort of way, at the bits of work in progress and memorabilia scattered everywhere: model cars, leopards, china cats, a picture of the last pope with a raised, slightly three-dimensional face, an image torn out of a magazine of a tarty-looking girl with her bum stuck out provocatively – a rear-view shot, cheap and tacky. The early seventies, I guessed, an aide memoire for Tracey's Margate childhood, a memory cue for her early childhood experiences: molestation by a stranger on the beach when she was 11, rape, lots of promiscuous and largely unwanted sex, psychological intimidation, violence, dark days of the soul. Years and miles away from the clean desert air of Arizona.

There was a pair of black knickers drying on the radiator, or it could have been a swimming costume. I knew that she was a keen swimmer. As the kettle boiled I turned the knickers over; it was a swimming costume. She arrived, looking fresh in a pale blue shirt, and made her way to the green couch and lay down, comfortable and still. I wanted to know what it was like to be Tracey Emin, the artist who exposes her life and her body so readily in the name of art. I began by asking her how she feels about people (and not just me) observing and analysing her because of the nature of the art she produces. 'Sometimes I feel all right about it, but sometimes I get really paranoid.' She spoke quietly, with frequent hesitant thinking pauses, some filled with 'ums' and long reflective silences. 'Sometimes I don't want people to see what I feel inside. A while ago I had to get on to an airplane, alone, and I was really crying. I didn't want people to see I was crying so I wanted to put my sunglasses on to cover it up. But this is a big problem. If I hadn't worn the sunglasses, the public would have said, "Tracey Emin's got no emotional control." If I wear the sunglasses they say, "Tracey Emin thinks she's the big celebrity artist."'

'Either way you get punished,' I said. She nods and smiles. What she was outlining was Bateson's 'classic' double bind: whatever response you choose in a situation like this you cannot escape punishment. No rational response is possible. You can't explain to everyone why you're putting the sunglasses on. So you put them on and try to hide, now doubly hidden with first the glasses and then the evasion, afraid of the responses of others, distrustful of how they might respond if they see you. She made a slight, uncomfortable movement.

'People don't realise how vulnerable I am. I really, really hate it when people come up to me in restaurants when I'm on my own and ask me for my autograph, because it's taken all my courage to go to the restaurant in the first place. I've psyched myself up to be there and suddenly I'm sitting there isolated in front of someone with their own view of me.'

I had read somewhere that she was voted the forty-first most disliked person in Britain. How does that make her feel? 'I was asleep on the sofa and suddenly I heard my name being mentioned on the TV and I woke up. I know these surveys are stupid, but it still dents your confidence. But you know how these things come about, it's all deliberate. The public ring up with people they want to nominate and the person on the other end of the line makes suggestions: "You want to nominate a pop star? We've got a lot of those already, what about an artist instead? You want to nominate Damien Hirst? A lot have gone for him already, what about a female artist? Yeah, Tracey Emin, that's a good one, I'll put her down." I know that it's all shit, but it doesn't make you feel good. You can rationalise it all you like, but it's still there.'

But her rationalisation is all in terms of unknown others deliberately manipulating lists to make her look and feel bad. The seeds of paranoid thought, I thought to myself. That place on the list wasn't to do with negative press that may have influenced people's perceptions of her but something more malevolent, intentional and enduring. Sly unknown others out to get her, and probably still out there, along with future humiliations.

I want to talk about her early experiences so I mention that I really enjoyed her memoir, *Strangeland*. 'It's not a memoir,' she responded defensively.

'But wasn't it based on diaries written over twenty-five years?' I asked.

'It wasn't diaries; it was writing I did over the past twenty-five years. I don't know much about nature and animals, but I do know about me and my life, so that's what I wrote about.'

'What I'm interested in as a psychologist,' I said slightly pompously, 'is what we remember and what we don't remember and the way memories change as we try to make sense of our experiences. Do you think that the conscious reflection behind writing about our early experiences can change our very memories of the experiences themselves?'

'Maybe,' she replied, cautiously. 'But you still know what the truth is. If we are both sitting here and someone throws a brick through the window then we both know that this has actually happened, but we see it from our own perspectives. These things happened, exactly as I described them, from my perspective.'

'So the brick comes through the window,' I continued, 'you might say that someone has thrown the brick through the window because they hate you and I might say someone has accidentally thrown the brick through the window. So our versions of the truth may differ considerably.'

'When I write things down it's the way I see them at that time, so it's the truth as I see it.' I asked her what she wanted me to call the 'memoir'. 'The book,' she replied forcefully. 'Call it the book.'

'OK, the book. Well, in the book there's a story about when you were eleven years old in Margate, swimming in the sea without your bikini top because you'd forgotten it. You saw some kids playing, and you wanted to join them. They called you over, but then one of them said: "See? I told you she was a boy." They pushed you down and got on top of you, chanting "Boy. Boy. Boy. Boy." Not long after that you came across "a big, brown hairy man" in the water. You write that he made you laugh and smile and told you that you were beautiful and like a tiny mermaid, and then you write, "And I pulled at his willy until a giant spray of white covered my limbs. I wasn't yet 12, but I knew it could feel lovely to be a girl."

'When I read that, I had a particular perception of the events that occurred,' I told her. 'It's the contrast between the two events which is significant. The young boys persecute you because of your lack of sexuality and the big brown hairy man desires you. But I read a subsequent interview where you said you were the instigator of the sexual act. But in the book you don't say that. In the book the earlier incident with the boys is critical, that is why you were feeling so vulnerable that you talked to the man in the first place. Your feeling of vulnerability is what he exploited. But in the interview, years later, you suddenly take responsibility for the whole thing.'

She seemed slightly irritated that I should question her in this way. Her articulated history of suffering infuses her work, and I seem to be questioning this, by suggesting that there are several different versions of the truth available directly from her. 'Look,' she said, 'let me be clear – it was me who was directing what happened with this man, but there are other things that happened when I was ten where it wasn't me directing it and I didn't want it. In the case of the man in the sea I liked it. But the man shouldn't have done it. Even if I was sat on his fucking face, he shouldn't have done it. He should have thought, "Hmm, this girl is in a lot of trouble here, maybe I should go to social services and find out why she is behaving like this." But it was the seventies, what was he supposed to do? Put it this way, if I had an eleven-year-old daughter and the same thing happened to her, then I would cut his balls off. It's wrong, wrong, wrong, wrong, wrong.'

I found this extraordinary. By taking personal responsibility for what happened with the man in the sea and excusing him ('It was the seventies, what was he supposed to do?') she is laying all the blame on her eleven-year-old self. She attributes motives to her younger self that may never have been there. But why? As a form of defence, so that, in her mind, she is taking control of critical incidents in her life in which she would appear to have been the victim of something bad? Or is it as an attempt to shock us – we cannot accept an eleven-year-old being blamed in this way for her own molestation so therefore we direct our shock and anger towards her? Does she need to feel these negative emotions, those negative emotions so reminiscent of her childhood, to spark her creative energies? Or is she doing it for both reasons? She continued:

'Some people who have reviewed the book have said my experiences are extraordinary and one reviewer said that the only sad thing is that the book should have been edited by someone who loved me. The problem is that I have no parameters so I give too much away. If I had somebody who loved me there would have been lots of stuff that wouldn't have appeared in the book. I have no one to advise me on what to put in and what to leave out. That is why it's so raw. I know I have to be responsible, but I can take that level of responsibility. OK, so I wanked off some bloke in the sea, so get over it. If I had somebody who really cared about me, who really cared about my vulnerability, then they could advise me. It really hurt me to make those admissions.'

I tried to say, 'I don't see why you would necessarily need someone who was in love with you ...' but she interrupted me. 'I don't think anybody would be in love with me.'

'Why?' I asked, overlapping slightly with her, to express my surprise.

'I've been on my own for so long now. It's not the book; it's about everything I do. I think I'm a bit full on. I think I've had certain types of experiences that put people off. Maybe not for you because you're a psychologist. I've got a friend who's a psychiatrist who works with the criminally insane and I say to him, "Have you had a good day at work today?" And he says, "Oh, one of my patients cut his dick off today." So what I'm saying is, it depends on what you're used to – people who are shocked by my revelations live sheltered lives. There's nothing in the book really.'

She was skilfully bonding with me, creating a strategic alliance of the two of us against the rest of the world. *You would not be shocked by my experiences; you would understand*, she is whispering to me. She is flattering me and I am responding. I ask her how she thinks being a twin has affected her psychological make-up.

'I think it's been quite stressful for me because I like hanging out with people. I think my overriding sense of loneliness is because I'm a twin. All of my smiling, all of my socialising is fuelled by alcohol. In reality, I would like the fire to be burning naturally. I don't want to keep cranking it up, but for me alcohol is like a firelighter. I really like that glow, but in the end it's not true energy. Drinking is a social vehicle that I ride out on. I've been drinking since I was thirteen, but there must be a reason why I do it. What is it that I am hiding from? Why is it that I have to get off my face? I've got so drunk that I've gone out dancing and had no memory of it whatsoever. There was one bloke I really fancied, and I kissed him, but I had no memory of it at all. It was my one and only chance with him and I just couldn't remember any of it. It was the forgotten kiss. I really wanted to know what it was like. The only time I would really want to give up drinking is when I fall in love.'

I smiled at her last comment, but make no response. She is putting a lot of emphasis on love as her potential salvation. Instead, I ask her about sex and creativity. In her opinion, when artists don't engage in sex so freely do they become more creative or less creative?

'I didn't have sex for two years, which is quite a long time. Then I did have sex, and I think the work that I've made in the past six months is the best work I've ever made. But I think I had to go without it for two years to understand the power of sex. People think that a lot of my work is about sex, but I make more work about God than I do about sex. People just get the sex thing because that's the easy bit. I made a fantastic piece of work called *Sleeping with You*. I sleep alone and get very afraid. I have recurrent nightmares – I wake up and think there's someone in the room. A friend advised me to sleep on my right side so that my heart would be free and my liver would be open, because otherwise I'm sleeping in a tight ball, squashing my heart and liver. And the liver is to do with the polar regions of your imagination. That's why when we get drunk we get disorientated. And it really works. So I made *Sleeping with You*, this collection of helixes with this lightning strike of neon above it, all intricate and beautiful. I love it. I've made something that is really beautiful, it's like I didn't make it, as if it was magic. And that all came about by me feeling that I was in love with someone. I could never have made that work if I was feeling down. I'd never have understood it. The work is to do with the weight of a relationship and the dependency and the vulnerability in a relationship and the fact that it's really difficult to sleep with people.'

I asked her whether she had the same nightmares when she was sleeping with somebody.

'I have done. I was with someone for six years and he said it was like sleeping next to the girl in *The Exorcist*, my face wobbling, me sitting bolt upright. I'm an insomniac as well, I take sleeping tablets, but I know it's bad to take them. I go to sleep quite early, but I wake up about four. If you have sleep deprivation you can't enjoy yourself, you can't smile, you're so dehydrated, you're awake twice as much as you should be. I don't think that I can't sleep because I'm unhappy, I think that I'm unhappy because I can't sleep.'

I realise that I am enjoying my time with her. She combines a curious mixture of precise perceptions of the physical and social world around us with this enduring belief in the unseen world that influences much of what we do. She can strike up an immediate rapport in conversation, which is surprising when you remember the dysfunctional background she is keen to tell us about. She has subconsciously worked on her early memories in a particular way, to allow her to be in control of much of her past. Not a frightened little girl in an incomprehensible adult world, but someone who could play the men on Margate beach at their own game. She was the instigator, the controller, or so she says now. The boys might have thought she was sexless, the hairy man knew different, and got what he desired. This reverberates in the present. Be careful about judging me, she says; others might not share your view and get much more.

Tracey Emin has been quite open in the past about her belief in the sixth sense, the twilight zone of the paranormal, fortune tellers and gypsies, the dead and dreams, sleeping on your liver and its effects on the imagination. She even told me that the second time she had an abortion, she knew that there was something wrong with the baby because 'it felt like green algae inside'.

I knew that she likes to read people from their keys, although she often declined to do this with interviewers. But nevertheless, despite my obvious scepticism, she agreed to read mine. 'You have a great affection for sweet, fluffy things, like Angora rabbits,' she says, 'because you're very analytic. People don't expect you to be sentimental, but you are. Your organisation skills irritate people. The reason I can tell this is because although you have a lot of responsibility you have very few keys. You're at the top of your field in a certain subject: the reason I know this is because you have a key with "Grand Master" on it. Who goes around with "Grand Master" on a key?'

I laughed. 'The university gave me that key.'

'But with all your organisation you have left something in a bit of a mess; you really have to go back and deal with it because it's quite painful for someone. You have to go back and clear it up. I don't know what it is, but it could be a crash.'

'But I've never had a crash,' I protested.

'But somebody will, and you will have to clear it up. The reason I can tell this is because this key here is stained, it's marked, and you're not the kind of person to leave stains on things.'

I find myself smiling at her desperate attempt to read something from nothing. But then she handed me her keys and asked what I could tell from hers. I threw her a beseeching smile, but realised I had to say something.

'Well, there are no little stains anywhere, so this person doesn't leave messes; and lots of keys, so there are many facets of your life, but you're not as well organised as me.'

She interrupted me, frowning with impatience. 'The first thing you should ask me is, "Do you use all these keys? If not, why do you have them all on your key ring?" What that should tell you is that I'm not very good at offloading stuff. It means I carry all this psychological baggage around with me. You should tell me to take the keys off now – you're the psychologist, just tell me to do it now. You should be saying that part of your problem is that you carry too much around with you and this builds pressure up inside you.'

I handed back her keys without comment, interested in why such an obviously intelligent person should believe in any of this. Is it just a party trick or is the second bit, where she asks me to read her keys, the significant moment? Is she trying to cue me in some way, to elicit certain advice, using her own keys? Is she trying to help me analyse her, to make my job easier? If so, why? Is it so I will feel better about myself and therefore like her even more?

I told her that I am fascinated by something she said in an interview: 'Shame on people who conjure up the face of another person when they are making love to a partner.' I asked her if she thought that people need certain fictions to keep them together? Did she not think that we need certain lies to bind us all together?

'Lies might bind you together with other people, but it's not what I do.'

'But do you think people can bear the truth all the time? For example, if someone says, "Do you still love me as much as you did when we first met?" what do you say? Most psychologists would say that the feeling of love dwindles eventually with time, that's a biochemical fact of life.'

'You should say firmly to anyone who asks, "No, I don't love you as much," or "I don't love you the same way, but I love you differently."'

I asked her whether she thinks, then, that as an artist she is telling the public some great uncomfortable and provocative truths about themselves. Truths that hurt. Truths that made people dislike her. Truths about a world where eleven-year-olds are made to feel the instigator of their own sexual molestation. Truths that are perhaps designed at some subconscious level to provoke hostility and alienate.

She smiled, but didn't answer. Her long pause forces me to ask her how lonely she feels at this particular point in time.

'Out of ten? Today? Nought. But on Monday, nine. I've had two relationships in the past fourteen years. I'm monogamous when I'm in a relationship. And that's one of my biggest failures. I wish I wasn't. I wish I could just sleep with different people, but I can't, because I did it when I was young. Let me tell you something else about myself,' she says. 'When I was in a relationship for six years I woke up every day thinking he'd leave me. So when he eventually did leave me, painful as it was, it was a relief because I didn't have to have that feeling anymore.'

'But the danger,' I say, 'is that this was a classic self-fulfilling prophecy – you expected him to leave, you subconsciously sent signals to this effect and he picked up on them. He thought to himself, "She somehow feels that I am going to leave and therefore I must not be right for her, and therefore I should leave."'

'It was all so sad,' she said. 'You could feel this separation happening, but what he liked in me was my feisty independence in the first place.'

She was clearly lonely and idealises the love relationship to such an extent as to make it virtually untenable. You can never fantasise about another person when making love, she says – never. Whether she likes it or not many relationships depend on small lies for their existence.

She told me that she would give up drinking if she were to fall in love, and if she were in love then she'd be able to display more emotional control and reveal less in her writing and, presumably, in her art. Love is the answer to her problems, she seems to think, but she appears to feel unworthy of it, and relieved when the love affair is over, because when she is in love she thinks her partner will leave her anyway.

'You see, I couldn't start clinging on like a limpet for dear life when I felt our relationship coming apart,' she says, sadly. 'He would have thought this was very scary, perhaps scarier than anything else in my whole world. And I couldn't really expose him to that.'

With slight embarrassment I glanced away and looked down at my notes at this intense moment of sadness, a sadness that was so often effectively masked by her obvious and malignant anger. And we both paused temporarily and let this sad moment slip away in the afternoon sun before I ask her about her unmade bed, and the blood and the shit and the tampon.

Jamie Pennebaker and the art and science of turning trauma into stories

Tracey Emin articulates her unconscious desires, her longings, her past, her sufferings; but the sufferings of everyday life in Margate she is keen to point out through her art in spontaneous, unconscious and unconstrained forms; and through language in her memoir, or 'the book' in (necessarily) more constrained forms using syntax and grammar and logical connectives. Both tell a story about trauma; both translate the trauma in different ways initially. *My Bed* (1998) with its dirty sheets, vodka bottles, knickers, used condoms and a bloody tampon, 'the real as a thing of trauma' (Ross 2006: 392), the art the result she says of a 'complete, absolute breakdown' where she spent four days in bed 'asleep and semi-unconscious. When I did eventually get out of bed I had some water, went back, looked at the bedroom and couldn't believe what I could see; this absolute mess and decay of my life.'

Here, 'the screen function of the image, which used to protect the viewer from the Real (the realm of the unrepresentable, of what lies outside the symbolic process) by only letting it obliquely emerge as a traumatic point (Jacques Lacan's tuché; Roland Barthes' punctum), has dissolved itself to reveal the real as traumatic and repulsive, truthful in its abjection' (Ross 2006: 392). But her art (especially after *My Bed* was shortlisted for the Turner Prize in 1990) is endlessly discussed ('So let's talk art.' Her life wraps around it like a supportive vive, or maybe it's the other way round. Why, I ask, is my unmade bed just an unmade bed while hers is art? 'Because … I have transferred what I feel on to someone else looking at it', see *The Scotsman*, 15 September 2008).

Her experiences and traumas revealed in the art are then encoded for a second time into language. And this is a complex process in many ways, from experience through fragments of autobiographical memory which may well be conflicted in detail, in terms of sequence, motivation, causal links and emotion, into multi-dimensional, multi-layered pieces of art, and then into logically interconnected discourse and talk and writing in numerous interviews, articles and books.

Tracey Emin's experiences are, in many ways, an interesting test case for one of the most significant 'methods' (or theories, depending on your point of view) developed in psychology in the last fifty years, namely the emotional disclosure paradigm of Jamie Pennebaker and why it is that 'When people put their emotional upheavals into words, their physical and mental health improved markedly.' Pennebaker writes that 'the act of constructing stories appeared to be a natural human process that helped individuals understand their experiences and themselves' (Pennebaker 2000: 3). This latter point is, of course, self-evident. But it can lead us to ask interesting questions about the sorts of stories that people tell, how they are assembled, and which stories assist our physical and mental health and which do not. Pennebaker's significant contribution is that he has consistently demonstrated throughout his research the clinical link between talking, and writing, about trauma and physical and mental health. Pennebaker (1982; Pennebaker and Beall 1986) proposed that if you do not 'confront' traumatic events, then both your physical and your mental health will suffer. The principal assumption behind this is that to inhibit thoughts, feelings, and behaviour requires considerable effort, and that if you do this over a significant period of time it puts considerable stress on the body and the mind, which are highly interconnected, of course, and makes you susceptible to stress-related diseases. Pennebaker et al. (1987) demonstrated that 'individuals classified as repressors, inhibitors, or suppressors demonstrate higher cancer rates (Kissen 1966), elevated blood pressure levels (Davies 1970; McClelland 1979), and more physical disease in general (Blackburn 1965) than do more expressive individuals' (see Pennebaker et al. 1987: 782).

Therefore, the argument continues, 'disinhibiting' or disclosing thoughts and feelings relating to past or present traumatic experiences should be associated with an improvement in physical and mental health. There is clear evidence to back this up. Derogatis et al. (1979) found that women who lived the longest after diagnosis of breast cancer were those who most openly expressed feelings of anger and depression. Pennebaker and Beall (1986) reported that those subjects who recounted the 'facts' surrounding a traumatic event in combination with their emotional feelings concerning the trauma evidenced great health benefits. These positive effects resulting from the disclosure of past traumatic events have been repeatedly reported in research carried out by Pennebaker and his colleagues (see Pennebaker 1989). Borkovec et al. commented that this is not that surprising given that this is the 'assumption upon which the majority of verbal psychotherapy rests' (1995: 47). As far back as 1895, Breuer and Freud (1966 [1895]) in their development of the cathartic method, stressed the importance of 'the talking cure' in the relief of hysterical patients' symptomatology by encouraging the patient to discuss earlier traumatic experiences and associated emotions. Later, Stiles (1995) stated that 'Across the many alternative psychotherapeutic approaches and theories, expression of private thoughts and feelings is understood as beneficial' (1995: 71). But this newer research suggests that the psychotherapist might be somewhat redundant in this whole process, or at the very least sometimes redundant. It is the translation of the experiences into language that seems to be most important, rather than the insights of the psychotherapist.

But what is it about talking about negative events that leads to health benefits, especially in the absence of a therapist? Pennebaker (1993) argued that 'Through language individuals are able to organise, structure and ultimately assimilate both their emotional experiences and the events that may have provoked the emotions' (Pennebaker 1995: 5). In other words, he believes that disclosure does three things. The first is essentially cognitive – talking about traumatic or negative emotional experiences necessitates giving these memories a sequential, organised structure. Second, it allows for the recognition, labelling and the expression of emotions concerning what happened. Third, it allows for the organisation and assimilation of an individual's perceptions and emotions about the event with their understanding of the event itself. Pennebaker has also stressed that 'translating traumas and their accompanying images and emotions into language demands that all features of the experience be encoded and stored in a more organized, coherent and simplified manner' (Pennebaker et al. 1997: 864). Therefore, it is also about 'simplifying' the account, and making it more 'coherent'. This will involve dealing with any conflicted aspects of the memory, which would be necessary in any process of simplifying the account.

Others, however, have placed the emphasis elsewhere. Stiles (1995) emphasised that disclosure 'helps relieve the distress – by catharsis and by promoting self-understanding. Thus, the relation of disclosure to psychological distress is analogous to the relation of fever to physical infection: both an indicator of some underlying disturbance and part of a restorative process' (1995: 82). Pennebaker would argue that this is only part of the process. Borkovec et al. (1995) concluded that the 'mechanisms by which either psychological or physical benefits occur through [the] verbal process remain as unclear as they are crucially important to identify' (1995: 47–48). There is *still* much disagreement about why it works.

However, perhaps what is surprising is that few researchers have focused in any detail on how people talk about trauma or negative emotional events in this paradigm of 'emotional disclosure', especially given the clinical evidence that this sort of disclosure is so beneficial. Pennebaker's own analyses here focus at the level of the individual word. Francis and Pennebaker (1993) devised a text analysis program, LIWC (Linguistic Inquiry and Word Count), which is an analysis of individual lexical items in these accounts. LIWC measures the percentage of negative and positive emotion words and the number of words suggesting 'self-reflection' or 'insight'. The number of words in the disclosure and the percentage of unique words are also counted. This is obviously a very crude measure of what can occur in any linguistic account. Pennebaker (1993) himself wrote that although 'the results from the LIWC are encouraging ... One problem with LIWC is that it can only give us a very rough conception of overall coherence, organisation and structure' (1993: 543). Unfortunately, 'such a strategy fails to capture people's use of irony, metaphor, and other subtle ways of communicating' (Pennebaker and Francis 1996: 622), which, of course, are crucial aspects of communication. Although LIWC has been developed in the years since it was introduced, it does not (and cannot) have the power to analyse what speakers do in talk. It is like trying to analyse why certain buildings work in terms of design or function by counting the number of bricks of different types. You need a different sort of approach, and you need to be explicit about the assumptions you make (people giving expression to their lives and their traumas in isolated words, and in such words *alone*, i.e. without nonverbal accompaniments, might be considered as one sort of assumption).

Using LIWC, Pennebaker and his colleagues have looked at changes in usage of positive and negative emotion words, insight words, and causal words from one day to the next over the course of an experiment and found that the most important factor that reliably predicted improved physical health was an increase in both causal and insight words. Pennebaker also reported that this increase in these causal and insight words can relate to broader evaluations of the construction of the story or narrative. But again this is like saying the use of certain types of brick may relate to the quality of the building. We may need, however, to understand more about the design of the building to work out why it really works.

There is significant disagreement as to why emotional disclosure works, which is perhaps not that surprising in the light of Pennebaker's comment that 'Most of the research on disclosure has been devoted to demonstrating its effectiveness rather than on identifying the underlying mechanisms' (1997: 164), and the types of analyses conducted on the data. So the question *still* remains: why is disclosure effective in bringing about such health-related changes? Pennebaker has argued that disclosing a traumatic experience does more than just allow for the reduction of inhibitory processes. He suggested that 'linguistically labelling an event and its emotions forces the experience to be structured. This structure promotes the assimilation and understanding of the event, and reduces the associated emotional arousal' (Pennebaker et al. 1997: 864). Clark (1993) argued that through talking, an individual

> attempts to communicate a coherent explanation of the situation, along with an account of his/her own reactions to it. The planful, creative nature of conversation may produce coherence, insights, emotional reactions, and a broadening of perspectives that directly enhance problem solving and interpretive coping.
>
> (Clark 1993: 49)

Pennebaker believes that verbalisation allows for the integration or cognitive reorganisation of the person's perceptions and feelings about an event. In other words, through verbalisation the person may discuss many different aspects of the experience and the mere act of putting one's thoughts and feelings into words may increase the person's understanding of the event. Clark stated that whilst expressing one's innermost feelings about a traumatic event can be important, as in catharsis, like Pennebaker, Clark also believes that 'it is also important that the individual have the opportunity to respond to his/her developing understanding of the problem as well' (1993: 37). Clark explained that

> In the act of creating and producing a communicative act, the speaker has the opportunity to react to the evolving product. In this 'product', the speaker's words give a reality to his/her thoughts and understanding beyond that which exists inside the mind. These processes make that particular version of

what happened seem more real. It seems plausible that creating an explanation for a listener of some event is also likely to make the speaker feel more confident about this version's 'reality'.

(Clark 1993: 37–38)

With respect to disclosure leading to beneficial health effects, Pennebaker stated 'It is hoped that psychologists specializing in language, cognition, social, and clinical psychology can work together in better understanding the basic mechanisms of this phenomenon' (1997: 165).

It is also interesting that although Pennebaker does discuss at times that 'improvements in psychosomatic conditions will most likely be achieved by allowing individuals to express traumatic experiences with both words and behaviors' (1993: 18), he has never examined the types of nonverbal behaviour that typically, and naturally, *accompany* such accounts, as opposed to nonverbal behaviour like dance which is independent of speech (see Pennebaker 2000: 8). Most studies examining the link between nonverbal behaviour and health-related activity have done so in the absence of verbal behaviour. There is clearly a significant gap in the literature with clinicians not recognising the essential multimodal nature of human communication (see Beattie 2016).

Clearly other approaches to this issue of why emotional disclosure might work are possible, but it is important to be more explicit about the theoretical underpinnings of these different approaches. 'Traditional' social psychologists have worked for many years with linguistic and textual material in the form of spoken responses relating to interview situations and written responses to questionnaires. However, the question then is, what standing should be given to this linguistic material? Coyle (1995) stated that

It is generally assumed [by traditional social psychologists] that language is a neutral, transparent medium, describing events or revealing underlying psychological processes in a more or less direct, unproblematic way. The possibility of self-presentational and other biases occurring within this material may be acknowledged but it is assumed that these can be eradicated or at least minimised by refining methods of data generation and collection.

(Coyle 1995: 244)

Indeed, many traditional social psychologists try to 'relate aspects of communication to features that are external to the communicative context', and thus Duncan (1969) 'has called this the "external variable" approach. Duncan contrasts this with what he calls the "structural" approach, where behaviour is analysed in terms of its sequential and hierarchical organisation' (Roger and Bull 1989: 3). An example of a structural approach is *conversation analysis*.

Conversation analysis, which owes so much to the pioneering ideas of Harvey Sacks (1963; 1992), has developed over the past fifty odd years originating within the framework of ethnomethodology. A central concern is the issue of the indexicality of language – that is the meaning of a word or utterance is dependent on its context of use. In other words, the study of what any utterance means requires an understanding of the occasion on which the utterance is used (see Potter 1996: 43). Garfinkel (1974) defined ethnomethodology as the 'study of practical reasoning underpinning everyday social life'. That is, ethnomethodology 'refers to the study of the ways in which everyday common-sense activities are analysed by participants, and of the ways in which these analyses are incorporated into courses of action' (Roger and Bull 1989: 3). The goals of conversation analysis, arguably the most important development within ethnomethodology, are to describe how communicators do things with and in talk (see Hopper 1989). In order to achieve such goals, conversation analysis examines the procedures used in the production of ordinary conversation. Conversation analysis is the study of the interactional organisation of social activities performed in talk. Within this framework, talk-in-interaction is viewed as a topic in its own right – it is not analysed with respect to wider sociological or psychological issues. Heritage (1989) argued that every detail of the conversation is *potentially* significant, and therefore cannot be dismissed 'a priori as disorderly, accidental or interactionally irrelevant' (Heritage 1989: 22). One might say that it is an obvious approach to apply to the study of emotional disclosure where people confront their traumatic experiences and memories by talking about them to a therapist, a friend or even to a researcher. The detailed description of the content and form of the utterances might hold a clue as to what the talk is doing. Pennebaker says that

> conveying a story to another person requires that the speech act be coherent. Linguistic coherence subsumes several characteristics, including structure, use of causal explanation, repetition of themes, and an appreciation of the listener's perspective ... conversations virtually demand the conveying of stories or narratives that require an ordered sequence of events.
>
> (Pennebaker 2000: 12)

Of course, they do all this, but there is clearly so much more to it than that.

Conversation analysis is interested in the ways in which the details of conversation 'can be represented as faithfully as possible in transcription. One primary reason given for this approach is that it provides readers with an opportunity to check for themselves the adequacy of the claims being made' (Roger and Bull 1989: 143). Conversation analysts (e.g., Sacks et al. 1974) rarely begin with a 'theory' – rather, they try to begin with data. Conversation analysts, therefore, favour the empirical approach to the study of social action. They typically rely on the detailed examination of the transcripts themselves relating to individual cases (however, see Heritage and Greatbatch 1986).

'From the outset, conversation analysts have aimed at grasping the organised procedures of talk as they are employed in real-wordly contexts between persons in real relationships whose talk has real consequentiality and accountability' (Heritage 1989: 23). Conversation analysis has been used to examine 'the phenomenon of the contextual determination of indexical speech activities' and 'the management of conversational turn-taking' (Sacks et al. 1974) (see Heritage 1989: 24). Conversation analysis is very diverse. For example, 'some analyses argue points of linguistic theory such as "questions" or "ambiguities" (Schegloff 1984) or "the sentence" (Goodwin 1979). Other analyses take the form of case studies (Sacks 1974), or descriptions of a feature in talk (Jefferson 1979)' (see Hopper 1989: 59). All studies attempt to identify organisational properties of talk and conversation.

Another approach to interpersonal communication, which is related to conversation analysis, is discourse analysis (Edwards and Potter 1992; Potter and Wetherell 1987; Wetherell and Potter 1992), 'a functionally orientated approach to the analysis of talk and text' (Edwards and Potter 1992: 27). Central to discourse analysis is again the idea of the functional nature of talk – the notion that talk is doing something – that all language, even description, has an action orientation (see Potter 1996: 108). Discourse analysis can trace its roots to other domains within social sciences such as speech act theories (Grice 1975; Searle 1969), and the most recent origins of discourse analysis are in the sociology of scientific knowledge (e.g. Ashmore 1989; Potter and Mulkay 1985), and applications of that to social psychology (e.g. Potter 1988; Potter and Wetherell 1987), which in turn had their origins in linguistic philosophy, 'where problems of knowledge had been reworked as problems of language and, specifically, as problems that could be fruitfully recast in terms of language use (Austin 1962; Wittgenstein 1953)' (see Edwards and Potter 1992: 27).

Discourse analysis deals with naturally occurring talk and text in all its forms. Potter and Wetherell (1987) explain that it is concerned with the content of talk, its subject matter, and its social rather than its linguistic organisation. Indeed, language in the form of discourses is viewed as constituting the building blocks of 'social reality'. The analysis of discourse emphasises how social reality is linguistically constructed and tries to achieve 'a better understanding of social life and social interaction from [the] study of social texts' (Potter and Wetherell 1987: 7). The 'emphasis on language as a constructive tool is one of the key tenets of discourse analysis' (Coyle 1995: 244). The individual producing a discourse is seen as selecting from the range of available linguistic resources, and using these resources to create a version of events. However, it should be noted that whereas conversation analysts deal with an extremely rich form of transcription in that they try to recreate from a very detailed transcript exactly what was said, the transcripts used by discourse analysts have traditionally been somewhat less detailed (although this has changed markedly in the past few years). Discourse analysts transcribe only at a level so that readers can make sense of the discourse and do not attempt to make a record of every single detail with respect to pauses, syllable elongation, and so on, on the assumption that such detail will not add a great deal to the meaning of the utterance (see, for example, Potter and Wetherell 1988). In other words, discourse analysts have often considered transcripts at a relatively less detailed level (however, see Potter 1996).

Over the past twenty-five years or so, efforts have been made to come up with a markedly psychological version of discourse analysis. 'This has resulted in what has been termed "discursive psychology", the central tenets of which have been described by Edwards and Potter (1992)' (Coyle 1995: 246). The features of discursive psychology have been summarised as the Discursive Action Model (DAM), which provides a conceptual scheme that captures some of the features of discursive practices and the relationships among them. It has three main components. First, the focus is on action, or function, rather than on cognition; that is, linguistic material is used to perform particular social functions such as justifying, questioning, and accusing, and it does this by employing a variety of rhetorical strategies. Second, there is a focus on the issue of dilemma of stake or interest that is encountered when constructing an account and how this may be negotiated by doing attributional work via reports. This dilemma can be characterised in the following way: 'The speaker of attitudes is caught in a dilemma of interest; that is, their attitude may be treated as having psychological motivations that are the subject of censure of some kind' (Potter et al. 1993: 392). Coyle (1995) stated that

> Any version of events is but one of a number of possible versions and therefore must be constructed as more persuasive than these alternative versions. Sometimes alternative versions will be explicitly mentioned and counteracted in a text but on other occasions they will be implicit.
>
> (Coyle 1995: 248–249)

Speakers, therefore, engage in a number of discursive practices to construct their particular versions as factual and thus external to them and their particular interests, desires, and concerns. For an account to be accepted as a factual report of an incident, or as a description of what really happened, the speaker has to engage in a good deal of constructive work (see Potter 1996). Third, there is a focus on how speakers attend to issues of agency and accountability in their reports of the accounts of reported events. The DAM differentiates between two aspects of accountability: the accountability of the actors whose actions are being described in the reports and the accountability of the speakers themselves. The construction of a version of an event can make available implications about the current speaker's accountability for that event. This could be crucial in emotional disclosure.

For these reasons and more, Vicky Lee, who was a postgraduate student at the time at the University of Manchester, and I became interested in the psychology of communicating past emotional events in a non-therapeutic setting drawing on these different strands. We were interested in issues of construction and function in people's accounts of significant personal emotional events, and in how

> the description is made to seem precisely that: a description rather than a claim, a speculation or indeed a lie. This is the force of saying that people do description ... and [in] how the description is used to accomplish a range of [social] activities.
> (Edwards and Potter 1992: 105)

Discursive psychology argues that the social meanings of events and the social identities of the actors in those events have to be actively constructed in talk. But, we were also interested in identifying specific features within the talk, which derives very much from the conversation analysis tradition. Our research, however, looks beyond the words and paralanguage to the nonverbal behaviour, in an attempt to offer a broader perspective on the analysis of talk about emotional experiences, to recognise the multimodal nature of human communication. Again traditionally, research has kept language and nonverbal behaviour quite separate on the basis of certain assumptions about function. For example, Argyle and Trower stated that 'Humans use two quite separate languages each with its own function' (1979: 21). Argyle (1978) outlined what he believed to be the four main functions of nonverbal communication (NVC): (1) communicating interpersonal attitudes; (2) communication of emotions; (3) regulating or supporting speech; and (4) self-presentation.

But notice immediately that the communication of emotions is listed as one of the primary functions of nonverbal behaviour. I have argued that although the above may be four functions of NVC, not one is unique to NVC. 'Language can and does fulfil all four functions. Sometimes NVC fulfils the specific function to a greater extent, sometimes it does not' (Beattie 1981b: 1173). I have suggested that 'the clear functional division between language and NVC, so long a cornerstone of the psychological literature, may be more illusory than real' and that instead of trying to uncover unique functions for language and NVC we should 'ask how they operate together' (1981b: 1177).

'Natural' speech in everyday life is never disembodied from nonverbal behaviour, therefore, it might well be necessary to include nonverbal behaviour in our present analysis and in so doing examine how the verbal and nonverbal systems of communication interact. With respect to psychotherapy and psychiatric interviews, Schelde and Hertz (1994) talked about the value of focusing on nonverbal as well as verbal behaviour. They stated that

> No doubt an important means in any kind of psychotherapy is the verbal communication between patient and doctor/ therapist. But equally important to this communication is the amount of nonverbal behaviour demonstrated by both parties that influences the interaction and the therapy to a considerable degree, not least of which is the establishment of a relationship of trust between doctor and patient.
>
> (Schelde and Hertz 1994: 383)

Indeed, Wierzbicka (1995), looking at the meaning of nonverbal behaviour, suggested that in order to 'understand human communicative behaviour, we need an integrated description of verbal and nonverbal communication' (1995: 247).

Early conversation analytic research 'gave little attention to the role of non-vocal behavior in interaction' (Heritage 1989: 32). Much of the early work was based on the study of telephone conversations, 'in order to simplify the work of analysis through "the automatic elimination of non-vocal conduct as an object of participants' orientations"' (Roger and Bull 1989: 146). One major problem with the inclusion of nonverbal behaviour in conversation analytic research was the sheer complexity of the issue. A coherent set of transcription procedures had evolved for some features of paralanguage and intonation (see Jefferson 1985), but no comparable set of procedures had been derived for other aspects of nonverbal behaviour. A small body of research in the conversation analytic tradition had attempted to incorporate some limited aspects of nonverbal behaviour, most notably eye gaze. For example, Goodwin (1979; 1981) focused on the ways in which eye gaze is organised with respect to the management of turn allocation and turn construction (see also Beattie 1983). Further, in examining the operations used by a recipient during talk, Goodwin focused on head nods and eyebrow lifts, but it should be noted that this work has always been the exception rather than the rule (except perhaps in the case of hand gesture, see McNeill 1992; Beattie 2003; 2016).

Nonverbal behaviour was conspicuously absent from research in discourse analysis for many years, which again may seem rather surprising given that nonverbal behaviour can completely alter the meaning or reading of any utterance. The statement 'I hate you', said with a particular intonation and with certain accompanying NV behaviour (smile, eye contact, etc.) changes dramatically the underlying meaning, and from a discourse analytic perspective, the action orientation of the utterance. That was why we wanted to take a discourse analytic focus on the action orientation of talk, but in addition, carry out some analysis of the accompanying nonverbal behaviour with some interpretation of how these behaviours are functioning with respect to talk. We chose to focus on a number of aspects of nonverbal behaviour. The first was the smile. There are a number of specific reasons for choosing to focus on smiles. First, it's very common, the smile is 'one of the most frequent of all the facial expressions' (Ekman 1985: 149); the second concerns its perceptual salience: '[the] smile is the easiest expression to recognise. We found ... smiles can be seen from further away (300 feet) and with a briefer exposure than other emotional expressions' (Ekman 1985: 149). Third, the smile is one aspect of NVC which has a very strong effect on the communication of interpersonal attitudes. In a study examining the communication of friendly and hostile attitudes by verbal and NV signals, Argyle et al. (1971) described a friendly NV style as consisting of a 'warm, soft tone of voice, *open smile*, [and] relaxed posture' (1971: 389; emphasis added). They stated that if the nonverbal cues are friendly, 'one then assumes the [speaker] to have a positive attitude (she likes me) towards one' (1971: 400; but see also Beattie 1981a). Further, subjects 'tended to see the performer as sincere, i.e. honest in intention' (Argyle et al. 1971: 400–401). In a related finding, Ekman (1985) stated that 'it is hard not to reciprocate a smile ... People enjoy looking at most smiles, a fact well known to advertisers' (1985: 149). The smiles (and eye gaze) are also of significance because these two forms of nonverbal behaviour have been shown to be central in the interpersonal communication of the intimacy of a relationship balancing with them verbal behaviours such as the intimacy of the topic (Argyle and Dean 1965).

However, the facial expression commonly referred to as 'the smile' is not, in fact, a single category of facial behaviour. Ekman (1985) concluded that there are 'dozens of smiles, each differing in appearance and in the message expressed. There are many positive emotions signalled by smiling – enjoyment, physical or sensory pleasure, contentment, and amusement ... [but] people also smile when they are miserable' (1985: 150). He noted that there are also 'false smiles', which are used to convince others that positive feelings are felt when they aren't, and 'masking smiles', which are made deliberately to hide the experience of negative emotion. However, Ekman (1989) stated that of the eighteen different smile types which he described in 1985, only one particular type of smile – the enjoyment smile – accompanies experienced positive emotions such as enjoyment, happiness, or pleasure. Frank and Ekman (1993) stated that 'while many types of smiles may occur in the course of ... experiments, it is the enjoyment smile that seems to manifest true felt enjoyment or happiness' (1993: 10).

It would seem, therefore, that failing to recognise that there are different types of smiles which may have led to some confusion and apparent contradictions in past research. Ekman (1992b) commented that such confusion 'might have been avoided if scientists in this century had read the work of French neuroanatomist G. B. Duchenne de Bologne, who wrote in 1862' (1992b: 36). Duchenne stated that the smile of enjoyment, which Ekman and Friesen (1982) have referred to as the 'felt' smile, and which Ekman (1989) later renamed the Duchenne smile in the Frenchman's honour, could be distinguished from deliberately produced smiles by considering two facial muscles. The first of these muscles, zygomaticus major, pulls the lip corners up at an angle towards the cheekbones. The second muscle, orbicularis oculi, encircles the eye and pulls the skin from the cheeks and forehead towards the eyeball, producing crow's-feet wrinkles beyond the eye corners. According to Duchenne, 'The first [zygomaticus major] obeys the will but the second [orbicularis oculi] is only put in play by the sweet emotions of the soul; the ... fake joy, the deceitful laugh, cannot provoke the contraction of this latter muscle ...' (1990 [1862]: 126).

Frank and Ekman (1993) suggested that the differences between enjoyment and other smiles originate in basic functional neuroanatomy. 'It appears that there are two distinct neural pathways that mediate facial expressions; one pathway is for voluntary, wilful facial actions, and a second for involuntary, emotional facial actions (Meihlke 1973; Myers 1976)' (see Frank and Ekman 1993: 12). As a result of this neuroanatomical foundation, in conjunction with Duchenne's observations, Ekman and Friesen (1982) predicted that the 'orbicularis oculi/zygomatic major configuration observed by Duchenne would be one among several morphological and dynamic markers that would distinguish smiles which are shown in concert with the emotion of enjoyment from smiles which are shown for reasons other than enjoyment' (Frank and Ekman 1993: 12). Enjoyment, of course, is a very general term that covers quite a variety of different positive emotional experiences, including sensory pleasure, earning praise, satisfaction at accomplishing a task, relief, contentment, or amusement; Ekman and Friesen (1982) nevertheless claimed that smiles in all such 'enjoyable' circumstances would be different from those shown in the absence of enjoyment.

Although Ekman and Friesen (1982) suggested other ways in which enjoyment smiles could be distinguished from other forms of smiles (mainly through 'bilateral symmetry', and the slow onset and offset of enjoyment smiles), it is Duchenne's proposal about the morphological features that has been most widely tested, replicated and documented. For example, in a laboratory setting, Ekman et al. (1990) found that people showed more Duchenne smiles when they were watching pleasant films than when they were watching unpleasant films, but there was no difference in the frequency of the other types of smiles. Depressed patients showed more Duchenne smiles when they were being discharged from hospital than when they were being admitted (Matsumoto 1987). Similarly, for psychotherapy patients who were judged to have improved, there was a corresponding increase in Duchenne smiling (Steiner 1986). In the present study, it is an examination of the occurrence of the smile characterised by the Duchenne marker (to be called the Duchenne smile) and any other form of smile which does not show the Duchenne configuration (to be known as non-Duchenne smile), that are of particular importance.

The next behaviour we chose to focus on was eye gaze. Again, one reason for focusing on eye gaze is its perceptual salience. 'When looking at photographs of people, subjects look mainly at their faces, and especially the eyes and mouth' (Argyle and Cook 1976: 18). Argyle (1974) stated that

> The typical pattern of eye-movements during a 2-person conversation, in Western culture, can be described, on the basis of studies by Nielsen (1962, Denmark), Exline and Winters (1965, USA) and Kendon (1967, England). Interaction is often started by a period of eye-contact, which seems to signal that each is ready to interact with the other (Goffman 1963). Once under way each person looks at the other in the region of the eyes intermittently, in glances of varying length, usually between 1 and 10 seconds.
>
> (Argyle 1963: 105)

The second reason for focusing on eye gaze is that it is a powerful interpersonal signal in social interaction, and has already been mentioned, critical to the signalling of interpersonal intimacy (Argyle and Dean 1965). Ellis and Beattie (1986) stated that 'eye-gaze is affected by the degree of liking between two or more people ... and becomes a powerful signal of sexual interest' (1986: 36). However, eye gaze does not necessarily reflect liking. 'It can express the opposite – aggression and hostility, and staring at someone, whether it be intentional or not, may also evoke aggression' (Ellis and Beattie 1986: 36). Eye gaze can also reflect dominance (see Mehrabian and Friar 1969), and sometimes shame or embarrassment (see Modigliani 1971). The amount of eye gaze in social interaction is, therefore, affected by a number of different factors and has come to be thought of as an important signal.

There have been relatively few attempts to describe the complex interrelationships between verbal and nonverbal behaviour until comparatively recently, which may seem rather surprising given the volume of research in each of these two areas separately (but see Beattie 1983; Goodwin 1979; 1981; and Kendon 1967, for some notable exceptions). With respect to eye gaze, Ellis and Beattie (1986) suggested that most of the early studies analysing speaker gaze during speech have

> tended to confine themselves to attempting to measure the amount rather than the precise patterning of this form of behaviour. The studies, which have explored the patterning of gaze with speech, have often employed rather ubiquitous and sometimes vague categories of language such as 'remark' or 'question'. As a result, the patternings of gaze which have been reported have shown considerable variation.
>
> (Ellis and Beattie 1986: 137)

Kendon (1967) carried out the most intensive early investigation of the patterning of gaze in conversation. He observed that speakers tended to look at listeners more during fluent speech than during hesitant speech. Kendon also described the patterning of gaze with respect to 'phrases' and 'phrase boundary pauses', which were some of the principal units in his analysis, and found that the speaker tended to look at the listener as the end of a phrase was approached, and carried on looking during the phrase boundary pause, but gaze was averted as the next phrase began. Kendon also noted that 'utterances' terminated with prolonged gaze. However, one major problem with this study was that the linguistic units – 'phrase', 'utterance', etc. – which were central to the analyses, were not defined.

I had earlier in my career analysed the distribution of gaze with respect to the units of planning of spontaneous speech, specifically 'temporal cycles', which include a hesitant phase and a fluent phase (Beattie 1979; 1981a; 1983). Using frame-by-frame analysis of video-recordings of natural dyadic verbal interactions, these investigations revealed that speaker eye gaze is connected in an

> intricate pattern with the flow of spontaneous speech. Speakers tend to look most at listeners during the most fluent phases of speech. If they fail to avert their eyes during the planning periods of spontaneous speech, there is a marked increase in speech disturbances, particularly false starts. The temporal cycles which seem to reflect some of the basic planning processes of spontaneous speech have a great influence on the patterning of speaker eye-gaze.
>
> (Ellis and Beattie 1986: 144)

Previous research on the relationship between verbal and nonverbal behaviour has approached this topic from a number of different theoretical perspectives. Back in 1983, I was interested in approaching this from a more cognitive science perspective (Beattie 1983), starting from the assumption that monitoring the behaviour of one's fellow interactants and planning speech were cognitively incompatible operations, and that one could predict the pattern of eye gaze with respect to speech from an understanding of the cognitive demands underlying the cognitive generation and production of speech (see also Kendon 1967). Conversation analytic work on the relationship between verbal and nonverbal behaviour approached this topic from a perspective essentially focusing on interactional management, and has been concerned with how verbal and nonverbal behaviour may be organised to accomplish certain interactional ends. In the research described here the focus was quite different. We were interested in the action orientation of talk, and thus we were interested in conceptualising nonverbal behaviour in these broad functional terms as well. The question we were asking was how can the nonverbal behaviour be used to affect the overall action orientation of the utterance?

There were three broad hypotheses that we chose to examine. The first hypothesis was that speech and the nonverbal behaviours of smiling and eye gaze work together in emotional disclosure, so that when the speech is positive, the nonverbal behaviour will also be positive (more smiles, more eye gaze). The second hypothesis is really the antithesis of the first – the two channels, speech and nonverbal behaviour, operate in opposition, so that when talk is very negative, speakers offset this negativity with positive nonverbal behaviours. This is rather like how postural congruence (Beattie and Beattie 1981), where people mimic each other's bodily posture, is sometimes thought to operate, with old friends showing higher levels of congruence when they are arguing to signal 'the ultimate continuity of their relationship' (Scheflen 1965). The third hypothesis we considered was that there is no *overall* relationship between verbal and nonverbal behaviour in emotional disclosure, but that nonverbal behaviour is most often used to mark important transitions within and between turns (Goodwin 1979; 1981; Kendon 1967).

In this research, which formed part of the basis for Vicky Lee's Ph.D., fifty-four university students were video-recorded talking about two events, one of which gave rise to a positive emotional experience and one to a negative emotional experience. Here, I re-present a detailed microanalysis of just one female subject ('S') from this project talking about an event to a researcher ('E') which evoked powerful negative emotions (see Lee and Beattie 1998; 2000 for more detail). The analysis here is an (extremely limited) single case study, but one that perhaps hints at how language, accompanied by a number of different types of nonverbal behaviour, is sometimes used in emotional disclosure. The analysis is very different to the type carried out when we apply LIWC to a corpus, but does, I think, tell us something interesting about the constructive and functional nature of language use in emotional disclosure, as revealed through the details of the talk and the interaction.

An account of a traumatic incident

The incident which the participant described here happened whilst she was working as a care assistant and nurse's aide in an American hospital. She had been asked to transfer a patient from his wheelchair to the bed. However, what should have been a relatively simple and smooth operation did not go according to plan. The patient tried to walk by himself; he fell, cracked two ribs, subsequently punctured his lung, and two weeks later he died.

We were interested in how this person actively constructed her account of the incident, including her emotional feelings about the event. We also examined the subtle and varied ways in which the description itself performed various social actions such as making attributions, assigning blame, and offering justifications. One particular focus in the verbal analysis was on how she, the nurse's aide, and he, the patient, are described and differentiated.

Her account is particularly interesting because

> in encountering an event, and encountering it as a witness or someone who in part suffered by it, one is entitled to an experience ... The teller owns rights to tell this story, and they give their credentials for their rights to tell the story by offering such things as that they saw it, and that they suffered by it.

> (Sacks 1984: 425)

In order for an emotional event to be classified as negative, it would have to deviate from, or be contrasted with, perceptions of day-to-day 'normality', in such a way as to result in the experiencing of less pleasant or less positive feelings than usual. But, the speaker also has to give an account that lets the listener infer what kind of person she is. As we shall see in this case-study analysis, she terminates her account by talking about her negative emotional feelings. Below, is a detailed transcript of her account, based on the conventions employed by Jefferson (1985); see Appendix on pages 237–8 for a description of the transcription conventions used.

Transcript

1 S: ↑U:m (0.5) well the ↑negative event happened when I was (0.3) I was

2   working at the same hospital in ↑ America. (0.7)

3   Em (0.6) I was working as a- a care assistant and °a nurse's aide,° (0.5)

4   and er I was supposed to trans:fer a <u>pati</u>ent from his wheelchair into the

5   bed

6 E: yyeh

7 S: and erm (0.2) I didn't <u>ac</u>tually know that this- this patient had a ((sort

8   of history of not doing what he was <u>to</u>:ld.)) ((*smiley voice*))

9 E: yeh

10 S: So em (0.7) I put him in his chair by the side of the bed, (0.5)

11   and I went out to call the nurse, (0.2) 'cos the nurse had to be present

12   when you did a transfer

13 E: right

14 S: and er (0.2) as I sort of left his side (0.2) he got up and decided to try

15   and walk by him↑self:: (0.9)

16   So em (0.4) when he got u::p (0.6) he er he ↑<u>fell</u>,

17   he fell sideways into em like- like er a bar alongside the ↑<u>wall</u>:

18 E: yeh

19   and err (0.2) he cracked two ribs. (1.0)

20   **And er I- I TURNED ROUND JUST IN TIME TO SEE HIM**

21   **FA:LLING,**

22   **SO I- I MANAGED TO GET THERE BEFORE HE HIT THE**

23   **FLOOR,**

24   **AND I MANAGED TO SORT OF CUSHION HIM as he hit** (0.2)

25   **you know, got down,**

26 E: right

27 S: **and em** (0.3) <u>hit</u> **the emergency cord, and called the doctors and**

28 **everything.**

29 **But em** (0.5) **then we found that he had these two broken ribs,**

30 **and em** (0.2) ↑<u>three</u> **days later** (0.2) **it em punctured his** ((<u>lung</u>

31 (0.4))) ((*laugh*)) **and he DI::ED** ((two weeks later)) ((*laugh*))

32 **and em** (0.2) **I felt like it was all** (0.3) <u>my</u> **responsibility and** <u>my</u> **fault**

33 **for having left him**

34 (0.3)

35 E: right

36 S: **and er** (0.2) **we had to have a** (0.1) **disciplinary council to** (0.4)

37 <u>vin</u>:**dicate me and say that it wasn't my fault,** (0.8)

38 and er (0.1) I just remember ((<u>be</u>:ing)) ((*smiley voice*)) re:ally really

39 down and really (0.2) feeling, (0.4)

40 apart from the fact that you know that I- I actually (0.6)

41 **I felt** <u>guilty</u> **for the fact that I hadn't** <u>been</u> **there and- and like to**

42 **help him,** (0.2)

43 E: right

44 (0.1)

45 S: **even though it wasn't really my fault 'cos I turned round and** (0.3)

46 **you know he did it on his** ↑ow↓**n.**

47 E: yeh

48 (0.4)

49 S: But I just remember feeling ab:solutely awful 'cos I felt

50 ((RESPO::NSIBLE)) ((*laugh*)) ((FOR HIM DYING)), ((*smiley voice*))

51 AND THEN I HAD ALL THIS ER (0.3) °palaver with the (0.1)

52 council, and had to go and give° (0.1) ((testi↑MONY:: and))

((*smiley*
53   voice)) ((all the rest)) ((*laugh*)) of it.
54   So (0.2) it was a real nightmare ((((1.2))) ((*laugh*))
      ((basically)).
55   ((*smiley voice*))
56   Em (0.6) and- and I had to go and see (0.5) em the council
      ↑every
57   ((couple of weeks)) ((*smiley voice*)) 'cos (0.3) I got really
      tearful and
58   °upset about it,° and it er (0.1) shook me up a bit.

Construction of credibility and the allocation of blame

The respondent begins her account by constructing herself in a positive light – a competent individual who cares about, and is willing to help sick people. After all, not everybody would choose to work as a care assistant in a hospital. She repeats the words 'I was working'.

1   ↑U:m (0.5) well the ↑negative event happened when I was (0.3) *I was*
2   *working* at the same hospital in ↑America. (0.7)
3   Em (0.6) *I was working* as a- a care assistant and °a nurse's aide,° (0.5)

This repetition serves to reinforce her construction as a caring and hard-working person. She wasn't there for the fun of it, but rather to hold down a responsible job. The issue of the dilemma of stake or interest encountered when constructing an account and how this may be negotiated by doing attributional work via reports, is of fundamental importance. Attributions are inferences about why a particular event in our social world occurred. The 'attribution process' is the term given by social psychologists to the inferential process linking the event in question to the resultant attribution. The most influential theoretical contributions to our understanding of the attribution process are those made by Kelley (1967). According to Kelley, in trying to answer the question 'why' about others' behaviour, we focus on three major dimensions:

(1) *Consensus*: the extent to which other people react in the same way as the target person to a particular stimulus. Thus, consensus information relates to variation across persons. If everybody reacts in the same manner as the target person, then consensus is said to be high. If only the target person reacts in the observed manner, consensus is said to be low.

(2) *Consistency*: the extent to which this person's behaviour is stable across time, i.e. the extent to which an individual reacts in a similar manner to the same stimulus on different occasions. Thus, consistency information relates to variation across time of action. If the person reacts in a similar manner to the same stimulus on different occasions, consistency is said to be high. If the person reacts in a different manner to the same stimulus on different occasions, then consistency is said to be low.

(3) *Distinctiveness*: the extent to which this person's behaviour is or is not specific to a particular stimulus, i.e. the extent to which the person reacts in a similar manner to different stimuli. Thus, distinctiveness relates to variation across stimuli. High distinctiveness means that behaviour is specific to that stimulus, whereas if the person reacts in the same way to a wide range of stimuli, distinctiveness is low.

Kelley's theory suggests that the combinations of consensus, consistency, and distinctiveness have certain effects on the outcome of the attributional process. Kelley's model holds that, in order for the target person's behaviour to be attributed to that person (i.e. a *person* or a *dispositional attribution*), both consensus and distinctiveness should be low, and consistency should be high. In contrast, high consensus, high consistency, and high distinctiveness should, according to the model, result in a stimulus *attribution*. Finally, any pattern of information including low consistency, and in particular low consensus, low consistency, and high distinctiveness, should, according to Kelley's model, result in a circumstance attribution.

In the account of the traumatic event, the nurse's aide says that:

4   and er I was supposed to trans:fer a <u>patient</u> from his wheelchair into the
5   bed

7 and erm (0.2) I didn't <u>a</u>ctually know that this– this patient had a ((sort
8 of history of not doing what he was <u>to</u>:1d.)) ((*smiley voice*))

The respondent can be construed as 'the person' (from the point of view of Kelley's model), and the patient can be construed as the 'stimulus' (again from the model's point of view). By saying that the patient had a 'history' of not doing what he was told, the speaker is implying that other nurses had also had a problem with this patient, i.e. other nurses had told him what to do and he wouldn't conform with their requests (in other words this was an example of 'high consensus'). The speaker is being explicit that this type of non-conformist behaviour on the part of the patient has happened before ('high consistency'), and implicit is the notion that most patients do not have a history of not doing what they're told ('high distinctiveness'). Thus, this is a way of discursively evoking Kelley's dimensions of high consensus, high consistency, and high distinctiveness in discourse, and therefore a way of discursively guiding the listener (and perhaps herself) towards a stimulus attribution – blame for this negative event resides with the patient himself. In other words, she achieves the subtle negotiation of blame, which might be attributed to her, onto the somewhat irresponsible patient, and in so doing has constructed a contrasting identity for herself (responsible, carefully follows instructions – 'supposed to transfer a patient', rule follower) to that of the patient (irresponsible, does what he likes etc., all the nurses have trouble with him). This is further reinforced by her next comments:

10 So em (0.7) I put him in his chair by the side of the bed, (0.5)
11 and I went out to call the nurse, (0.2) 'cos the nurse had to be present
    when you did a transfer
12 when you did a transfer

Through the description of her understanding of the necessity to follow instructions, she portrays herself as someone who does everything by the book. She is explaining why it was necessary to leave the room in the first place: ''cos the nurse had to be present when you did a transfer', and her desire to do what she was told.

This is in stark contrast to the patient, who has been presented as somewhat irresponsible and as someone who (habitually) breaks the rules. Further, she pre-empts any potential blame directed at herself by attributing the responsibility for her not staying with the patient to the necessity to comply with the rules laid down by the medical authority itself. In other words, she implies that she would have stayed with the patient at all times, but out of necessity 'went out to call the nurse, ''cos the nurse had to be present ...' Thus, her reason for not staying with the patient is presented via the use of role talk. She acted as a member of the medical team, legitimately and under orders (see Halkowski 1990). The deployment of group membership categories, presently by an implicit role description, is an indirect way of performing important attributional work. In this way, she is able to downplay her own agency in the course of this event.

14 and er (0.2) as I sort of left his side (0.2) he got up and decided to try
15 and walk by him↑self:: (0.9)
16 So em (0.4) when he got u::p (0.6) he er he ↑<u>fell</u>,
17 he fell sideways into em like- like er a bar alongside the ↑<u>wall</u>:
19 and err (0.2) he cracked two ribs. (1.0)

The phrase 'sort of' is in direct contrast to the verb 'decided'. By saying 'and er as I sort of left his side', she is displaying her unsureness or indecisiveness regarding her actions. It is as if she knows she shouldn't really leave the patient, but has no option as she must comply with the rules which say a nurse has to be present in such situations. However, the patient, she says, 'got up and decided to try and walk by himself'. The verb 'decided' implies a conscious decision on the part of the patient, therefore intimating that he has a wilful character. Thus, again we have a contrast between her, the caregiver, defenceless as a result of having to abide by the rules, and he, the patient, actively breaking them.

Contrastive pairs

There is variability within the carer's own personal agency and self-construction reflected through the use of a number of verbal formats known as 'contrastive pairs' (e.g. Atkinson 1984). A contrastive pair consists of two consecutive items or parts of discourse, which contrast with one another in some way. Contrastive pairs are recurrent, rhetorical structures which are significant devices used in many types of 'persuasive' communication, including those used by market traders and politicians (see Beattie 1988). In his work on the language of politicians, Atkinson argued that 'as so much political debate involves assertions and counter-assertions about "us" and "them", it is hardly surprising that making a contrast between two items is an extraordinarily adaptable and widely used technique for packaging and delivering ... messages' (1984: 73). Atkinson believes that if a speaker can present an audience with some sort of puzzle, then the speaker 'stands a good chance of arousing their curiosity, and thus giving them more of an incentive to pay attention' (1984: 73). A major advantage of these verbal formats is that 'they provide a way of formulating the gist of a message which is both brief and complete in itself' (1984: 158), and they also 'provide an economical way of formulating rival positions' (1984: 159). Atkinson had concluded that details which are typical of the way contrasts are produced are the similarities in length, content, and grammatical structure of the two parts. There are a number of contrastive pairs in the particular account analysed here. Note that **(N)** means negative and **(P)** means positive, which relate to the speaker's own personal agency in the course of the event within each contrastive pair.

1st contrastive pair

A1   'And er I– I TURNED ROUND JUST IN TIME TO SEE HIM FA:LLING, **(N)**

B1   SO I– I MANAGED TO GET THERE BEFORE HE HIT THE FLOOR, **(P)**

2nd contrastive pair

A2 AND I MANAGED TO SORT OF CUSHION HIM as he hit
(0.2) you know, got down, and em (0.3) <u>hit</u> the emergency cord,
and called the doctors and everything. **(P)**

B2 But em (0.5) then we found that he had these two broken ribs, and
em (0.2) ↑<u>three</u> days later (0.2) it em punctured his ((<u>lung</u> (0.4)))
((*laugh*)) and he DI::ED ((two weeks later)) ((*laugh*)) **(N)**

3rd contrastive pair

A3 and em (0.2) I felt like it was all (0.3) <u>my</u> responsibility and <u>my</u>
fault for having left him, **(N)**

B3 and er (0.2) we had to have a (0.1) disciplinary council to (0.4)
<u>vin</u>:dicate me and say that it wasn't my fault', **(P)**

4th contrastive pair

A4 'I felt <u>guilty</u> for the fact that I hadn't <u>been</u> there and- and like to
<u>help</u> him, (0.2) **(N)**

B4 even though it wasn't really my fault 'cos I turned round and (0.3)
you know he did it on his ↑ow↓n'. **(P)**

Both parts of the first contrastive pair (A1 and B1) are marked in
a loud voice. In the first part of the contrast (A1) she says that she
turned round 'just in time to see him falling'. Here, she presents
herself as more of an observer. She, herself, is much less active, as it
is 'he' who is falling. The words 'just in time' imply that she was
not, however, slow to react, and the phrase as a whole suggests that
she could not have gone too far from the patient in her care. This
observer role is in contrast to the much more active role presented
in the second part of the contrast (B1). Here, there is much more
active agency on the part of the speaker. Because she hadn't gone
too far, she 'managed to get there before he hit the floor'. Thus, she
portrays herself as a responsible person: she had to leave out of
necessity, but didn't go too far.

The first part of the second contrast (A2) reflects the continuation of her active agency as she describes the positive actions that she performed. She says that she 'managed to sort of cushion him', which suggests that the fall would have been much worse if she hadn't been there. 'As he hit, you know, got down' serves to de-dramatise the incident: as he hit the floor with a 'thump' or a 'thud', might lead to a somewhat different interpretation of the event. The positive actions that she performed are contrasted in the second part (B2) with the rather negative consequences that occurred as a result of the fall. She says that 'then we found that he had these two broken ribs ...' The word 'we' is very important in her self-presentation as a person 'in the know' with respect to medical matters, and as an accepted and valued member of a medical team. She positions herself, in a medical discourse, within a caring medical context. Through the description of her understanding of the conditions he suffered, she portrays herself as someone who is knowledgeable about medical matters, and as one to whom medical officials chose to divulge information about the patient's condition. In presenting herself as one who has a 'category related speaking entitlement' (Edwards and Potter 1992: 160), she makes her account difficult to undermine. Thus, in the first two contrastive pairs she uses contrasts between her own active and positive role as she describes the actions she performed (B1 and A2) and the negative consequences of events out of her control (A1 and B2).

In the third contrastive pair, the acceptance of some responsibility in the first part ('I felt like it was all my responsibility and my fault for having left him') is contrasted with the shift of responsibility evident in the second part ('we had to have a disciplinary council to ... say that it wasn't my fault'). Note that she stresses the word 'my'. There is also variability in her own self-construction. On the one hand she constructs herself as this medical 'expert' by using the word we, and on the other hand portrays herself as peripheral to the medical team, when she says '*I* felt like it was all my responsibility and my fault for having left him'. She could have said '*they* felt that it was all my responsibility', but she doesn't. So in this sense the choice of the word 'I' serves to play down any potential blame attributable to her because even though she feels like it was her responsibility and her fault, the medical officials – people with expert knowledge within the medical field – are not saying so.

According to Potter and Wetherell (1987), one way of throwing light upon the functions of discourse is through the study of such variability in what is being said. Variation occurs within an individual's discourse, dependent upon the action orientation of the particular utterances. They have claimed that mainstream approaches to psychology, in their search for individual consistency, have looked to minimise or explain away intra-individual variation. Discourse analysis, on the other hand, actively seeks it out. 'As variability arises from the different functions that the discourse may be fulfilling, the nature of the variation can provide clues to what these functions are' (Coyle 1995: 249). Thus, presently, the attribution of responsibility has been offset by her description, demonstrating how variable self-construction can be related to function in talk. She is presented as unequal to the medical officials when her status as a blameless and somewhat naive caregiver is to be established but elsewhere in the account is presented as 'in the know', as a credible member of the team.

The three contrastive pairs above follow in succession, and together form items in a three-part list. The three-part list is a construction which has been shown to be rhetorically important in different types of discourse, for example, political speeches (Atkinson 1984), courtroom dialogue (Drew 1990), and everyday talk (Jefferson 1990). 'Jefferson (1990) has emphasized that lists, particularly three-part lists, can be used to construct descriptions which are treated as complete or representative' (Edwards and Potter 1992: 163). Here, the three contrastive pairs are separated from the fourth by a section of talk relating to her own feelings. Thus, having just described the unfortunate incident, she reiterates the kind of person she is: a caring person who is capable of experiencing certain feelings (e.g. 'being really really down'). The fourth contrastive pair is similar to the third, in that she starts with a description of her feelings which could be associated with an acceptance of blame ('I felt guilty'), and a subsequent denial of blame through the statement 'it wasn't really my fault'. She goes on to justify why she wasn't to blame, and this is twofold. First, she 'turned round' which implies that she was in some way trying to right the situation or at least trying to lessen the gravity of possible consequences. Second, she says that the patient 'did it on his own'. She has therefore shifted responsibility away from herself and onto the patient. Thus, she uses the third and fourth contrastive pairs to indicate that while she feels a degree of responsibility (A3 and A4), the facts of the incident, and medical authorities, absolved her of blame (B3 and B4).

She ends her account by saying how upset she was over the whole affair. She reiterates her feelings and an acceptance of some responsibility for the patient dying.

Nonverbal behaviour in emotional disclosure

In terms of the nonverbal behaviour, we examined the way that both Duchenne smiles and non-Duchenne smiles, and eye-gaze, were organised within these contrastive pairs. The analyses are set out in Tables 6.1 and 6.2.

We hypothesised that nonverbal behaviour could have a number of possible interactional functions with respect to these contrastive pairs. Non-Duchenne smiles and eye gaze could:

(1) *Augment the contrast.* Nonverbal behaviour could be operating to highlight the positive content of the verbal message, if higher levels of non-Duchenne smiles and eye gaze were evident in the positive part (P) of the contrastive pair than in the negative part (N).

(2) *Mark the transition.* Nonverbal behaviour could be operating to highlight the transition between the two parts of the contrast.

(3) *Ameliorate the contrast.* Nonverbal behaviour could be operating to lessen the effects of the negative content, if higher levels of non-Duchenne smiles and eye gaze were evident in the negative part (N) of the contrastive pair than in the positive part (P). An interesting additional question is where the Duchenne smiles

occur, as they are much less intentional and associated with genuine emotional expression.

We measured the total duration of both parts of each contrastive pair, and then measured the duration of Duchenne and non-Duchenne smiles and eye gaze within both parts (see Table 6.1). The percentage of total time that the nonverbal behaviour was displayed (on and off) within each part of the contrastive pair was calculated (see Table 6.2).

TABLE 6.1 Total duration of both parts of each contrastive pair and time duration of Duchenne smiles, non-Duchenne smiles, and eye gaze within

		DURATIONS (seconds)						
		Total time	D smile ON	D smile OFF	Non-D ON	Non-D OFF	Gaze ON	Gaze OFF
1st contrastive pair	A1 (N)	2.7	2.7	0	0	2.7	1.8	0.9
	B1 (P)	1.8	0	1.8	0	1.8	0.5	1.3
2nd contrastive pair	A2 (P)	7.0	2.7	4.3	1.5	5.5	2.2	4.8
	B2 (N)	9.4	4.4	5.0	2.9	6.5	4.9	4.5
3rd contrastive pair	A3 (N)	4.8	4.8	0	0	4.8	3.1	1.7
	B3 (P)	4.8	1.6	3.2	0.8	4.0	3.1	1.7
4th contrastive pair	A4 (N)	3.1	0.9	2.2	0	3.1	2.7	0.4
	B4 (P)	3.4	1.2	2.2	0	3.4	3.0	0.4

TABLE 6.2 Percentage of total time that Duchenne smiles, non-Duchenne smiles, and eye-gaze are on and off within both parts of each contrastive pair

		D smile ON	D smile OFF	Non-D ON	Non-D OFF	Gaze ON	Gaze OFF
1st contrastive	A1 (N)	100	0	0	100	67	33
pair	B1 (P)	0	100	0	100	28	72
2nd contrastive	A2 (P)	39	61	21	79	31	69
pair	B2 (N)	47	53	31	69	52	48
3rd contrastive	A3 (N)	100	0	0	100	65	35
pair	B3 (P)	33	67	17	83	65	35
4th contrastive	A4 (N)	29	71	0	100	87	13
pair	B4 (P)	35	65	0	100	88	12

Analysis of Duchenne smile

1st contrastive pair

A1 ʼAnd er, I- I TURNED ROUND JUST IN TIME TO SEE HIM FA:LLING, (N)

B1   SO I- I MANAGED TO GET THERE BEFORE HE HIT THE FLOOR,ʼ   (P)

The Duchenne smile was observed throughout the (N) part of the contrast, but not at all during the (P) part.

2nd contrastive pair

A2 ʻAND I MANAGED TO SORT OF CUSHION HIM as he hit (0.2) you know,

← D.SMILE —

got down, and em (0.3) <u>hit</u> the emergency cord, and called the doctors and

everything. (P)

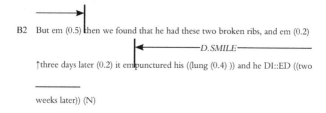

B2   But em (0.5) then we found that he had these two broken ribs, and em (0.2)

↑three days later (0.2) it em punctured his ((lung (0.4))) and he DI::ED ((two

weeks later)) (N)

Although the Duchenne smile occurred in both parts of the contrast, there was relatively more smiling in the (N) part than in the (P) part. The smile became most intense when she discusses the consequences, and she laughed when she said 'lung and he died two weeks later'.

3rd contrastive pair

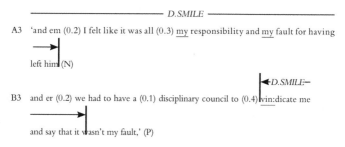

A3   'and em (0.2) I felt like it was all (0.3) <u>my</u> responsibility and <u>my</u> fault for having

left him (N)

B3   and er (0.2) we had to have a (0.1) disciplinary council to (0.4) <u>vin:</u>dicate me

and say that it wasn't my fault,' (P)

She displayed a Duchenne smile throughout the (N) part of the contrastive pair and less during the positive part (P).

4th contrastive pair

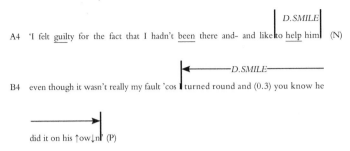

A4 'I felt guilty for the fact that I hadn't been there and- and like to help him (N)

B4 even though it wasn't really my fault 'cos I turned round and (0.3) you know he

did it on his ↑ow↓n' (P)

Here, there was relatively more Duchenne smiling in the (P) part of the contrastive pair than in the (N) part.

Analysis of non-Duchenne smiles

2nd contrastive pair

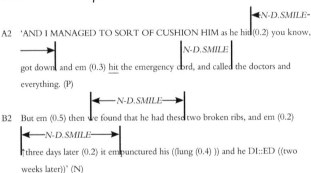

A2 'AND I MANAGED TO SORT OF CUSHION HIM as he hid (0.2) you know,

got down and em (0.3) hit the emergency cord, and called the doctors and

everything. (P)

B2 But em (0.5) then we found that he had these two broken ribs, and em (0.2)

↑three days later (0.2) it em punctured his ((lung (0.4))) and he DI::ED ((two

weeks later))' (N)

Similar to the Duchenne smile, there was a relatively greater occurrence of non-Duchenne smiles in the (N) part of the contrastive pair than in the (P) part.

3rd contrastive pair

A3   'and em (0.2) I felt like it was all (0.3) <u>my</u> responsibility and <u>my</u> fault for having
       left him (N)

B3   and er (0.2) we had to have a (0.1) disciplinary coun|cil to (0.4)|<u>vin</u>:dicate me
       and say that it wasn't my fault,' (P)

$$\left|\begin{array}{c} N\text{-}D.SM \end{array}\right|$$

Here, there was only a brief non–Duchenne smile which occurred in the positive part of the contrastive pair.

Analysis of Duchenne and non-Duchenne smiles together

1st contrastive pair

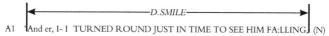

A1   'And er, I- I TURNED ROUND JUST IN TIME TO SEE HIM FA:LLING, (N)

B1   SO I- I MANAGED TO GET THERE BEFORE HE HIT THE FLOOR,' (P)

2nd contrastive pair

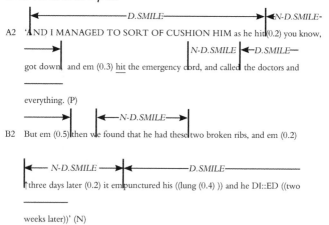

A2   'AND I MANAGED TO SORT OF CUSHION HIM as he hit (0.2) you know,

       got down| and em (0.3) <u>hit</u> the emergency cord, and called the doctors and

       everything. (P)

B2   But em (0.5) then we found that he had these two broken ribs, and em (0.2)

       three days later (0.2) it em punctured his ((lung (0.4))) and he DI::ED ((two

       weeks later))' (N)

What we found surprising at the time was the amount of smiling, whether it be Duchenne or non–Duchenne, which occurred throughout this contrastive pair. It is also interesting to note that the non-Duchenne smile often occurred just before or just after the Duchenne smile, as if the build-up to a Duchenne smile involved this form of nonverbal behaviour.

3rd contrastive pair

A3 'and em (0.5) I felt like it was all (0.3) <u>my</u> responsibility and <u>my</u> fault for having

left him (N)

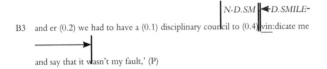

B3 and er (0.2) we had to have a (0.1) disciplinary council to (0.4) vin:dicate me

and say that it wasn't my fault,' (P)

4th contrastive pair

A4 'I felt <u>guilty</u> for the fact that I hadn't <u>been</u> there and- and like to <u>help</u> him   (N)

B4 even though it wasn't really my fault 'cos I turned round and (0.3) you know he

did it on his ↑ow↓n. (P)

Analysis of eye gaze

1st contrastive pair

A1   'And er, I- I TURNED ROUND JUST IN TIME TO SEE HIM FA::LLING (N)

B1   SO I- I MANAGED TO GET THERE BEFORE HE HIT THE FLOOR,' (P)

Eye gaze was on relatively more during the (N) part of the contrast than during the (P) part. One possible hypothesis is that it could have an ameliorating effect.

2nd contrastive pair

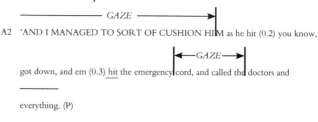

A2   'AND I MANAGED TO SORT OF CUSHION HIM as he hit (0.2) you know,

got down, and em (0.3) hit the emergency cord, and called the doctors and

everything. (P)

B2   'But em (0.5) then we found that he had these two broken ribs, and em (0.2)

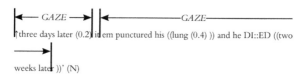

three days later (0.2) it em punctured his ((lung (0.4))) and he DI::ED ((two

weeks later))' (N)

Similar to the first contrastive pair, eye gaze was on more in the (N) part of the contrast than during the (P) part.

3rd contrastive pair

A3   'and em (0.2) I felt like it was all (0.3) my responsibility and my fault for having

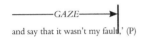

left him (N)

B3   and er (0.2) we had to have a (0.1) disciplinary council to (0.4) vin:dicate me

and say that it wasn't my fault,' (P)

Eye gaze occurred here equally often within both parts of the contrastive pair.

4th contrastive pair

A4   I felt guilty for the fact that I hadn't been there and- and like to help him, (N)

B4   even though it wasn't really my fault 'cos I turned round and (0.3) you know he

did it on his ↑ow↓n' (P)

Eye gaze occurred equally often within both parts of the contrastive pair.

Analysis of Duchenne and non-Duchenne smiles and eye gaze

1st contrastive pair

A1 'And er, I- I TURNED ROUND JUST IN TIME TO SEE HIM FA:LLING, (N)

B1 SO I- I MANAGED TO GET THERE BEFORE HE HIT THE FLOOR,' (P)

2nd contrastive pair

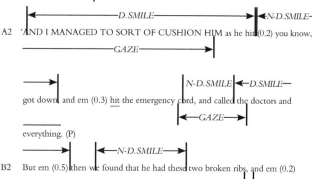

A2 'AND I MANAGED TO SORT OF CUSHION HIM as he hit (0.2) you know,

got down, and em (0.3) hit the emergency cord, and called the doctors and everything. (P)

B2 But em (0.5) then we found that he had these two broken ribs, and em (0.2)

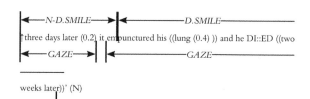

↑three days later (0.2) it em punctured his ((lung (0.4))) and he DI::ED ((two weeks later))' (N)

3rd contrastive pair

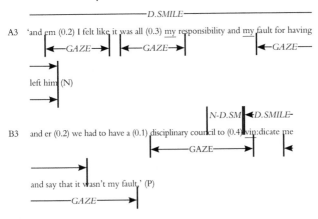

A3 'and em (0.2) I felt like it was all (0.3) my responsibility and my fault for having

left him (N)

B3 and er (0.2) we had to have a (0.1) disciplinary council to (0.4) vin:dicate me

and say that it wasn't my fault,' (P)

4th contrastive pair

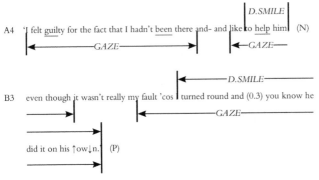

A4 'I felt guilty for the fact that I hadn't been there and- and like to help him (N)

B3 even though it wasn't really my fault 'cos I turned round and (0.3) you know he

did it on his ↑ow↓n. (P)

We found that Duchenne smiles (but not non–Duchenne smiles) tended to occur more in the negative parts of the contrastive pairs. There was also a tendency for eye gaze to occur more throughout the negative parts of the contrastive pairs. Furthermore, Duchenne smiles in particular, and eye gaze to a lesser extent, terminated at the exact juncture between the negative and positive components of the contrastive pairs, thus operating to highlight the transition between the two parts of the contrast.

So what does occur during emotional disclosure?

This exploratory analysis has suggested one way of trying to determine what occurs in emotional disclosure and why it might work, in terms of its psychological and medical benefits. This was essentially an account about responsibility for an accidental death. If one heard an impartial account of the event being discussed, an event in which a patient in a hospital fell, cracked two ribs, subsequently sustained a punctured lung, and died, and also learned that this event happened not in the presence of the nurse's aide who should have been present, then one might assume that the patient was a victim of medical negligence. Blame could therefore lie with our speaker, the nurse's aide, for leaving the patient unattended whilst she went to call the nurse. However, in our analysis, using discourse analysis, we identified a number of ways in which the speaker used the talk to skilfully negotiate blame away from herself, and present herself, rather than the patient, as the *victim* of an event which did not go according to plan.

What we also tried to do was move outside the somewhat narrow and constricted boundaries of (traditional) discourse analysis, to get a broader picture of the communication. As 'natural' speech in everyday life is never disembodied from nonverbal behaviour, we thought it might be informative to include some forms of nonverbal behaviour in the analysis and examine how the verbal and nonverbal systems of communication interact in this account. Our results show that undifferentiated smiling and eye gaze did not occur randomly within the contrastive pairs that operated as the basic structuring devices in the account. Rather, these forms of nonverbal behaviour occurred primarily within the 'negative' parts of the contrasts. In other words, our subject showed more overall smiling and eye gaze whilst talking about the most negative parts within her account, with respect to her own personal agency. For example, whilst describing how the patient 'punctured his lung and he died two weeks later', and whilst describing her own internal state at that time – 'I felt like it was all my responsibility and my fault for having left him' – she smiled constantly, simultaneously showing high levels of eye gaze. How could such results be interpreted? Nonverbal behaviour might well be part of this process of self-construction as a generally good and responsible person, and to show that she could deal with these things. She, after all, had a good story to tell, in which any personal blame and responsibility for the accident was being fully negotiated away from her. With respect to smiles, at first glance it may seem surprising and somewhat contradictory that the occurrence of Duchenne and non-Duchenne smiles should be so prevalent in an account about a past negative event. However, LaFrance and Hecht (1995) have pointed out that 'smiling can attenuate judgments of possible wrongdoing' (1995: 207), a phenomenon which they termed the 'smile-leniency effect'. In an interesting study, LaFrance and Hecht (1995) investigated the social significance of human smiles and specifically this smile-leniency effect with respect to a possible case of academic misconduct, examining both what mediated the effect and whether different types of smiles (Duchenne, false, and miserable) generate different degrees of leniency. Their results showed that smiling targets were given more leniency than non-smiling targets, although, interestingly, they were not viewed as being less guilty. The type of smile did not significantly moderate the amount of leniency shown – one smile was in effect as good as any other. Of the variables evaluated for mediating the smile-leniency effect, 'such as perceiving the target as more likable, submissive, or diplomatic' (1995: 207), the one that best accounted for the effect of smiling on leniency was perceiving the target as a trustworthy person. LaFrance and Hecht (1995) stated that such a result 'makes sense given that the case involves a possible transgression. The most relevant dimension seems to be whether the target is perceived as an honest and good person, and smiling serves to increase perception of those qualities' (1995: 212). They concluded that these results have important implications 'for people attempting to manoeuvre their way out of a transgression situation: If in doubt, smile' (1995: 213). It is possible that our speaker smiled more within the most negative parts of her talk, in order to construct herself as a good and trustworthy person and thus ameliorate judgements of possible wrongdoing.

However, it is important to note that here it was the Duchenne smile which occurred primarily within the negative parts of the contrastive pairs, whereas non-Duchenne smiles occurred far less frequently and approximately equally often within negative and positive parts. LaFrance and Hecht would say that smile type is not a significant factor in terms of the smile-leniency effect. But how would Ekman interpret this finding? After all, Ekman (1989) posited that the Duchenne smile – the enjoyment smile – accompanies experienced positive emotions such as happiness, pleasure or enjoyment. Indeed, Frank and Ekman (1993) stated that 'it is the enjoyment smile that seems to manifest true felt enjoyment or happiness' (1993: 10). Would Ekman argue that when our speaker talked about this negative event she was giving genuine smiles? Does this mean that she was feeling genuine positive emotions when she was talking about such negative things? One might think that if Ekman's (1989) distinction holds true then we would expect to witness more non-Duchenne smiling whilst talking about the most negative parts of the account. However, Ekman et al. (1990) have also pointed out that 'Duchenne smiles are the signal for any positive emotions, such as ... *relief* (1990: 350, emphasis added). Ekman (1992a) stated that he 'used the term enjoyment as a gloss to cover amusement, *relief*, sensory pleasure, pride in achievement, the thrill of excitement, satisfaction and contentment' (1992a: 190). Ekman proposed that these different positive emotions could be considered to be members of the enjoyment family. 'The thrill of excitement, relief, contentment, might all be different variations on a common theme, just as annoyance, fury, resentment, and outrage are all members of the anger family' (Ekman 1992a: 190). The research participant here might well have been experiencing genuine relief whilst talking about some of the worst aspects of the event.

As well as showing more Duchenne smiles whilst talking about the most negative parts of the trauma, our speaker also sometimes showed more eye gaze. Argyle and Cook (1976) have pointed out that 'a number of studies have found that people who look more are seen as more truthful or credible' (1976: 91). For example, filmed performers have been judged to be more effective or have produced more attitude change or information gain when they looked more (Cobin and McIntyre 1961). Argyle and Cook (1976) have argued that, in general, 'the research supports the proposition that people who look more (and with longer glances) create a more favourable impression and are liked more' (1976: 91; see also Exline and Winters 1965; Mehrabian and Friar 1969). Thus, our speaker could have been using increased eye gaze as part of her self-construction process, in which she constructs herself as a credible person. In Graham and Argyle's (1975) terms, eye gaze could have been used to strengthen her self-construction. However, although Rutter and Stephenson (1979) did not question the relationship between gaze and affiliation, they argued that the primary function of eye gaze is to monitor information from others, rather than to communicate affect. Thus, the increased levels of eye gaze during the recounting of the most negative parts of the disclosure could well be attributable to this desire to see how these were being received. Emotional disclosure in the presence of another person is, after all, an interactive process, whether it be your best friend, a therapist or an experimenter. We have to understand both eye gaze and smiling as part of that process.

Our participant here gave a detailed account of an incident where many might well blame her for what occurred – the death of a patient in her care. In her telling of the story, however, she was not to blame, her constructed account assigned responsibility, using a variety of means as we have seen, to the patient himself. She did not necessarily get everything off her chest, what she did instead was to get a particular account off her chest. Duchenne smiles, presumably of relief, were present when she recounted some of the worst bits of the story, and during those periods she watched the researcher carefully to see how the story was going down. This, I think, possibly tells us something about the psychological mechanisms underpinning emotional disclosure.

So what does happen in emotional disclosure? Pennebaker puts it like this: 'The net effect of constructing a good narrative is that our recollection of emotional events is efficient – we have a relatively short, compact story – and undoubtedly biased' (Pennebaker 2000: 13). He goes on to say

> Ironically, then, good narratives can be beneficial in making
> our complex experiences simpler and more understandable

> but, at the same time, they distort our recollection of them.
> Translating distress into language ultimately allows us to forget
> or, perhaps a better phrase, move beyond the experience.
>
> (Pennebaker 2000: 13)

But this set of claims does beg a lot of questions. What constitutes 'a good narrative'? What degree of bias can we tolerate? How is the degree of conflict in our memory related to how we construct our account and our ability to 'move beyond the experience'? What our case study (and other analyses, see Lee and Beattie 2000) demonstrated is that issues to do with *why* things occurred are every bit as important as to *what* things occurred. Any *coherent* narrative needs to contain this element, and especially when it is encoded into a 'short, compact story' form. However, it is neither efficient, nor accurate, to attempt to describe the process in terms of a word count of certain linguistic categories (as in the LIWC). That, quite simply, is not how language works. Our nurse's aide built her story around a patient who wilfully did what he liked, in contrast to herself. This was not a case of medical negligence, but a case of two contrasting individuals, with responsibility for the accident and for the death firmly residing within the patient himself. The nonverbal behaviour of the speaker helped in this construction of her as the decent, caring aide who did everything she could in the circumstances. But there may be other clues in that laughter and those Duchenne smiles that we, as psychologists, have not fully (or even partially) understood, as she described the worst bits of the unfolding event. Her eye gaze at these points in the disclosure narrative was presumably functioning to see how her account was being received (which was well) and her Duchenne smiles might well have been an expression of relief that she had arrived at an account that worked socially and in terms of its attributional responsibilities. She was not to blame for what occurred – that was paramount in her telling.

But perhaps the most important lesson of all from this case study is that it suggests that this process of emotional disclosure is not a cognitive or emotional process, as Pennebaker and others have so readily assumed, or at least not primarily, it is a social *interactional* process. If we construct an account of personal trauma that nobody accepts then my guess is that we do not get better, either physically or psychologically. This is, of course, an empirical issue which some in the future might well try to resolve. Critical to the production of the emotional disclosure I discussed here, is the monitoring by the speaker of the reception of the message by the experimental confederate (simply acting in a supportive and encouraging manner to facilitate the disclosure process), and the genuine smiles of relief on the speaker's part as these critical parts of the message were received and accepted.

Similarly, Tracey Emin's story about that day in the sea in Margate, sexually abused as an eleven-year-old, is a story primarily about responsibility. In some senses, it has to be. That's what is involved in the telling. Tell me what happened; implicitly, tell me *why*, that's always in there somehow. But in Tracey Emin's case, it seems to be a desperate *search* for responsibility, where in some tellings (in different contexts) she was, somehow, the instigator of the sexual act, with clear responsibility for the act happening, but this was not the case in her memoir. In her memoir, an earlier incident with some boys involving cruel teasing is critical, that was why she felt so vulnerable and talked to the man in the first place. Her feeling of vulnerability is what *he* exploited. In interviews elsewhere, however, she takes responsibility for the whole thing in a way that would shock most people. After all these years there is still uncertainty, inconsistency, danger (and not just with this event in her life). Understanding 'why' gives you some control. So how would this fit with the Pennebaker method, where she would be asked to say the story over and over again (just three times, please) until she can 'forget' and 'move beyond the experience'. Or is she the exception that proves the rule? A conflicted memory that resists ease of encoding, and maybe that's why she needs the used condoms, and the vodka bottles and the dirty knickers to signal that the unconscious does not allow assimilation into the conscious stream of language quite that easily. And that sometimes we need bad narratives as well as good ones to survive personally, emotionally and psychologically.

Chapter summary

- If you do not talk about any traumatic experiences over a period of time, you may suffer from both mental and physical health problems.
- Inhibiting traumatic experiences is stressful.
- Individuals classified as repressors, inhibitors, or suppressors 'demonstrate higher cancer rates, elevated blood pressure levels, and more physical disease in general than do more expressive individuals'.
- Disinhibiting or disclosing thoughts and feelings relating to past or present traumatic experiences seems to improve health outcomes.
- Jamie Pennebaker has presented considerable clinical evidence to suggest that individuals who recounted the facts surrounding a traumatic event in combination with their emotional feelings concerning the trauma evidenced great health benefits.
- Pennebaker has also stated that 'Most of the research on disclosure has been devoted to demonstrating its effectiveness rather than on identifying the underlying mechanisms'.
- Even today, the question remains: Why is disclosure effective in bringing about such health-related changes?
- Pennebaker has used an analysis of individual words in these accounts to answer this question.
- This may well not be the whole story.
- A case study of emotional disclosure was analysed using conversational analysis with detailed transcription of eye gaze and smiles and how they connected to the speech.
- An account of why the event occurred and the negotiation of individual responsibility for the actions was paramount.
- This was part of the 'effort after meaning'.
- Nonverbal behaviours, like eye gaze and smiling, were central to the construction and delivery of a suitable account.

- Our participant monitored carefully how her account was being received as she recounted the worst bits and displayed genuine Duchenne smiles (of relief) during these phases.
- How one's account of any traumatic incident is regarded by others could be a critical issue for psychological recovery.
- This might well suggest that emotional disclosure is an *interactional* as well as a cognitive or emotional phenomenon.

Appendix

Transcription conventions, taken from Potter (1996: 233–234), adapted from Jefferson (1985)

1   C: Was that the time that you left? =
2   W: = He left the:n that was – [nearl] y two years ago.
3   C: [°Yeh°]
4   W: He <u>walked out</u> then. Just (.) literally walked out.
5   (0.8)
6   C: ↑Oka↓y. So, (0.5) for me list↓enin:g, (.) you've
7   got (0.5) rich an:d, (.) complicated lives,
8   I nee:d to get some his [tory to put –]
9   W: [Yyeh. mmm, =]
10   [Mmm. (.) Ye:h (.) Oh ye:h.]
11   H: [= Yeh. (.) that's (.) exactly wha]t ih °um°</list>

- Underlining (<u>walked out</u>) indicates words or parts of words which are stressed by the speaker.
- Colons mark the prolongation of the sound immediately before (the:n); more colons would show a longer prolongation (Ah:::).
- Arrows precede marked rises and falls in intonation (↑Oka↓y).
- The question mark in line 1 marks a questioning intonation (there is no necessary correspondence with utterances that participants treat as questions).

- The full stop (for example, in line 2) marks a completing intonation (not necessarily a grammatical full stop).
- The comma in line 6 marks a continuing intonation (not necessarily a grammatical comma).
- A dash (for example, Thanks– Tha:nksgiving) marks a noticeable and abrupt termination of a word or sound.
- The brackets across lines 2 and 3, 8 and 9, 10 and 11 mark the onset and completion of overlapping talk.
- Where one turn runs into another with no interval this is marked by an equals symbol (lines 1 and 2, 9 and 11).
- Numbers in brackets (0.5) are the times of pauses in tenths of a second; where there is just a full stop in a bracket (.) this is a pause which is audible but too short to measure.
- Talk that is quieter than the surrounding talk is enclosed by degree symbols: °yeh°.
- Talk that is louder than the surrounding talk is capitalised (WHERE).
- Clarificatory comment is placed in double parentheses: ((laughs)). (stands up)).

7

CONFLICTED ROLES

New Year's Eve was always special, ever since David was a boy, ever since his father was alive. His father, dark like Clark Gable his mother said, knocking on the neighbours' doors in that little grey street on the stroke of midnight, carrying a wee bit of coal, with his wee son beside him. A drink in every house for the first footer; people who had nothing in those little damp, mill houses of North Belfast, sharing what little they had.

However, that seemed a long time ago.

He picked up the little bit of silver foil from the Formica table in the back room and opened it up, checking again. Maybe they dissolve if they get too hot. He counted the little pink tabs, laying them out in a neat line with regular gaps between them. He knew there would be a row if he lost one, maybe worse than a row. They had trusted his friend Rob with their money and he'd scored, round the back of the City Hall, after standing there for hours with the pelting rain full in our face. This was David's first time with him and it showed. He was very nervous. Rob was an old hand at this; he was always doing deals of one sort or another. He had a lot of front.

He insisted that David go with him that night into town, 'for the company' was how he put it. There was always a lot left unsaid, and an implicit threat in these requests. Rob said that he had to pop into town to see an old friend, 'I want you to come along ... *just for the company*'. It was a Sunday night, the night when everything was closed in Belfast, including the pubs, when the swings in the parks were still chained on a Sunday lest children enjoy themselves too much on the Lord's Day. David had been to church twice that day, he was a junior churchwarden at the time.

Rob was very good at getting people to do what he wanted by being very vague about what it was that you were actually going to do. You agreed with the smaller things he asked you to do, until eventually you could see the whole picture opening up in front of you, before it dawned on you, and then it was too late, far too late. There was no backing out. He didn't explain in advance what they were going to do that night in the town centre. The 'friend' was a business acquaintance, the transaction was over in seconds. David stood as far away as he could, without drawing attention to himself, chewing on the cord of his duffle coat, and with a little bit of heavy encouragement, he slipped them into the left pocket of his duffle coat, his lucky pocket, the one without a hole. That was Rob's idea, of course. He said that David looked more innocent than him. He couldn't argue with him. 'Stick them in your pocket,' Rob said. David didn't even nod back; he just did it. It was as direct as that. This, I suppose, was an order of sorts.

There was a lot of security on the streets in Belfast at that time. The Troubles had sealed off the town centre, bombs more or less every night. The buses might be off the road. They might have to take their chance and walk home. They might get pulled. The police or the army would be looking for weapons, of course, not little bits of silver foil. David was rehearsing what he might say. 'Love hearts', that's all that he could think of. Crushed love hearts. His heart was pumping furiously. Rob joked away, but then again he was clean. David was the one with the drugs on him. 'I hope you've got your story right,' Rob said. 'You're an Academy boy, you'll be alright. You look plausible.' That was also one of David's mother's words, 'plausible'. 'You'd better get our story right,' and Rob laughed at David's discomfort.

David's 'reward' was this – a free tab, fatter than the rest for going with him and for 'looking after' the drugs in his bedroom. Rob said that his mother searched his and that David had to hide them for him in below the school books on Latin and physics, the silver foil peeking out to remind him where they were. It would be his first time. David had told him that he didn't want to drop any acid. Rob replied that he had no choice. 'We're all in this together,' he said.

So here he was, examining them carefully on the table in the back room. He could hear his mother cleaning upstairs, the brush digging in frustration at the corner of my bedroom. He put the silver foil in his pocket and hurried up. It was no place for prying eyes. School books everywhere, posters on every wall, pictures torn out of magazines drooping down from the ceiling, and the drawers full of different things that he was 'looking after' for Rob, with little choice on his part. You couldn't open the drawers they were so full.

'Look at this mess,' his mother would say. 'You make this house look like a right hole.'

'It's a hole anyway', he said, 'without my help.'

There had been talk about an IRA ceasefire that Christmas. The UDA said they would stop killing if the IRA did, just like kids, but in the end, 'nobody bothered their arse', his mother said. So the bombs continued and somebody was found with his throat cut up some entry. According to his mother, his head was hanging on by a single thread. But he wasn't going to let this ruin his mood. 'How can your head hang by a thread? There are no threads in your head,' and he remembers laughing at his own cleverness, the cleverness of an Academy boy.

The night before, however, was bad. His mother left her bedroom door open, which she always did when she sensed trouble. 'That blast was very close, I'd say Smithfield. What do you think?'

'I'm trying to sleep,' he shouted back. 'That's what I think. It's bad enough living here without a running commentary every bloody night.'

'I'm only trying to make conversation,' she said. 'You never talk to me anymore; it wasn't like this when your father was alive.' Then the sobbing started. He lay there thinking about his dad, until he too felt like crying, but privately, then another blast snapped him out of it. Probably Smithfield, he thought.

Moke called about seven the next night. His mother answered the door, hovering around, pretending to tidy. 'You two off out tonight to bring in the New Year? I wish I was going.'

'Just a few beers,' said Moke, and David pushed past her onto the street, touching his lucky pocket, mumbling a goodbye.

'Rob's aunt is out for the New Year,' said Moke. 'We've got the house to ourselves. What did you get? Purple Haze?'

'They're more pink than purple,' said David, 'but genuine.'

'They'd better be,' said Moke threateningly.

'Rob actually scored them,' he replied. 'He made the call. I'm just looking after them for him.'

He knew that would shut him up.

The gang were all there already; Jack Bruce from Cream was singing 'Born under a Bad Sign.' One lad had brought five cans of Harp lager with him, having obviously drunk one already on the way. 'No beer,' said Rob. 'I've heard it stops it working.' David handed the silver foil to him. He knew that Rob would be the master of ceremonies. He knew that Rob would be in charge; Rob liked the theatre of it all.

Rob uncurled the silver foil and handed them out slowly, and with some little flourishes of the hands. 'Can I wash mine down with Harp?' said the boy with the lager.

'Just swallow it,' said Rob, 'without the lager. Use your own spit.' 'Here's yours,' he said to David. 'Take it.' David did as he was told.

And there they all sat for the next hour, in another small dark, damp room, the only sort of room that they'd ever known, but this one lit with a candle, all cross-legged, all waiting silently for something to happen.

It was John who first noticed the flickering after-image when somebody moved. 'Jesus,' he said, laughing hysterically, as much in relief as anything else. Then, by a process of magic contagion, the euphoria worked through the little group, all hunched up in their duffle coats and pants with heavy wet flared bottoms. Time slowed, the flame of the candle danced with the music, finding the beat within minutes, and lit the grinning faces, pulsating red then green.

Belfast was finally at peace. Rob started swaying gently with a slight sardonic grin on his face, and they all watched him attentively.

'What did I tell you?' he said. 'I said that I would get the good gear. We could all move to London and become big dealers, except for your man over there. He's going to go off to university and leave us all behind. Free trips all round for the rest of us.' And they all laughed hysterically at this. David felt mellow, melting into the cushions, now soft and luxuriant. The room had been transformed. They were in a cave, with a flickering light, messages from the changing shadows appeared on the walls. David sat trying to interpret them out loud. He thought that some of them were in Latin. He read the Latin inscriptions out slowly to the group. 'Look at your man trying to show off,' said Rob. 'Fucking Academy boy.'

The night stretched out into this long, luxuriant night of pleasure. All the cushions, cheap and stained, were now made of soft yielding velvet. David looked round at his friends, some giggling, and some tracking their hands in space, some following the colours up and down the walls. But then suddenly, and without any warning at all, the door swung open. A tall figure in a long coat stood there aghast. Everybody giggled at the joke, somebody was dressing up, nobody stirred, but David's heart was racing with the unexpected nature of this sudden spectacle. Then the lights went on and somebody shouted that it really was his aunt back early. All David remembers was trying to get onto his feet and the pushing and shoving as the rest tried to get up as well. They stumbled down the stairs and onto the street. She was shouting after them. David half-ran one way, his heart pumping louder than he had ever heard it, the others disappeared into the dark. The rain stopped, and he paused to get his breath, the puddles were now emerald green. He had never seen anything so beautiful; he can remember them to this day. He stamped in one and the splashes, like radiant sparks caught by the streetlights, hung in the air. He stood there in the empty street, jumping into puddles, staring at magical patterns of light, giggling like a child.

A sapphire Black Taxi glided up beside him. Somebody was obviously lost. Maybe they would like to trip out, that was his thought. He wanted to be kind. After all, he had still one tab left to share.

He trod carefully over the ground rolling now like the deck of a ship. There were two other men in the taxi with red balloon faces that might pop. He leaned towards them, unsteady on his feet, trying to hear what they wanted, trying not to giggle. One man reached out and grabbed him forcefully by the collar.

'Thanks mate,' he said. 'I thought I might fall.'

'What's going on?' the man said. He looked at David carefully. 'Your man's taken something,' he said to the others. 'There's terrorists roaming the streets of Belfast, and this little fucker decides to wander through this magic wonderland of North Belfast.' They were all laughing. David was still giggling. Helpless. They told him that it would be too dangerous for him to walk home, they knew from his address that he was on their side ('Where do you live again? Above or below the library?' The library in Ligoniel was the invisible territorial marker of religion and community that guaranteed his safety). That was the beauty of the Troubles – when you have enemies, you automatically, it seems, have friends or allies that are prepared to look after you.

Nobody said a word on the drive but David watched every street light changing colour and glowing towards the heavens like searchlights. And there was Rob sitting on his front step waiting for him. They knew Rob, of course. That didn't surprise David. That added to Rob's charisma and power. Rob tried to hide his own true state the best he could. He didn't want them to know that he was tripping as well. But they laughed at the helplessness of the two boys and drove off in this old, spluttering diesel taxi. They both sat there on the step until the morning until the acid wore off.

Rob had arrived a few months earlier from somewhere on the Shankill and taken over their little gang. David met him with two of his friends at a pop concert at Dunmore greyhound stadium. He remembers how trendy he looked compared to the rest of them. There was just something about him. He and his friend Bill were with two girls that they didn't know well. Rob didn't know them, but maybe vaguely recognised them, but perhaps jealous that they were with someone. So after a few minutes' innocuous chat, he pulled a hatchet out of his denim jacket and swiped it at Bill's head. Bill ducked and then stumbled and fell off this balcony. He just lay there moaning. There had been no argument, or fight, it was all completely unprovoked. The two girls ran off shrieking. Rob turned to David and said 'you're next.' He just stood there, frozen with fear. Rob stared at him for a few seconds that seemed to go on forever, his facial expression didn't change, and then he burst out laughing. He and his friends just turned and walked off; David's right leg was trembling of its own volition for several minutes as he just stood there watching them getting smaller and smaller, wondering what had just happened. He ran down to help his friend up. That was the first time he met Rob. The next night he turned up at his house (he had never given him my address) and he spent an hour chatting to his mother whilst he was out running. He has to this day no idea how he got his address. 'What a lovely lad,' his mother said, when he got back, the sweat dripping off him. 'He's got a lot to say for himself, unlike you. You just stand there sweating and not saying anything.'

Rob was unpredictable. One night at the corner, he turned on one of his old, long-term friends and in some 'play fighting' dragged him around the street for about twenty minutes. The lad was in a head lock and dragged backwards along the grimy street. One of his shoes came off. It just went on for so long that it made the whole thing really humiliating to even watch. But it was his unpredictability and his knowledge that facilitated his ascent in this little street gang. At that time in Belfast unpredictability could be a serious advantage. Life was becoming much more violent on the streets, and if people were wary of you this gave you some advantage. You never knew what they might do. He had a dangerous authority about him. You didn't challenge his statements or plans. And he knew how to get things; he could be a great facilitator. He told David that he wanted him to go shopping with him. He could tell that he needed some new gear. So they started in Burtons in Royal Avenue and made their way around a number of shops. Shops where David would look longingly through the windows. Rob shoplifted a pair of wrangler jeans and a leather jacket. To celebrate they went to Wimpey's for lunch. David told that him that he had no money; he had already spent my pocket money. Rob said that you don't need money. They had a double cheeseburger each and two cokes right in the middle of the restaurant. When they finished Rob asked for the bill, and then told David to go with him to the toilet. Rob had stolen a waitress' pad of bills and he simply wrote a bill out for two coffees. 'You hand it over at the checkout,' Rob said. It was a test of sorts. Of course, David did what he was told. Rob just stood glowering at the lady behind the checkout, and threw a few coins onto her little table. She said that she had seen them eating. Rob denied it. 'I wouldn't eat the crap in here, if you paid me,' he replied. Incredibly, she let us go without paying for the meal. Wimpey's became their regular Saturday treat.

To bring the two sides together in the Troubles, the local church had decided to organise a disco for the local Protestants and Catholics. David could sense that this was going to be trouble, especially because two of the local senior churchwardens were going to be doormen. They were both very nice, his mother always said, young Christian men, well out of their depth for this. Rob seemed to feel that he had something to prove to them all, and within ten minutes of the disco starting, he chose some random Catholic boy to knock out with one punch. He just walked up to him and punched him. The force made him fall on top of the lad. One of the group said that the lad wouldn't have gone down in the first place, if Rob hadn't fallen on him. The churchwardens ran around switching on all the lights and the disco finished very early. But David's most vivid memory of that awful night was some Catholic lad that he trapped down by the bottom gate of St Mark's church. Rob made them crowd around in a little tight semi-circle. The lad was terrified. Rob punched him first. His lip started to bleed. He had gone white as a sheet. Rob held his arms down by his side; he told them that they all had to hit him. 'We're all in it then together,' he said. But there was a momentary hesitation in the group. Not because the rest of the gang were unused to fighting, far from it, it was just the situation they didn't like, the unfairness, that look of helplessness, maybe the instantaneous thought of where this might lead in that one moment. None of them could do this *automatically* at that point. To this day, David can remember the facial expression of his friend Ray, slightly puzzled, slightly questioning, it didn't have the harsh meanness of Rob, even though Ray himself was a great fighter. This expression echoed around the group, challenging Rob's authority.

'Nah,' said Ray. 'Nah. Let's just give him one for good luck and then let him go. It's not worth it.'

Rob was angry. He paused. His second punch was vengeful in its ferocity. The lad's nose spurted blood. Rob was muttering under his breath as he walked off. 'Not worth the trouble anyway.' He wasn't used to not being listened to.

Nobody seemed to want to go home. But David could sense that there was going to be serious trouble so he eventually did. 'Home early tonight,' his mother said. 'How was the disco?'

David heard the next morning that one of their lads from the corner had got stabbed later that night in the knee of all places, and had to hijack a bus to take him to hospital with the knife still stuck in his knee. Everyone remembers that. It was a joke for years about the corner. He went on to join a Protestant paramilitary organisation, the Ulster Volunteer Force, and make bombs that killed innocent Catholics. He made a bomb that was planted at a funeral. He got eight life sentences for his part in six murders and two attempted murders and a further twenty years for a series of thirteen bombings and possession of explosives, guns and ammunition.

If the truth be told, *I* saw all of this unfold and became fascinated by orders and directives and human suffering, and, of course, obedience to authority, but mindful of the fact that authority takes many forms and is realised and constructed in particular ways in everyday social life. Rob was not after all a conventional authority figure, but within *our* social group because, of course, I was there, he had considerable authority. But why do we go along with what people tell us to do, even when we know that it is wrong? And under what conditions do we dissent? Why didn't they, why didn't we, all lay into that poor terrified lad that night by the gates of St Mark's? How did David escape? How did I?

Stanley Milgram and conflicted roles in the obedience experiments

The classic research on obedience in psychology was carried out by Stanley Milgram, that great showman of psychology. His research on obedience was carried out at Yale in the early 1960s, and this is one of the best known, and indeed infamous, experiments in psychology. He found that when presented with a learning task where a 'teacher' (the actual participant in the research) had to give electric shocks to a 'learner' (the confederate of the experimenter) every time the learner made a mistake, that 65 per cent of the participants would continue following the teacher's directives ('each time he gives a wrong answer, you move up one switch on the shock generator'; 'if the learner doesn't answer in a reasonable time, about 5 seconds, consider it wrong'; 'please continue'; 'please go on'; 'you have no choice, you *must* go on'). They would continue to do this up to the maximum voltage on the electric shock machine beyond the 'Danger: Severe Shock' zone and into the very ominous sounding 'XXX' zone (see Milgram 1963). Milgram's research would seem to suggest that we all have a propensity to simply follow orders when there is a (conventional) authority figure prepared to accept responsibility for the act itself.

In the first variation of the study the 'learner' was in a separate room out of sight of the 'teacher'. In a second variation, a 'voice-feedback' condition, Milgram had the learner play pre-recorded complaints which got more and more desperate as the voltage increased. Here, 62.5 per cent of the participants continued to the maximum 450-volt maximum. When the learner was in the same room as the teacher, acting out the pain and voicing his complaints, 40 per cent continued to the maximum voltage. In the final variation of the study, the teacher had to use physical force, pushing the learner's hand onto the electric plate. In this condition, 30 per cent of participants continued to the very end. Milgram's conclusion was that ordinary people without any apparent sadistic or psychopathic tendencies could continue to give intense enough shocks to kill a stranger, merely as a function of being directed to do so by an authority figure, who took responsibility for the act.

Milgram describes in detail the behaviour of some of his obedient participants. 'Bruno Batta' was a 37-year-old welder, who progressed all the way to the end. Milgram writes:

> At the 330-volt level, the learner refuses not only to touch the shock plate, but also to provide any answers. Annoyed, Batta

turns to him and chastises him: 'You better answer and get it over with. We can't stay here all night.' The scene is brutal and depressing: his hard, impassive face showing total indifference as he subdues the screaming learner and gives him shocks. He seems to derive no pleasure from the act itself, only quiet satisfaction at doing his job properly. When he administers 450 volts, he turns to the experimenter and asks: 'Where do we go from here, Professor?' His tone is deferential and expresses his willingness to be a cooperative subject, in contrast to the learner's obstinacy.

(See Blass 2004: 96)

Milgram was apparently in doubt from the start about the potential significance of his research. In a letter to Henry Riecken, head of Social Science at the National Science Foundation, he wrote:

The results are terrifying and depressing. They suggest that human nature – or more specifically, the kind of character produced in American society – cannot be counted on to insulate its citizens from brutality and inhumane treatment at the direction of malevolent authority. In a naïve moment some time ago, I once wondered whether in all of the United states a vicious government could find enough moral imbeciles to meet the personal requirements of a national system of death camps, of the sort that were maintained in Germany. I am now beginning to think that the full complement could be recruited in New Haven. A substantial proportion of people do what they are told to do, irrespective of the content of the act, and without pangs of conscience, so long as they perceive that the command comes from a legitimate authority.

(From Blass 2009: 100)

The analogy with death camps and the Nazis had been there from the start of his research. He wrote:

[My] laboratory paradigm .... gave scientific expression to a more general concern about authority, a concern forced upon members of my generation, in particular upon Jews such as myself, by the atrocities of World War II ... The impact of the Holocaust on my own psyche energized my interest in obedience and shaped the particular form in which it was examined.

(From Blass 2004: 62)

The specific idea for his research followed from Solomon Asch's conformity experiments, which had demonstrated that in a series of perceptual judgement tasks (often about the length of particular lines) naive participants would make erroneous judgement decisions in the face of a bogus majority decision. Milgram wrote:

I was trying to think of a way to make Asch's conformity experiment more humanly significant. I was dissatisfied that the test of conformity was judgments about *lines*. I wondered whether groups could pressure a person into performing an act whose human import was more readily apparent, perhaps behaving aggressively toward another person, say by administering increasingly severe shocks to him. But to study the group effect ... you'd have to know how the subject performed without any group pressure. At that instant, my thought shifted, zeroing in on this experimental control. Just how far *would* a person go under the experimenter's orders? It was an incandescent moment ...

(Reprinted in Blass 2009: 62)

Thomas Blass suggests that this 'incandescent moment' was, in fact, occasioned by the abduction of Adolf Eichmann from his home in Buenos Aires on 11 May 1960 to stand trial in Israel for the murder of six million Jews (the obedience experiments apparently were not mentioned in a letter to his research mentor Gordon Allport in March 1960 in which he outlined his research plans, but were mentioned to Asch in June of that year). Blass also noted dryly that Eichmann's execution occurred shortly before midnight on 31 May 1962, four days after Milgram concluded his obedience study. Milgram may well have devised this new paradigm to mirror this significant world event:

in this alignment the 'experimenter' would play the role of the bureaucratic Eichmann, following orders, and then giving orders for others to follow. Milgram's language is hardly neutral at times when it comes to the descriptions of his own participants. He wanted to study the 'hard, impassive faces' of those 'moral imbeciles' who could follow the orders to the end 'without pangs of conscience' in response to commands that came from a 'legitimate authority'. And it looked like the concept of legitimate authority did not have to be that elegantly constructed. The experimenter in a grey lab coat rather than white (so that participants would not be confused that this was in any way a medical experiment), deadpan directives ('please continue'), even when the experiment was staged in a location in downtown Bridgeport, far removed from the ivory towers of Yale (although here it should be noted that full obedience dropped from 65 per cent to 47.5 per cent). Milgram explained:

> It is possible that if commands of a potentially harmful or a destructive sort are to be perceived as legitimate they must occur within some sort of institutional order. But it is clear from the study that it need not be a particularly reputable or distinguished institution. Our subjects may consider one laboratory to be as competent as another, so long as it is a scientific laboratory.
>
> (Reprinted in Blass 2009: 109)

But in many ways this is an odd conclusion to draw from a set of observations that if a man that you have never met before standing there in a grey lab coat, asks you to apply a series of graded shocks to another stranger (a pudgy 47-year-old Irish American, 'mild mannered and submissive, not at all academic', 'perfect as a victim', according to Milgram) to a level that is indicated on the machine as above the danger level, you will do so because of 'instructional order'. What sort of institutional order is this? Do institutional orders not consist of pre-existing hierarchies in which individuals work and where they know and appreciate the explicit and implicit rules that govern their operation? These participants were strangers, temporary visitors, trapped by the moment, presumably bound only by a temporary contract (they had after all applied to the ad and signed up to the experiment), presumably wanting to know how to get out of this bizarre situation as quickly as possible. Perhaps, the most obvious way that opened up before them was to continue doing what was asked. Arguments, after all, often do take some time.

Why do I describe the situation as bizarre? First, because the situation is so improbable. Why would you be giving electric shocks to a mild mannered 47-year-old with a heart condition in the first place? Second, because this strange scientist experimenter (Mr Williams) in the grey lab coat (what sorts of scientists wear grey lab coats?) shows no emotional response to the tape recorded pitiful screams and insistent demands to be let out by the 'learner'. Third, the 'scientist' says the same four prompts over and over again with no emotion. 'Please continue'; 'please go on'; 'you have no choice'; 'you *must* go on.' What kind of responsible scientist is that? Fourth, the scientist, Mr Williams, clearly breaks his own rules. Williams after all has explained to the 'learner' that although the shocks might be painful, they are not dangerous. And yet, in a matter of minutes he is directing the 'teacher' to apply shocks to the 'learner' that the machine indicates are in the 'danger: severe, shock zone.' These two propositions are clearly mutually contradictory. The shocks are either dangerous or they are not. So either the scientist was lying to the 'learner', or he was lying to the 'teacher' or he was lying to both. So what kind of institutional authority is this? There are only minutes to establish this authority as the participant in this research is introduced to the experimental set-up and to the 'learner'. Artefacts may well play some role in establishing some form of institutional context and institutional order, the name of the setting (Yale University; 'Research Associates of Bridgeport'), the scientific apparatus and (grey) lab coat, but equally important is the communication and behaviour of the scientists. This scientist showed no real human response to the apparent suffering of the 'learner', none at all in fact, his responses never wavered and showed no contextual shaping, he appeared to contradict himself in his instructions to the learner and in his behaviour. So how does this combination working together establish the kind of institutional authority that would lead to blind obedience?

Milgram speculates on why there was not a greater difference when the experiment was carried out at Yale and in downtown Bridgeport. He says that

> it is clear from the study that it need not be a particularly reputable or distinguished institution … It is possible that the category of institution, judged according to its professed function, rather than its qualitative position within that category, wins our compliance … our subjects may consider one laboratory to be as competent as another, so long as it *is* a scientific laboratory.
>
> (Blass 2009: 109)

This is an odd argument. It would suggest that if you simply assert that you are a scientist, participants will follow your orders. This, in my view, is implausible in the extreme. This was all about stagecraft, there was no memory experiment, there was no real participant, there was no shock machine, but there were conflicting cues, and there was a real human participant who had entered into an agreement to be part of this and was exposed to these conflicting cues.

Other psychologists in the past have made a similar point. Martin Orne, from the University of Pennsylvania, has spent a significant part of his career investigating the 'demand characteristics' of human participants, when participants work out what is required in an experiment and play along with it. They do after all usually arrive at the experiment wanting to cooperate, to be helpful. They want to be a good participant. The scientist in the grey coat is telling them how to be a good participant. They go along with the charade because they don't want to ruin the experiment. According to Blass, Milgram's response was 'Orne's suggestion that the subjects only feigned sweating, trembling, and stuttering to please the experimenter is pathetically detached from reality, equivalent to the statement that haemophiliacs bleed to keep their physicians busy' (see Blass 2009: 120).

But, of course, it does not have to be this black and white, either a willing protagonist in lab-based arbitrary torture or part of a bit of play acting. What happens if the participants *sensed* that things were not quite right in this situation? What happens if they picked up on the unwavering flat emotional tones of the scientist, immutable in emotional valence, despite the screams and cries of the 'learner'? What happens if the pre-recorded cries did not sound quite right in their timings in that context? After all we can be very sensitive to the naturalness and appropriateness of 'conversational' latencies, like the exact timing of screams and cries in response to a shock. What happens if they sensed that the experiment did not make much actual sense? What kind of learning experiment kills the learner? (What is the other person going to learn if he's dead?) What happens if they sensed that the transformation of the scientist from a rational and just figure to something clearly unjust and irrational did not really add up? But at the same time, they have listened to the carefully worded introduction to the experiment. They have understood the roles ascribed to them and the apparent ideological rationale behind why they are there (science and the pursuit of knowledge). They have understood the instructions and rationally followed these instructions for the low voltages at least. And rationally, they have agreed to enter into this temporary contract, which makes the breaking of it a little embarrassing. Here we may see another aspect of the inner conflict of the participants. Not just, or not necessarily, a conflict between individual moral conscience and institutional order but a conflict between System 1 and System 2 of the participants, between the quick, intuitive system that was telling them that things were not quite right here, and the slower rationale system that had listened carefully to what the scientist had explained to them, and decided that they had a role to play in this research. How would the 'sweating, trembling, and stuttering' of some participants be affected by this? Milgram does not consider this option. But it is clear that a significant number of participants reported some uncertainty about what actually was going on (William Mendel, for example, said that he had doubted whether the 'thing was real or not … But it was so well done … I bought the whole thing').

In other words, I am suggesting that there are several factors that are potentially operating in this Milgram situation, and that neither Milgram nor those that followed on reflecting on this paradigm (e.g. Zimbardo 2007) have tested these two possible hypotheses against each other to determine their relative effects on compliance rates and nonverbal behaviour.

Milgram submitted the first article on the obedience experiments on 27 December 1961 to the *Journal of Abnormal and Social Psychology*. It was rejected. Edward E. Jones, editor of the *Journal of Personality* rejected it for a second time in 1962 for not having any theory to explain his findings. According to Thomas Blass, Jones dismissed it as 'a kind of triumph of social engineering'. It was eventually published in 1963 after an invitation to resubmit to the first of these two journals.

The *New York Times* published an article on the research soon after its publication, and news of this research quickly spread around the world. The rest is history, as they say. The ethics of the research troubled many, but not apparently Milgram himself. He wrote

> I do not think I exaggerate when I say that, for most subjects, the experiment was a positive and enriching experience. It provided them with an occasion for self-insight, and gave them a first-hand and personalized knowledge of the social forces that control human conduct.
>
> (Blass 2009: 115)

According to Blass (2004: 115), Milgram wrote that 'relatively few subjects experienced greater tension than a nail-biting patron at a good Hitchcock thriller'. His experimental participants evidently disagreed. William Menold said that during the experiment he was 'hysterically laughing, but it was not funny laughter.... It was so bizarre. And, I mean, I completely lost it, my reasoning power.' He described himself as an 'emotional wreck' and a 'basket case'. Herbert Winer reported that he went home extremely angry at having been deceived in this way and embarrassed that he hadn't stopped earlier. Milgram is reported as being 'totally astonished' by the criticism of his work in the media and elsewhere.

Milgram had always said that in his research he wanted to study actual behaviour (actual behavioural compliance in the obedience experiments rather than merely asking them what they would do; for example, people actually posting a 'lost letter' rather than reports of what they might do), as opposed to questionnaire responses or what people might say (see Blass 2009: 143). But to defend himself against these criticisms of the ethics of his research, Milgram reported a follow-up questionnaire (attached to a report of the study itself) which suggested, he said, no long-term harm in his participants. He wrote that 43.5 per cent of his participants reported that they were 'very glad to have been in the experiment'; only 10.2 per cent reported that they were extremely upset in the experiment; 63.6 per cent reported that they were not bothered at all by the experiment, which is odd given that 60.2 per cent were distressed during the experiment itself. Blass does not appear to see the irony or the contradiction in Milgram gravitating to the 'relativism and ambiguity inherent in many other types of measures (like self-report questionnaires)' for the defence of his own obedience research.

It seems that the obedience experiments were meant to be a prelude to a larger project into obedience to authority in the German character, as he indicated in a letter to his mentor Gordon Allport on 10 October 1960 (see Blass 2009: 65). Milgram had, after all, conducted his Ph.D. research into conformity and national character (contrasting Norway and France) using Asch's bogus majority paradigm and its effects on perceptual judgements. But this work was never carried out. Perhaps it was due to the controversy and the bad publicity surrounding the new research on obedience. Perhaps it was the fact that the level of obedience in his American participants left little room for 'improvement' in a German sample, thus leaving him with no opportunity to say that there was something distinctive about German culture that allowed the Holocaust to happen in the first place.

What Milgram did do instead, some twelve years after completing the obedience experiments, was to present a theory to bind together his empirical observations, a theory which drew upon both evolutionary theory and cybernetics. He hypothesised about the evolutionary advantages of authority-dominated social groups in hostile environments, where individual members can override their individual consciences to act in a more aggressive manner for the leader. Groups cannot act in coordinated ways if everyone follows their own individual conscience and mores. The transition from an autonomous state to a systemic mode of operation requires the individual entering an 'agentic state', where responsibility for one's actions is relinquished. Milgram wrote:

> From a subjective standpoint, a person is in a state of agency
> when he defines himself in a social situation in a manner that
> renders him open to regulation by a person of higher status.
> In this condition the individual no longer views himself as
> responsible for his own actions but defines himself as an
> instrument for carrying out the wishes of others.
>
> (See Blass 2004: 216)

But as Blass and others have noted, this does not explain the
variation in level of obedience as a function of experimental
condition. After all, they are still being regulated by a person of
higher authority in each condition. But there is a much more
pressing question. Did Milgram really study hostile environments,
where survival is threatened (like on the streets of Belfast in the
1970s) and where we can see the limits of compliance and obedience?
Or did he just study individuals in odd conflicting situations that
may make some sense for a few minutes and then instinctively stop
making any sense? What are the events, and conditions and directives
that lead to one outcome rather than another? Milgram after all had
written to a government agency in 1960 seeking research funding
that 'Given that a person is confronted with a particular set of
commands .... we may ask which conditions increase his compliance,
and which make him less likely to comply'. Milgram had found that
in his obedience experiments the most effective antidote was the
support of others, signalled in his studies through active dissent. On
the streets of Belfast, I got some schooling into this. That night by
the gates of the church I saw how that might work. But it was all
done in the briefest of looks, but looks that have stayed with me.
That was what undermined Rob's power. Those fleeting nonverbal
signals which told us all that none of us, apart from Rob himself,
wanted to go through with this. The active dissent followed on
from that. It was conditional on that; it was part of a process. But we
know nothing about how these nonverbal signals work in real
environments of any significance.

It is a pity that the great showman who was Stanley Milgram
didn't consider these subtle everyday signals that make us go in one
direction rather than another. The subtle signals that tell others how

we feel. It is a pity that instead of producing a piece of stagecraft (which he then committed to an even more theatrical film) he did not try to study these processes in real situations so that we may understand human beings better and see how they really resolve their inner conflicts. It is a pity that he did not leave the laboratory. Milgram thought that he had provided some startling conclusions about the essence of human beings, about the power of situations, about the banality of evil. But the situation wasn't real, and at some level, I believe, all of his participants knew that. We are still waiting for answers in this most important of areas.

But what was really going on?

Of course, it was only a matter of time before Milgram's research was scrutinised in a way that was always going to be required. Unfortunately, the matter of time in this case was fifty years. This scrutiny was especially important, given what Muzafer Sherif speaking in 1975 had said about Milgram's work: 'Milgram's obedience experiment is the single greatest contribution to human knowledge ever made by the field of social psychology, perhaps psychology in general' (cited in Takooshian 2000: 10). A number of eminent psychologists critically evaluated Milgram's legacy, amongst them Stephen Reicher, Alexander Haslam and Arthur Miller writing in the *Journal of Social Issues* in 2014. They begin the article by saying 'we outline the rationale for re-examining Milgram's explanation of how ordinary people can become perpetrators of atrocity' (Reicher et al. 2014: 393). On the fiftieth anniversary of Milgram's first publication of his Yale studies they say that the aim of their articles was to examine

> the contemporary relevance of Milgram's studies and the way that they help advance our understanding of one of the most pressing of all social questions: when do people do the bidding of authority? In particular, when do they follow instructions to commit atrocities? Do we have the conceptual tools to answer these questions and hence to prevent future atrocities?
>
> (Reicher et al. 2014: 394)

I found this a surprising way of starting a critical article on Milgram because, of course, the point about Milgram's research is that his participants never became perpetrators of any violent act, let alone an atrocity. They were taking part in a psychological experiment where no actual harm was done to the learner in this experimental situation. So whatever Milgram's research tells us, it tells us nothing about how ordinary people can become perpetrators of atrocity. It may tell us about how participants in psychological research can engage in sanctioned 'acts' which might (potentially) disturb them in many ways because of the paradoxical and highly puzzling nature of the situation. Logic would, after all, seem to indicate that you cannot help people learn by giving them electric shocks when they have stopped responding and who are (all the indicators seem to be telling us) apparently already dead. What kind of Shelleyan science did the scientist in the grey coat practise? But this is how they frame their paper. Even when they critique 'the moral dangers' of Milgram's work as well as the 'analytic weaknesses' inherent in it, they still seem to assume that it can shed light on the instigation of actual violence where suffering is both believed and believable. With this firmly in mind, they say

> before Milgram, we could retain some comfort from the assumption that perpetrators were a breed apart. They might well appal us, but we could dismiss their acts as having minimal self-relevance. After Milgram, no such comfort was available. His results showed that we ourselves could be perpetrators. We are thereby drawn into the drama not only as an audience but also as potential participants. We cannot watch without asking what would we do in the same circumstances? Would we (as we would like to believe) refuse to comply or would we (as we fear) continue shocking?
>
> (Reicher et al. 2014: 397)

I think that this question needs to be reframed. The question is, how would we respond when confronted with a paradoxical situation? Would we play along with what an experimenter was asking us to do, no matter how odd?

Reicher and colleagues point out that in these 'obedience' experiments 'the proportion of people who were completely compliant varied from 100% in the "no-feedback" pilot … to 0% in at least three of the studies … These are not just studies of obedience. They are also studies of *dis*obedience' (2014: 398). This, of course, is a very important point. They also query Milgram's theoretical account of why individuals might behave in a certain way and critique Milgram's use of the concept of the 'agentic' state. They say that there are a number of weaknesses with this concept – it cannot account for the varying levels of compliance in the different versions of the study because Milgram presented no theoretical evidence that variations in the level of the agentic state could possibly underlie these variations in rate of compliance. They also highlight the fact that the experimental participants were most likely to stop conforming to the experimenter's requests or demands at exactly those points when the learner most forcefully voices protests to what was going on. They raise the question of why this might be the case if the experimental participants were totally 'focused on their obligations to the experimenter and ignore all else' (2014: 398). Why then would they start listening to the participants? They go on to make the very important point that if you look more closely at the prods used in this experiment they were not all direct orders, far from it. Three of them were, in fact, 'polite requests or justifications for continuing in terms of the needs of the experiment ("Please continue," "The experiment requires that you continue," "It is absolutely essential that you continue")' (2014: 399). Only the fourth constituted a clear order – '"You have no other choice, you must go on"' (Reicher et al. 2014: 399).

In re-evaluations of Milgram's actual data, the evidence seems to show that every time a direct order was used, participants failed to comply (see Burger 2009; Reicher et al. 2012). It seems clear that when experimental participants were presented with this direct order they responded fairly negatively. Milgram himself gives the example of one 'teacher' who said "If this were Russia, maybe, but not in America" (Milgram 1974: 65).

In other words, whatever Milgram's experiment does tell us, it does not tell us anything about how people follow *direct orders* when told to inflict *actual harm* on another human being. Although, of course, there is a possible confound here – by the time the direct order was issued the participants had already made up their mind that they were not going to continue, so this direct order might have seemed like an act of desperation on the part of the experimenter.

Reicher et al. do remind us that the Milgram paradigm was an experiment, like all other experiments, which almost invariably involves a short-term interaction between strangers (Beattie 1982), completely unlike the settings of real violence or atrocities which are necessarily longer-term, and fuelled, defined and characterised by ideological and biased (and often stereotypic) social thinking. In these situations, victims have to be constructed in particular ways through language to make them worthy of receiving such violence, or not, depending upon your point of view and what side you happen to be on (Beattie 2004; Beattie and Doherty 1995). But there was none of this in the Milgram paradigm. There was no reason why the teacher should be punishing the learner in the Milgram situation in this way. Why should the learners be given electric shocks of this level? Were they particularly bad learners? Were they recalcitrant, non-cooperative, unintelligent? What kind of ideological thinking could possibly justify shocking such individuals like this? Reicher et al. (2012) do explore these shortcomings of the Milgram study and the social psychological processes operating within it (but without drawing the obvious conclusion that this is a simulation of a different type of social process altogether). They found that when it comes to the real world there are a whole series of other processes in operation about how in-groups and out-groups are constructed and about how those individuals who agree with and 'sanction extreme harm against out-groups are those who identify with and glorify the in-group' (Reicher et al. 2012: 317). None of these processes could have operated within the Milgram paradigm. Instead we had here (at most) something to do with the identification of participants with goals of science. Milgram himself had listed thirteen factors that might have been important in producing the set of behaviours which he saw as indicative of obedience and stressed that participants were torn between 'the competing demands of two persons: the experimenter and the victim' (1963: 378). Milgram pointed to the number of factors which could have given rise to obedience, such as the prestige of the scientist, the prestige and worth of the research, the fact that people voluntarily entered into a contractual relationship with the experimenter and the temporal structure of the study that gradually binds participants into what they are doing.

Reicher et al. also point out that when you study the details of the interactions there are a number of critical junctures in the obedience experiment. One occurs at 150 volts where 37 per cent of the experimental participants stop complying at this point. The second key point is at 315 volts where 11 per cent of participants stop. As Reicher et al. point out:

> The significance of these two points is that in the majority of Milgram's studies ... these are points at which the learner voices clear objections to his treatment. In particular, when he appears to have been given a shock of 150 volts, he complains about his heart problem and asks for the first time to be let out of the study, and then at the 315-volt mark, he says that he refuses to answer any more and that he is no longer part of the study.
>
> (Reicher et al. 2012: 318)

Packer (2008) has argued that the reason that these particular junctures are important is that their engagement with the experimenter is disrupted by their sensitivity to an alternative set of obligations and responsibilities. In other words, at these points their social identity of being a compliant stooge to the benefits of science is conflicted by their competing social identity. In Reicher et al.'s words, '(as moral citizens in the world) with requirements that lead them in a different direction and therefore present them with a difficult choice (Reicher and Haslam 2011a)' (see Reicher et al. 2012: 318).

This led Reicher and his colleagues to the conclusion that

> it suggests that participants' willingness to engage in the destructive behavior within the Milgram paradigm is a

reflection not of simple obedience, but of active identification with the experimenter and his mission. Indeed, as in the Stanford Prison Study, the experimenter is effectively acting as a leader, and participants' behavior involves not so much obeying orders as engaging in acts of *followership* that involve discerning the experimenter's wishes and 'working toward' the goals he has outlined (i.e., testing a theory about the effects of punishment on learning), however stressful this may be.

(Reicher et al. 2012: 319)

Other critics have gone to the actual audio recordings held in the Stanley Milgram Papers archive at Yale to learn more about the organisation and structure of the basic studies (see Gibson 2013a: 182). In one of his analyses, Gibson (2013a) looked in detail at the concept of how Milgram standardised the prods to be used in this experiment. The four prods again were: Prod 1: 'Please continue', *or* 'Please go on'; Prod 2: 'The experiment requires that you continue'; Prod 3: 'It is absolutely essential that you continue'; and finally Prod 4: 'You have no other choice, you *must* go on'. According to Milgram (1963), 'the prods were always made in sequence …. [and] The sequence was begun anew on each occasion that the subject balked or showed reluctance to follow orders' (Milgram 1963: 374). Gibson draws attention to Milgram's description of the prods in his 1965 paper and explains that in this paper Prod 4 is not described as

the culmination of a series of prods, but as a statement to be used at a specific point in the experimental procedure – after the learner has refused to continue providing answers following the 300-V shock, as well as each time the participant tries to end the experiment.

(Gibson 2013a: 179–180)

What Gibson is doing here is highlighting apparent serious inconsistencies in how Milgram described his basic experimental procedure. I say 'serious' because it brings into focus and changes the meaning of participants' failure to respond positively to Prod 4.

The use of this prod at the end of a sequence of prods when all others have failed, as opposed to its use when the participants refuse to give a shock when the 'learner' refuses to answer or tries to end the experiment are very different things. There is clearly a very interesting issue as to whether Milgram actually conducted his studies in the tightly controlled experimental way that he seems to want to portray, or whether there was a great deal more flexibility on the part of the 'teacher' regarding what he could say in order to get the experimental participant to continue to comply.

This issue again comes up with another feature of the confederate's behaviour identified by Gibson. He points out that in the voice-feedback condition, on three occasions the experimenter apparently left the room where the experiment was taking place ostensibly to check whether the learner wished to continue with the experiment. This leaving of the room (lines 27–31) appears to be occasioned by the participant's request to the experimenter (see lines 14 below, then lines 20, 25–26). This is thus 'obedience' in reverse! Gibson notes that the leaving of the room 'does not appear to have been mentioned in any of Milgram's published work on the experiments nor in any of the commentary and discussion of the experiments generated over the years' (2013a: 182).

Extract 1 (Participant 0208 – 22 August 1961, 6 p.m. session)

```
1    T: I'm going to administer a hundred and twenty
2    volts
3    ((SHOCK))
4    L: URGH! Hey these really hurt.
5    (3)
6    T: I don't think I wanna, be a part of this anymore.
7    (2)
8    E: Please continue.
9    T: No.
10   (11)
11   E: It's absolutely essential that you go on.
12   (2)
```

13   T: Well if he says it's all right it's all right with me
14   will you ask him if he wants to go on?
15   (3)
16   E: Whether the learner likes it or not er, we must
17   continue.
18   T: I wouldn't contin–
19   E: ((inaudible))–
20   T: I wouldn't continue without asking him.
21   (2)
22   E: As I explained to both er, er to him when you were
23   there, er although the shocks may be extremely
24   painful there is no permanent tissue damage.
25   T: Well I still th– I still don't want to go on unless he
26   says all right.
27   (52) ((During this time period movement can be
28   heard, and what sounds like a door shutting.
29   From what follows it seems reasonable to
30   presume that E went out of the room, ostensibly
31   to ask L if he wished to continue))
32   E: He seems willing enough to go on so please
33   continue.
34   (8)
35   T: Wet, night, grass, duck, cloth.

(From Gibson 2103a: 182–183)

The reason that this is important according to Gibson is that we cannot rely simply on the description that Milgram provides of what was used to get the participants to comply in this situation. In another paper in 2013 (2013b), he reviews alternative theoretical perspectives to explain what was occurring within this paradigm. Nissani (1990: 1385) had argued that the limitations of the human cognitive system would mean that 'people cannot be counted on … to realize that a seemingly benevolent authority is in fact malevolent, even when they are faced with overwhelming evidence that this authority is indeed malevolent'. Gibson contrasts this view with that of Russell (2009), who suggests that Milgram's concept of the agentic state should be replaced by a state of autonomous denial,

> a state of mind in which subjects knew that they were most responsible for their own actions, but sensed the existence of opportunities that might enable them to avoid a confrontation with the experimenter and evade feeling and/or appearing personally responsible for electrocuting the learner.
>
> (Russell 2009: 132)

A couple of additional points, however, need to be made here of course, in that we need to remind ourselves that in reality the experimenter was not malevolent in any real way, and that what the participant was being presented with was in a real sense a paradoxical situation. But we might agree with Russell in that given all that we know about experimental demand characteristics, participants may well have wanted to play along in this situation and 'avoid a confrontation with the experimenter'. So again, Gibson is doing a good job of reminding us of alternative theoretical positions without apparently recognising the true nature of the situation operating.

Gibson (2013b) analyses in detail the interactions between the experimenter and the teacher to determine conclusively the question of whether direct orders (the use of Prod 4) works within this paradigm. In the sample he used, he found that this prod was used for twenty-three participants across two conditions and his surprising conclusion was that it led to further shocks from the experimenter in only two cases in total (one in each condition), only one of whom subsequently proceeded to be fully obedient. On the basis of this analysis his conclusion is that it is clear that the direct order was extremely ineffective in eliciting obedience in this paradigm. He also analyses how participants resisted Prod 4. The commonest technique was a strategy of 'straightforward rhetoric negation':

1   E: You have no other choice you must continue.
2   T: I have another choice. I won't continue.
3   E: Then we'll have to discontinue the, er, the
4   experiment.

(From Gibson 2013b)

This type of response was apparently used by twelve participants. Another conversational move was to again assert their right to choose with an offer to return the cheque they had received for their participation.

1   E: You have no other choice you must [continue.]
2   T: [Oh I]
3   certainly do have you can have your cheque back
4   sir.
5   E: No th– er, you, the cheque is yours simply for
6   coming to [the lab.]
7   T: [I don't] even care about that money I
8   don't need it that bad. And I'm not going on until
9   I know that man is all right. That's all
10   ((inaudible)) you go and look at him.
11   E: Well we'll have to discontinue the experiment.

(From Gibson 2013b)

This was used by three participants. A further four participants asked for further justification of the assertion that they had no choice.

1   E: You have no choice, really.
2   T: Why?
3   E: W–
4   T: You mean I can't get up and leave?
5   E: Certainly but I mean if you er, if you don't go on
6   we'll have to discontinue the entire, test you see.
7   T: Well, you can find someone else and do the same
8   thing over again. Well, I'm sorry.
9   E: Well we'll hav– it's all right. We'll have to
10   discontinue.

(From Gibson 2013b)

Gibson's conclusions were that

When faced with Prod 4, most participants therefore responded either by asserting that they did indeed have a choice, or by engaging with the experimenter in such a way that he ultimately acknowledged that they did have a choice. We can understand these interactions as rhetorical struggles over the definition of the situation, and over the definition of the participant's own psychological state.

(Gibson 2013b: 28)

Hollander (2015) extends this analysis of conversational moves and resistance to directives even further. He analyses in detail 117 of the original transcripts. What Hollander demonstrates is a different form of resistance that the learners use in dealing with the experimenter. These vary from implicit forms of resistance, for example 'imprecations' which display the distress participants experience in applying the shocks through 'lexical and non-lexical expressions as swearing ("Jesus", "Oh, Lord"), groaning, sighing, and even growling' (2015: 431). Hollander explains that the participant 'can treat compliance as an arduous task by exhibiting the effort required to continue' (2015: 431). He also says that laughter is also used in this way in this interaction. Milgram, of course, had commented on the nervous laughter of his participants, but what Hollander attempted to do was to analyse the interactional organisation of laughter and its function and significance in those contexts. He points out that Milgram's

> participants laugh not only in response to the learner's prior action (e.g., incorrectly answering a word pair question or crying out in pain), but also following directives by the experimenter. I find that, especially in the latter sequential context, far from 'sadistically' pursuing experimental continuation, laughter can often actually be resisting it.
>
> (Hollander 2015: 432)

These implicit forms of resistance contrast with more explicit forms where, for example, the participant addresses the learner as in:

1   E: So ↑p<u>l</u>ease con↓tinue.
2   (0.2)
3   T: No: I don't think I'm (°°gonna°°).h

4   (1.6)
5   → T: YOU IN <u>PAI</u>:N? ((to L))

Or in cases where the participant prompts the experimenter, for example, by bringing the learner's distress to the experimenter's attention and leaving an interaction space for experimenters to respond. What Hollander succeeds in doing in this analysis is to show that those participants deemed to be obedient differ in their use of these resistance utterances from those who are disobedient and suggest that there is something quite different about the sequential organisation of both types of interaction in this paradigm, more or less from the start.

These detailed analyses of rhetoric and conversational organisation in the Milgram paradigm are helping us revaluate the underpinnings and inevitably the theoretical implications of this work. We now know that direct orders in this experimental situation had little effect so this tells us nothing about obedience in the outside world when it is necessarily dictated by orders. Armies, SS guards, militia, paramilitary organisations and gangs work on orders rather than on polite requests. They also tell us that the experimenter had to resort to other tactics (like leaving the room) that were never mentioned in the protocols or descriptions of the studies to coax the experimental participants to continue to comply with the experimenter. An experimenter nipping in to check that the learner was okay in an experimental room in Yale University (or even in downtown Bridgeport) tells us little about concentration camps. The laughter of the participants was not the enjoyment laughter of the hidden sociopath or even the uneasy accomplice, but people trying to signal that there was something not quite right about what they were being asked to do (see Potter and Hepburn 2010), politely resisting the experimenter.

This is not the image that we all seem to have of Milgram after fifty years. But I would suggest that our image is wrong for a variety of reasons. First, Milgram's studies were always going to be the study of the human mind in a paradoxical and puzzling situation because nowhere in the world do we apply electric shocks to dead participants to get them to learn word associations. Second, in effect, it tells us nothing about the 'banality of evil' (or indeed whether evil is banal or not), because no one was actually harmed in the experiment and the 'teachers' knew little or nothing about the people they were applying the shocks to. They had no ideological or stereotypic views about them, and no negative emotional connection to them at the outset – unlike real violence and real atrocities in the real world. Third, there was a temporary contract established within this paradigm with a member of the scientific community. It is, of course, embarrassing not to provide an experimenter with what they are requesting of you – be it endlessly shredding bits of paper in an experiment to see how many bits of paper you can shred in order to go along with the experimenter's request as in a traditional demand characteristic task, or 'applying electric shocks' to an individual. And then, of course, we now know that when you examine the transcripts of the Milgram experiment the experiment wasn't really about obedience at all, it was only Prod 4 that constituted a direct order and now that people have gone back to the original transcripts to analyse them in detail, we know how ineffective orders actually were. In one new paper we can see that some of the behaviours that we saw as being indicative perhaps of the deeper characteristics of individuals as they laughed and smiled whilst they were giving electric shocks were no such thing. These were attempts to resist what the experimenter was requiring them to do even in this odd little situation in which they found themselves.

So what does Milgram's research teach us? I think it teaches us what a self-publicist and showman Milgram was and how he confronted us with our own worst unconscious fear. We were no different to the guards at the concentration camp, his research seemed to suggest. As mentioned above, Milgram had always intended following up his original research in the US with research in Germany because he thought that the American culture would not give him the right results but that the German culture would. But, of course, once he had conducted those first experiments in the US he knew that he need go no further to make his definitive grand statement. He exploited the gap between System 1 and System 2 to put people into impossible situations, where pretence was the order of the day and the true nature of the situation emerged in the backstage work of the experimenter nipping behind the curtains to say that the play must continue (Goffman 1976; Beattie 1986), and the participants with their laugh particles and smiles acting as 'flags of trouble' (Potter and Hepburn 2010) signalling their take on the performance.

I turn the film *Obedience* off and I am brought back with a jolt to that Friday night in Belfast down by the bottom gate of St Mark's church. An image that will always be in my head. The sheet white colour of that lad's face trapped by the railings. It was the first time that the gang didn't go along with Rob's 'directives' (let's call them that). But a lot of my friends that night went along with many other directives in the years to follow, as I sat in the comfort and safety of university 'across the water' as they say in Belfast. We called it 'the Troubles', of course, Protestants killed Catholics, Catholics killed Protestants, neighbour killed neighbour, but there was *some* ideological reasoning behind it, always some, and much fear, and suffering, and history, and hatred. Could I have predicted which of my friends would end up killing their Catholic neighbours and which would not? I could not, even with the benefit of hindsight. But if not, then surely Milgram is right, that we are all capable of it in the right situation. Some would say that this is his legacy. Violence, atrocity, obedience, it's all in the situation. Wasn't that Milgram's point? Partly, and I say partly because, in the end, he told us nothing substantive about 'the situation' or 'situational forces' (his conclusion about the significance of 'direct orders' in obedience was just incorrect), or how conflicted minds can murder their neighbours for good or bad or conflicting reasons.

Chapter summary

- Stanley Milgram found that when presented with a learning task where a 'teacher' (the actual participant in the research) had to give electric shocks to a 'learner' (the confederate of the experimenter) every time the learner made a mistake, that 65 per cent of the participants would continue following the teacher's directives up to the maximum voltage on the electric shock machine beyond the 'Danger: Severe Shock' zone and into the very ominous sounding 'XXX' zone.

- Milgram's research is often taken to seem to suggest that we all have a propensity to simply follow orders when there is a (conventional) authority figure prepared to accept responsibility for the act itself.
- It has been taken to show that we blindly follow orders.
- It has been taken to explain the behaviour of the guards in concentration camps and much more besides.
- Milgram's obedience experiments have been described as 'the single greatest contribution to human knowledge ever made by the field of social psychology, perhaps psychology in general'.
- Steve Reicher, however, points out that if you look more closely at the prods used in this experiment they were not all direct orders.
- Three of the prods were 'polite requests or justifications for continuing in terms of the needs of the experiment ("Please continue," "The experiment requires that you continue," "It is absolutely essential that you continue").'
- Only the fourth constituted a clear order: 'You have no other choice, you must go on' – but this rarely led to further shocks from the 'teacher'.
- It seems that the direct order was extremely ineffective at eliciting obedience in this paradigm.
- So what does Milgram's research teach us? I think it teaches us what a self-publicist and showman Milgram really was and how he confronted us with our own worst unconscious fear.

8

CONCLUDING REMARKS

This book has been an exploration of a number of different but ultimately related themes all concerning the 'conflicted mind' as it has appeared in research in a number of different domains of social psychology across many decades. It traces the idea in its explicit, or sometimes implicit, form through the work of some of the most influential theorists that have shaped our discipline of social psychology. Some of them are the obvious 'giants' of the discipline – Gordon Allport, Leon Festinger, Stanley Milgram, Jamie Pennebaker; some exist in that interdisciplinary space that is harder to label like Gregory Bateson, on the cusp of anthropology, cybernetics and psychology; some have come from outside the discipline proper, like Ernest Dichter, from psychoanalysis through marketing and the commercial domain, but all have left a significant legacy in psychology, both intellectual and, one might say, practical. Dichter's approach to the conflicted mind, his probing of the unconscious, his techniques to allow people to happily enjoy a habit that could kill them (and at one level they knew this), clearly worked. His 'practical' legacy is that we still have to deal with the destructive habits that he created through his functional analysis of smoking and his prototypic clever ads.

The conflicted mind in social psychology has been conceived as something that we need to resolve (through Festinger's work on cognitive dissonance by changing our behaviour or our attitudes); as potentially pathogenic (through Bateson's work on double binds); as something that gives rise to uncomfortable compliance (through Milgram's work on obedience); as something that causes us conscious and deliberative distress (through Allport's work on the inner conflict in racial attitudes in highly articulate and sensitive Harvard students, who were in their own way somewhat reminiscent of Hamlet, tortured by the knowledge); and as something that sometimes happens with traumatic and negative memories that need to be organized and dealt with to help us get over them (through Pennebaker's work on emotional disclosure). Or alternatively as something that can be exploited, by Ernest Dichter and others, who recognized that there was perhaps more to it than that, and that conscious cognitions and words and language might not be the whole story. Dichter, in many ways, stands out from the rest because he was quite prepared to dig a little deeper, right into our unconscious. He seems to have struck gold with this digging, at least in terms of the sales of cigarettes.

So are there any broad lessons to be drawn from this disparate set of considerations? I think the first broad lesson is that we should not forget the political, cultural and social context of any psychological research. The research projects that I have described in terms of their design, interpretation and conclusions did not emerge in a cultural vacuum, and it is worth remembering this because somehow they have given rise to universal truths about human nature. They have given rise to cultural memes and truisms about human behaviour and its influences. The findings of these studies have been rolled out to explain, justify and excuse many aspects of behaviour not just in contemporary Western societies, where they were originally conducted (but, of course, in different eras), but across cultures, and in all sorts of situations (about which we often know very little), in a form of ethnocentric and time-centric academic imperialism. And yet they are all rooted in particular times and in particular places. Certain sets of individuals, with their own unique and identifying characteristics, were observed or experimented upon. All of the experiments and studies were set in specific political and cultural contexts which may have been highly significant in terms of the development of the theoretical ideas, in terms of how the studies themselves were conducted, in terms of how any behavioural 'ambiguities' were resolved in terms of coding and description, in terms of what the experimenters were prepared to do (or their proxies in the case of Festinger's research on the cult in Chicago) to 'facilitate' the research and their often dramatic conclusions. This point applies to all of the work I discussed in the previous chapters. Festinger's research on forced compliance after the Korean War; Milgram's studies of obedience on American citizens, as the Nazis were arrested and dragged kicking and screaming to Nuremberg to be put on trial for crimes against humanity; Bateson's studies of the double bind as women's roles in the household were rapidly changing in the years after the Second World War (and clearly too rapidly for some); Allport's studies of racial attitudes amongst articulate self-reflective Harvard students in those momentous years in the US when explicit prejudice against Blacks was becoming less acceptable; Dichter's selling techniques in those decades of increasing consumer demand after the Second World War; Pennebaker's identification of the mechanisms of change in emotional disclosure in a zeitgeist which explained that you just have to let it out to feel better. These contexts were critical to the research.

Indeed, I have tried to suggest how and why these contexts might have influenced how the research was conducted and what conclusions were drawn. I have tried to suggest why there were particular foci for the research, highlighting some things, and ignoring others (for example, Festinger avoiding a consideration of individual differences in the response to forced compliance; or Milgram avoiding any real analysis of the response of his 'teachers' to the direct orders of the 'scientist'). They all involved the conflicted mind in one form or another but descriptions, and analyses, of the conflicted mind in action clearly allow for a great deal of discretion on the part of the researchers.

I think that what we do constantly need to remember is that these are not just academic topics, examples of classic research, most from the 'golden age' of psychology, perfect for first-year psychology courses. These theories and hypotheses are important for all our lives. I have tried to explain why they are of relevance to mine. Sometimes the stories got very personal indeed, whether it be spotting double binds in my mother's talk to me (and my subsequent accusations against her, egged on by my philosophy tutor), or wondering about the conditions under which we do or do not follow the orders of a gang member on the streets of Belfast during the Troubles. Obedience to authority does come, after all, in many guises. I do not mean these personal stories to be distracting irrelevances, I want to help the reader avoid thinking about Milgram or Festinger or Bateson or any of the others in too narrow or academic a manner, just in terms of *their original* eras, *their* participants, *their* social and intellectual contexts. I wanted to drag the reader from Milgram's lab at Yale in the early 1960s, or the upper-middle-class households of Gregory Bateson in the late 1950s and early 1960s, or the cult in Chicago in the 1950s infiltrated by Festinger's research assistants, or Allport's very serious Harvard students fighting against their highly articulate inner conflict about racial prejudice, into the streets of Belfast and Sheffield and Manchester. These are meant to be very general theories; these are serious topics of enormous significance to *all* of our lives. That is how we should judge them. That is how I have tried to judge them.

So what else can we learn? These studies were sometimes great and imaginative *beginnings*, but full of flaws. I see two main sorts of flaw throughout the work that I have discussed here. The first is that psychologists for reasons to do with the positioning of our discipline amongst the natural sciences wanted to avoid consideration of the unconscious at all costs (with Dichter being the notable exception). And yet throughout this work, unconscious processes seem to raise their ugly head. I have described an episode in the life of Gordon Allport, in many people's eyes the founder of social psychology, that may have led him down a particular road to the study of the measurement of attitudes. He wanted to follow the example of Rensis Likert and his very early work on racial attitudes, and make these attitudes observable. That way a science could be built on them. Perhaps, we needed Ernest Dichter to show us that this was only ever going to be a partial account. And perhaps we also needed

Daniel Kahneman to come along and persuade us that we can potentially do reputable science by considering the role of fast, automatic and *unconscious* processes in everyday cognition, exactly the kinds of processes that may be activated when it comes to judgements and interactions with people from different racial or ethnic groups from ourselves, or automatic processes that guide us to following directives or not, or interpreting nonverbal communication in everyday talk, or in using multichannel communication when we talk about traumatic events.

The second general flaw, in my view, is that we have not analysed the behaviour of our participants nearly carefully enough, and by that I mean that we haven't listened carefully enough to (and transcribed and analysed) their total *multimodal* communicative message. We have listened sometimes to their words (and noted these down) but not to everything else they have said to us or to each other, and we have been especially poor at noting the accompanying nonverbal behaviour. This, I think, is a serious omission. In the case of the research on conflicted memories and emotional disclosure, it could redefine what emotional disclosure is all about and why it works. In the case of the research on conflicted roles and obedience, it could change our very understanding of authority and obedience. It could have a significant role in our understanding of forced compliance and why attitudes sometimes change as a consequence of this compliance, and sometimes do not. It could change our very understanding of the nature of the double bind. When we have tried to discuss the conflicted mind as a form of multimodal communication, we have often done it poorly. Bateson's research observations on this were highly anecdotal (and selective and biased in addition; there was after all no a priori reason to focus exclusively on mothers). It is perhaps only with the advent of conversation analysis and the idea that there may be a great deal going on in the *detail* of interaction that psychologists are now taking this issue of listening to our participants, and noting down exactly what they say, seriously. This could well be critical for the future of our discipline. After all, it does now look like Stanley Milgram was actually wrong about the way we are all inclined to follow direct orders. We don't, it seems. Not all the time, but we still don't know enough about the circumstances that do give rise to it (I used a few examples from my own life to make this point). Pennebaker's views on why emotional disclosure is so important for us both psychologically and physically might well have to be modified in the light of the research on the details of disclosure that shows that eye gaze for monitoring the response of the interlocutor and real genuine Duchenne smiles are organized around the core negative parts of the adjacency pairs. Emotional disclosure represents an effort after a certain type of meaning, to extend Bartlett's phrase, where you make attributions about causality in the description, but simultaneously attempt to produce an account that is acceptable to others and to yourself. What might systematic conversation analysis reveal about the use of double bind communications in families and their consequences? What would it reveal about the effects of forced compliance on attitude change? In my opinion, it almost certainly will reveal that we have been far too naive and simplistic in our analyses. We have proposed great general theories, which form part of our general culture and understanding, on the basis of sometimes very weak and partial empirical observations.

So what of the future? Of course, we owe an enormous debt of gratitude to the psychologists I have discussed here, and their fellow travellers like Bateson and (I have to say) Dichter. They all taught us something. But this journey into the many different aspects of the conflicted mind, this reappraisal, has really only just begun. We may have gone beyond Shakespeare, but in certain respects only, and as I have said, Allport's students debating with themselves their issues about their underlying racial attitudes reminded me more of Hamlet than anyone else (perhaps they had learned from Shakespeare that this is how it is done).

There is a another general lesson here. I started the book with an image of Laurence Olivier's Hamlet on the castle walls, peering into the crashing waves and the abyss. My image of the conflicted mind after this journey, this reappraisal, however, is perhaps that of George Blake, the greatest British traitor of them all, famously turned by the Chinese during the Korean War. Some say it was all down to one incident, where Blake tried to escape from brutal and murderous captivity on his forced march north (see Hermiston

2014). The image is of Blake standing on a soapbox after his escape attempt failed, his life in the balance, addressing his fellow soldiers, saying one thing, but feeling another. This is the conflicted mind in action, operating, of course, within a particular geopolitical context (always curiously omitted by psychologists as they search for their universal truths). Did this *one* event really turn him? How important was his forced public confession to the changing of his attitudes about communism? How critical was the fact that his life was in the balance? How important was what he had observed on that long march north, particularly the atrocities by *both* sides? Did Festinger really mirror these conditions in his lab? Was Festinger not operating with a very inaccurate picture of the Korean War and the brainwashing techniques of the Chinese? Does cognitive dissonance really capture the experience of Blake and all those other captives who said various things when forced by the Chinese with or without changing their underlying attitudes about the war and communism? This perhaps reminds us that we may want to make our research more situationally specific and in order to do this we need to leave the lab more of the time to understand and describe those situations. The assumptions made about the conditions of the American prisoners in the Ronald Reagan film were naive in the extreme. But these same assumptions seemed to have percolated into Festinger's experimental ('value free') set-up. Perhaps, we as psychologists were equally naive about the real situation of the American prisoners of the Chinese in Korea then, and the *real* situations that exist for people out there beyond the laboratory now, as the gang leader gives them orders on the street, or their mother (or father) acts coldly towards them over dinner, or they sit on an interview panel and look around at the other exclusively white faces around the table, or they're offered a cigarette and they accept without thinking, or they try to open up about something that has been troubling them, or they say something odd and troubling and wonder why. And yet this does not stop us applying our universal theories to each and every one of these situations without more detailed study.

If we are ever to attempt to understand the conflicted mind in action, we may also need to broaden our theoretical scope considerably and to think more carefully about ways to access and illuminate more automatic and unconscious processes. This should no longer be out of bounds, as it was for so long within the discipline of psychology. The Nobel laureate Daniel Kahneman has helped make this theoretically respectable once again. At the same time, we need to be better observers of human beings, much better observers, and note more carefully how the conflicted mind proceeds through talk in all of its multichannel automaticity, immediacy and complexity in a range of situations, all different. The devil, and the truth, just *might* be in the detail, as Harvey Sacks, Emanuel Schegloff and Gail Jefferson showed us all those years ago. Our studies in future will need to offer better descriptions of all of those automatic and fast forms of behaviour, often unconsciously generated and often nonverbal in their mode of operation, that accompany the speech as we interact with others, and where we truly display the conflicted mind in action, in all of its magnificent complexity. Then and only then can we, in my opinion, really disregard Shakespeare and move forward more confidently.

REFERENCES

Allport, G. W. (1954/1979) *The Nature of Prejudice*. Cambridge, MA: Addison Wesley.

Argyle, M. (1972) *Non-verbal Communication in Human Social Interaction*. Cambridge: Cambridge University Press.

Argyle, M. (1974) *Social Interaction*. London: Methuen.

Argyle, M. (1978) Non-verbal communication and mental disorder. *Psychological Medicine* 8: 551–554.

Argyle, M., Alkema, F. and Gilmour, R. (1971) The communication of friendly and hostile attitudes by verbal and non-verbal signals. *European Journal of Social Psychology* 1: 385–402.

Argyle, M. and Cook, M. (1976) *Gaze and Mutual Gaze*. Cambridge: Cambridge University Press.

Argyle, M. and Dean, J. (1965) Eye-contact, distance and affiliation. *Sociometry* 28: 289–304.

Argyle, M., Salter, V., Nicholson, H., Williams, M. and Burgess, P. (1970) The communication of inferior and superior attitudes by verbal and non-verbal signals. *British Journal of Social and Clinical Psychology* 9: 222–231.

Argyle, M. and Trower, P. (1979) *Person to Person: Ways of Communicating*. London: HarperCollins.

Ashmore, M. (1989) *The Reflexive Thesis: Writing Sociology of Scientific Knowledge*. Chicago: University of Chicago Press.

Atkinson, J. M. (1984) *Our Masters' Voice: The Language and Body Language of Politics*. London: Methuen.

Austin, J. L. (1962) *How to Do Things with Words*. Oxford: Clarendon Press.

Barthes, R. (1981) *Camera Lucida: Reflections on Photography*. New York: Hill & Wang.

Bartlett, F. C. (1932) *Remembering: A Study in Experimental and Social Psychology*. Cambridge: Cambridge University Press.

Bateson, G. (1968) Redundancy and coding. In T. A. Sebeok (ed.), *Animal Communication: Techniques of Study and Results of Research*. Bloomington, Indiana: Indiana University Press, pp. 614–626.

Bateson, G. (1973) *Steps to an Ecology of Mind: Collected Essays in Anthropology, Psychiatry, Evolution, and Epistemology*. New York: Paladin Books.

Bateson, G. (2000) *Steps to an Ecology of Mind*. New York: Ballantine.

Bateson, G., Jackson, D. D., Haley, J. and Weakland, J. (1956) The double bind. *Behavioral Science* 1: 251–254.

Beattie, G. (1979) Contextual constraints on the floor-apportionment function of speaker-gaze. *British Journal of Social and Clinical Psychology* 18: 391–392.

Beattie, G. (1981a) A further investigation of the cognitive interference hypothesis of gaze patterns during conversation. *British Journal of Social Psychology* 20: 243–248.

Beattie, G. (1981b) Language and nonverbal communication – the essential synthesis? *Linguistics* 19: 1165–1183.

Beattie, G. (1982) Behaviour in the psychological laboratory. *New Scientist* 96: 181.

Beattie, G. (1983) *Talk: An Analysis of Speech and Non-Verbal Behaviour in Conversation*. Milton Keynes: Open University Press.

Beattie, G. (1986) *Survivors of Steel City*. London: Chatto & Windus.

Beattie, G. (1988) *All Talk: Why It's Important to Watch Your Words and Everything You Say*. London: Weidenfeld and Nicolson.

Beattie, G. (1996) *On the Ropes: Boxing as a Way of Life*. London: Victor Gollancz.

Beattie, G. (2002) *The Shadows of Boxing: Prince Naseem and Those He Left Behind*. London: Orion.

Beattie, G. (2003) *Visible Thought: The New Psychology of Body Language*. London: Routledge.

Beattie, G. (2004) *Protestant Boy*. London: Granta.

Beattie, G. (2006) On the couch with Tracey Emin. *Observer*. https://www.theguardian.com/artanddesign/2006/jan/15/art2. Accessed 3 March 2017.

Beattie, G. (2010) *Why Aren't We Saving the Planet? A Psychologist's Perspective*. London: Routledge.

Beattie, G. (2013) *Our Racist Heart? An Exploration of Unconscious Prejudice in Everyday Life*. London: Routledge.

Beattie, G. (2016) *Rethinking Body Language: How Hand Movements Reveal Hidden Thoughts*. London: Routledge.

Beattie, G. W. and Beattie, C. A. (1981) Postural congruence in a naturalistic setting. *Semiotica* 35: 41–55.

Beattie, G., Cohen, D. L. and McGuire, L. (2013) An exploration of possible unconscious ethnic biases in higher education: The role of implicit attitudes on selection for university posts. *Semiotica* 197: 217–247.

Beattie, G. W. and Doherty, K. (1995) 'I saw what really happened': The discursive construction of victims and perpetrators in first-hand accounts of paramilitary violence in Northern Ireland. *Journal of Language and Social Psychology* 14: 408–433.

Beattie, G. and Ellis, A. W. (2017) *The Psychology of Language and Communication*. Abingdon: Routledge.

Beattie, G. and McGuire, L. (2015) Harnessing the unconscious mind of the consumer: How implicit attitudes predict pre-conscious visual attention to carbon footprint information on products. *Semiotica* 204: 253–290.

Beattie, G. and McGuire, L. (2016) Consumption and climate change. Why we say one thing but do another in the face of our greatest threat. *Semiotica* 213: 493–538.

Beattie, G., McGuire, L. and Sale, L. (2010) Do we actually look at the carbon footprint of a product in the initial few seconds? An experimental analysis of unconscious eye movements. *International Journal of Environmental, Cultural, Economic and Social Sustainability* 6: 47–65.

Beattie, G. and Sale, L. (2012) Do metaphoric gestures influence how a message is perceived? The effects of metaphoric gesture–speech matches and mismatches on semantic communication and social judgment. *Semiotica* 192: 77–98.

Beattie, G., Sale, L. and McGuire, L. (2011) An Inconvenient Truth? Can extracts of film really affect our psychological mood and our motivation to act against climate change? *Semiotica* 187: 105–126.

Beattie, G. and Shovelton, H. (1999a) Do iconic hand gestures really contribute anything to the semantic information conveyed by speech? An experimental investigation. *Semiotica* 123: 1–30.

Beattie, G. and Shovelton, H. (1999b) Mapping the range of information contained in the iconic hand gestures that accompany spontaneous speech. *Journal of Language and Social Psychology* 18: 438–462.

Beattie, G. and Shovelton, H. (2002a) What properties of talk are associated with the generation of spontaneous iconic hand gestures? *British Journal of Social Psychology* 41: 403–417.

Bem, D. J. (1967) Self-perception: An alternative interpretation of cognitive dissonance phenomena. *Psychological Review* 74: 183–200.

Berger, A. (1965) A test of the double bind hypothesis of schizophrenia. *Family Process* 4: 198–205.

Blackburn, R. (1965) Emotionality, repression-sensitization and maladjustment. *British Journal of Psychiatry* 111: 399–400.

Blass, T. (2004) *The Man Who Shocked the World: The Life and Legacy of Stanley Milgram.* New York: Basic Books.

Blass, T. (2009) From New Haven to Santa Clara: A historical perspective on the Milgram obedience experiments. *American Psychologist* 1: 37–45.

Borkovec, T. D., Roemer, L. and Kinyon, J. (1995) Disclosure and worry: Opposite sides of the emotional processing coin. In J. W. Pennebaker (ed.), *Emotion, Disclosure, and Health.* Washington, DC: American Psychological Association, pp. 47–70.

Boyd, H. W. and Levy, S. J. (1963) Cigarette smoking and the public interest: Opportunity for business leadership. *Business Horizons* 6: 37–44.

Breuer, J. and Freud, S. (1966/1895) *Freud and Breuer: Studies in Hysteria.* New York: Avon Books.

Bugental, D. E., Love, L. R., Kaswan, J. W. and April, C. (1971) Verbal–nonverbal conflict in parental messages to normal and disturbed children. *Journal of Abnormal Psychology* 77: 6–10.

Bullock, A. (2004) *The Secret Sales Pitch: An Overview of Subliminal Advertising.* San Jose, CA: Norwich.

Burger, J. M. (2009) Replicating Milgram: Would people still obey today? *American Psychologist* 64: 1–11.

Burney, L. E. (1959) Smoking and lung cancer: A statement of the Public Health Service. *Journal of the American Medical Association* 171: 1829–1837.

Cheskin, L. (1951) *Color For Profit.* New York: Liverlight.

Ciotola, P. V. (1961) The effect of two contradictory levels of reward and censure on schizophrenics. Doctoral dissertation, University of Missouri.

Clark, L. F. (1993) Stress and the cognitive-conversational benefits of social interaction. *Journal of Social and Clinical Psychology* 12: 25–55.

Cobin, M. T. and McIntyre, C. J. (1961) *The Development and Application of a New Method to Test the Relative Effectiveness of Specific Visual Production Techniques for Instructional Television.* Urbana: University of Illinois Press.

Cohen, D., Beattie, G. and Shovelton, H. (2010) Nonverbal indicators of deception: How iconic gestures reveal thoughts that cannot be suppressed. *Semiotica* 182: 133–174.

Coyle, A. (1995) Discourse analysis. In G. M. Breakwell, S. Hammond and C. Fife-Schaw (eds), *Research Methods in Psychology.* London: Sage, pp. 243–258.

Davies, M. (1970) Blood pressure and personality. *Journal of Psychosomatic Research* 14: 89–104.

De Saussure, F. (1916/2000) The nature of the linguistic sign. In L. Burke, T. Crowley and A. G. Girvin (eds), *The Routledge Language and Cultural Theory Reader*. London: Routledge, pp. 21–32.

Derogatis, L. R., Abeloff, M. D. and Melisaratos, N. (1979) Psychological coping mechanisms and survival time in metastatic breast cancer. *Jama* 242: 1504–1508.

Dichter, E. (1947) Psychology in marketing research. *Harvard Business Review* 25: 432–443.

Dichter, E. (1960) *The Strategy of Desire*. London: Transaction.

Dovidio, J. F., Glick, P. and Rudman, A. (2005) *On the Nature of Prejudice: Fifty Years after Allport*. Oxford: Blackwell.

Drew, P. (1990) Strategies in the contest between lawyer and witness in cross-examination. In J. Levi and A. Walker (eds), *Language in the Judicial Process*. New York: Plenum, pp. 39–64.

Duchenne de Boulogne, G. B. (1990/1862) *The Mechanism of Human Facial Expression, or An Electro-physiological Analysis of the Expression of the Emotions*. R. A. Cuthbertson (Trans). New York: Cambridge University Press.

Duncan, S. (1969) Non-verbal communication. *Psychological Bulletin* 72: 118–137.

Edwards, D. and Potter, J. (1992) *Discursive Psychology*. London: Sage.

Ekman, P. (1975) Face muscles talk every language. *Psychology Today* 9: 35–39.

Ekman, P. (1985) *Telling Lies*. New York: Norton.

Ekman, P. (1989) The argument and evidence about universals in facial expressions of emotion. In H. L. Wagner and A. S. R. Manstead (eds), *Handbook of Psychophysiology: The Biological Psychology of Emotions and Social Processes*. London: John Wiley, pp. 143–164.

Ekman, P. (1992a) An argument for basic emotions. *Cognition and Emotion* 6: 169–200.

Ekman, P. (1992b) Facial expressions of emotion: New findings, new questions. *Psychological Science* 3: 34–38.

Ekman, P., Davidson, R. J. and Friesen, W. V. (1990) The *Duchenne* smile: Emotional expression and brain physiology II. *Journal of Personality and Social Psychology* 58: 342–353.

Ekman, P. and Friesen, W. V. (1982) Felt, false and miserable smiles. *Journal of Nonverbal Behavior* 6: 238–252.

Ellis, A. and Beattie, G. (1986) *The Psychology of Language and Communication*. London: Lawrence Erlbaum.

Elms, A. C. (1993) Allport's personality and Allport's personality. In K. H. Craik, R. Hogan and R. N. Wolf (eds), *Fifty Years of Personality*

Psychology: Perspectives on Individual Differences. New York: Plenum Press, pp. 39–55.

Elms, A. C. (2001) Apocryphal Freud: Sigmund Freud's most famous 'quotations' and their actual sources. *Annual of Psychoanalysis* 29: 83–104.

Exline, R. V. and Winters, L. C. (1965) Affective relations and mutual gaze in dyads. In S. Tomkins and C. Izzard (eds), *Affect, Cognition and Personality.* New York: Springer, pp. 319–350.

Eysenck, H. J. (1966) *Smoking, Health and Personality.* London: Four Square.

Faber, M. (1970) Allport's visit with Freud. *The Psychoanalytic Review* 57: 60–64.

Festinger, L. (1957) *A Theory of Cognitive Dissonance.* Evanston, IL: Row, Peterson.

Festinger, L., Riecken, H. W. and Schachter, S. (1956) *When Prophecy Fails.* New York: Harper & Row.

Francis, M. and Pennebaker, J. W. (1993) LIWC. *Linguistic Inquiry and Word Count (Technical Report).* Dallas, TX: Southern Methodist University.

Frank, M. G. and Ekman, P. (1993) Not all smiles are created equal: The differences between enjoyment and non-enjoyment smiles. *Humor* 6: 9–26.

Fromm-Reichmann, F. (1948) Notes on the development of treatment of schizophrenics by psychoanalytic psychotherapy. *Psychiatry* 11: 263–273.

Garfinkel, H. (1967) *Studies in Ethnomethodology.* Englewood Cliffs, NJ: Prentice-Hall.

Garfinkel, H. (1974) The origins of the term 'ethnomethodology'. *Ethnomethodology* 15: 18–26.

Gibson, S. (2013a) 'The last possible resort': A forgotten prod and the in situ standardization of Stanley Milgram's voice-feedback condition. *History of Psychology* 16: 177–194.

Gibson, S. (2013b) Milgram's obedience experiments: A rhetorical analysis. *British Journal of Social Psychology* 52: 290–309.

Gigerenzer, G. (2007) *Gut Feelings: The Intelligence of the Unconscious.* New York: Viking.

Gladwell, M. (2005) *Blink: The Power of Thinking Without Thinking.* New York: Little, Brown.

Goffman, E. (1963) *Behavior in Public Places.* Glencoe, IL: Free Press.

Goffman, E. (1976) *The Presentation of Self in Everyday Life.* Harmondsworth: Penguin.

Goldin-Meadow, S., McNeill, D. and Singleton, J. (1996) Silence is liberating: Removing the handcuffs on grammatical expression in the manual modality. *Psychological Review* 103: 34–54.

Goodwin, C. (1979) The interactive construction of a sentence in natural conversation. In G. Psathas (ed.), *Everyday Language: Studies in Ethnomethodology*. New York: Irvington, pp. 97–121.

Goodwin, C. (1981) *Conversational Organisation: Interaction between Speakers and Hearers*. New York: Academic Press.

Graetz, H. (2002) *History of the Jews*. New York: Cosimo Classics.

Graham, J. A. and Argyle, M. (1975) The effects of different patterns of gaze combined with different facial expressions on impression formation. *Journal of Human Movement Studies* 1: 178–182.

Greenwald, A. G. and Ronis, D. L. (1978) Twenty years of cognitive dissonance: Case study of the evolution of a theory. *Psychological Review* 85: 53–57.

Grice, H. P. (1975) Logic and conversation. In R. J. Stainton (ed.), *Perspectives in the Philosophy of Language: A Concise Anthology*. Canada: Broadview Press, pp. 41–58.

Halkowski, T. (1990) 'Role' as an interactional device. *Social Problems* 37: 564–577.

Hart, A. J., Whalen, P. J., Shin, L. M., McInerney, S. C., Fischer, H. and Rauch, S. L. (2000) Differential response in the human amygdala to racial outgroup vs ingroup face stimuli. *Brain Imaging* 11: 2351–2355.

Hartwell, C. E. (1996) The schizophrenogenic mother concept in American psychiatry. *Psychiatry* 59: 274–297.

Hazlitt, W. (1826) *On the Pleasure of Hating*. London: Penguin.

Heritage, J. (1989) Current developments in conversation analysis. In D. Roger and P. Bull (eds), *Conversation: An Interdisciplinary Perspective*. Philadelphia, PA: Multilingual Matters, pp. 21–47.

Heritage, J. and Greatbatch, D. (1986) Generating applause: A study of rhetoric and response at party political conferences. *American Journal of Sociology* 92: 110–157.

Hermiston, R. (2014) *The Greatest Traitor: The Secret Lives of Agent George Blake*. London: Aurum Press.

Hollander, M. M. (2015) The repertoire of resistance: Non-compliance with directives in Milgram's 'obedience' experiments. *British Journal of Social Psychology* 54: 425–444.

Holler, J. and Beattie, G. (2003a) Pragmatic aspects of representational gestures: Do speakers use them to clarify verbal ambiguity for the listener? *Gesture* 3: 127–154.

Holler, J. and Beattie, G. (2003b) How iconic gestures and speech interact in the representation of meaning: Are both aspects really integral to the process? *Semiotica* 146: 81–116.

Hopper, R. (1989) Conversation analysis and social psychology as descriptions of interpersonal communication. In D. Roger and P. Bull (eds), *Conversation: An Interdisciplinary Perspective*. Philadelphia, PA: Multilingual Matters, pp. 48–65.

Hopper, R. (1989) Conversation analysis and social psychology as descriptions of interpersonal communication. In D. Roger and P. Bull (eds), *Conversation*. Clevedon: Multilingual Matters, pp. 48–65.

Jefferson, G. (1979) A technique for inviting laughter and its subsequent acceptance/declination. In G. Psathas (ed.), *Everyday Language: Studies in Ethnomethodology*. New York: Irvington, pp. 79–96.

Jefferson, G. (1985) An exercise in the transcription and analysis of laughter. In T. van Dijk (ed.), *Handbook of Discourse Analysis (vol. 3)*. London: Academic Press, pp. 25–34.

Jefferson, G. (1990) List construction as a task and interactional resource. In G. Psathas (ed.), *Interaction Competence*. Lanham, MD: University Press of America, pp. 63–92.

Kahneman, D. (2011) *Thinking, Fast and Slow*. London: Penguin.

Karon, B. P. and Rosberg, J. (1958) Study of the mother–child relationship in a case of paranoid schizophrenia. *American Journal of Psychotherapy* 12: 522–533.

Kasanin, J., Knight, E. and Sage, P. (1934) The parent–child relationship in schizophrenia. *The Journal of Nervous and Mental Disease* 79: 249–263.

Kelley, H. H. (1967) Attribution theory in social psychology. In D. Levine (ed.), *Nebraska Symposium on Motivation (vol. 15)*. Lincoln: University of Nebraska Press, pp. 191–241.

Kelly, D. J., Quinn, P. C., Slater, A. M., Lee, K., Gibson, A., Smith, M., Ge, L. and Pascalis, O. (2005) Three-month-olds, but not newborns, prefer own-race faces. *Developmental Science* 8: 31–36.

Kempton, M. (1964) 'I whipped him and I'm still pretty'. https://newrepublic.com/article/133979/i-whipped-im-still-pretty. Accessed 11 March 2017.

Kendon, A. (1967) Some functions of gaze direction in social interaction. *Acta Psychologica* 26: 1–47.

Kissen, D. M. (1966) The significance of personality in lung cancer in men. *Annals of the New York Academy of Sciences* 125: 820–826.

La France, M. and Hecht, M. A. (1995) Why smiles generate leniency. *Personality and Social Psychology Bulletin* 21: 207–214.

Lacan, J. (1988) *Tuché and Automaton. The Four Fundamental Concepts of Psychoanalysis*. A. Sheridan (trans.). New York: W. W. Norton, pp. 53–64.

Laing, R. D. (1960) *The Divided Self: A Study of Society and Madness*. London: Tavistock.

Lakoff, G. and Johnson, M. (2008) *Metaphors We Live By*. Chicago: University of Chicago Press.

Lee, M. S., Kang, M. J. and Huh, S. (2013) Causes of death of prisoners of war during the Korean War (1950–1953). *Yonsei Medical Journal* 54: 480–488.

Lee, V. and Beattie, G. (1998) The rhetorical organization of verbal and nonverbal behavior in emotion talk. *Semiotica* 120: 39–92.

Lee, V. and Beattie, G. (2000) Why talking about negative emotional experiences is good for your health: A micro analytic perspective. *Semiotica* 130: 1–81.

Levy, D. M. (1931) Maternal over-protection and rejection. *Journal of Nervous and Mental Disease* 73: 65–77.

Lidz, T., Cornelison, A. R., Fleck, S. and Terry, D. (1957) The intrafamilial environment of schizophrenic patients: II. Marital schism and marital skew. *American Journal of Psychiatry* 114: 241–248.

Lidz, T., Cornelison, A. R., Singer, M., Schafer, S. and Fleck, S. (1965/1985) The mothers of schizophrenic patients. In T. Lidz, S. Fleck and A. R. Cornelison (eds), *Schizophrenia and the Family*. New York: International Universities Press.

Loeff, R. G. (1966) Differential discrimination of conflicting emotional messages by normal, delinquent, and schizophrenic adolescents. *Dissertation Abstracts* 26: 6850–6851.

Matsumoto, D. (1987) The role of facial response in the experience of emotion: More methodological problems and a meta-analysis. *Journal of Personality and Social Psychology* 52: 769–774.

McClelland, J. L. (1979) On the time relations of mental processes: An examination of systems of processes in cascade. *Psychological Review* 86: 287–330.

McGuire, L. and Beattie, G. (2018) Talking green and acting green are two different things: An experimental investigation of low carbon choices. *Semiotica*, in press.

McNeill, D. (1992) *Hand and Mind: What Gestures Reveal about Thought*. Chicago: University of Chicago Press.

Mehrabian, A. (1971) *Silent Messages*. Belmont, CA: Wadsworth.

Mehrabian, A. and Ferris, S. R. (1967) Inference of attitudes from nonverbal communication in two channels. *Journal of Consulting Psychology* 31: 248–252.

Mehrabian, A. and Friar, J. F. (1969) Encoding of attitude by a seated communicator via posture and position cues. *Journal of Consulting and Clinical Psychology* 33: 330–336.

Mehrabian, A. and Wiener, M. (1967) Decoding of inconsistent communications. *Journal of Personality and Social Psychology* 6: 109–114.

Meihlke, A. (1973) *Surgery of the Facial Nerve*. Philadelphia, PA: Saunders.

Meyer-Lindenberg, A., Hariri, A. R., Munoz, K. E., Mervis, C. B., Mattay, V. S., Morris, C. A. and Berman, K. F. (2005) Neural correlates of genetically abnormal social cognition in Williams syndrome. *Nature Neuroscience* 8: 991–993.

Milgram, S. (1963) Behavioral Study of obedience. *Journal of Abnormal and Social Psychology* 67: 371–378.

Milgram, S. (1974) *Obedience to Authority: An Experimental View*. New York: Harper Perennial.

Modigliani, A. (1971) Embarrassment, face work and eye-contact: Testing a theory of embarrassment. *Journal of Personality and Social Psychology* 17: 15–24.

Myers, R. E. (1976) Comparitive neurology of vocalization and speech: Proof of a dichotomy. *Annals of the New York Academy of Sciences* 280: 745–757.

Nielsen, G. (1962) *Studies in Self Confrontation*. Copenhagen: Munksgaard.

Nissani, M. (1990) A cognitive reinterpretation of Stanley Milgram's observations on obedience to authority. *American Psychologist* 45: 1384–1385.

Oreskes, N. and Conway, E. M. (2010) *Merchants of Doubt*. London: Blomsbury.

Orne, M. T. (1962) On the social psychology of the psychological experiment: With particular reference to demand characteristics and their implications. *American Psychologist* 17: 776.

Packard, V. (1957) *The Hidden Persuaders*. London: Macmillan.

Packer, D. J. (2008) Identifying systematic disobedience in Milgram's obedience experiments: A meta-analytic review. *Perspectives on Psychological Science* 3: 301–304.

Pennebaker, J. W. (1982) *The Psychology of Physical Symptoms*. New York: Springer.

Pennebaker, J. W. (1989) Confession, inhibition and disease. *Advances in Experimental Social Psychology* 22: 211–244.

Pennebaker, J. W. (1993) Putting stress into words: Health, linguistic, and therapeutic implications. *Behaviour Research and Therapy* 31: 539–548.

Pennebaker, J. W. (1995) *Emotion, Disclosure and Health*. Washington, DC: American Psychological Association.

Pennebaker, J. W. (1997) Writing about emotional experiences as a therapeutic process. *Psychological Science* 8: 162–166.

Pennebaker, J. W. (2000) Telling stories: The health benefits of narrative. *Literature and Medicine* 19: 3–18.

Pennebaker, J. W. and Beall, S. K. (1986) Confronting a traumatic event: Toward an understanding of inhibition and disease. *Journal of Abnormal Psychology* 95: 274–281.

Pennebaker, J. W. and Francis, M. E. (1996) Cognitive, emotional, and language processes in disclosure. *Cognition and Emotion* 10: 601–626.

Pennebaker, J. W., Hughes, C. F. and O'Heeron, R. C. (1987) The psychophysiology of confession: Linking inhibitory and psychosomatic processes. *Journal of Personality and Social Psychology* 52: 781–793.

Pennebaker, J. W., Mayne, T. and Francis, M. (1997) Linguistic predictors of adaptive bereavement. *Journal of Personality and Social Psychology* 72: 863–871.

Pettigrew, M. P. and Lee, K. (2011) The 'father of stress' meets 'big tobacco': Hans Selye and the tobacco industry. *The American Journal of Public Health* 101, 411–418.

Pitt, N. (1998) *The Paddy and the Prince: Making of Naseem Hamed*. New York: Four Walls Eight Windows.

Potash, H. (1965) 'Schizophrenic interaction and the double bind'. Doctoral dissertation, Michigan State University.

Potter, J. (1988) Cutting cakes: A study of psychologists' social categorizations. *Philosophical Psychology* 1, 17–33.

Potter, J. (1996) *Representing Reality: Discourse, Rhetoric and Social Construction*. London: Sage.

Potter, J., Edwards, D. and Wetherell, M. (1993) A model of discourse in action. *American Behavioral Scientist* 36: 383–401.

Potter, J. and Hepburn, A. (2010) Putting aspiration into words: 'Laugh particles', managing descriptive trouble and modulating action. *Journal of Pragmatics* 42: 1543–1555.

Potter, J. and Mulkay, M. (1985) Scientists' interview talk: Interviews as a technique for revealing participants' interpretative practices. In M. Brenner, J. Brown and D. Canter (eds), *The Research Interview: Uses and Approaches*. London: Academic Press, pp. 247–269.

Potter, J. and Wetherell, M. (1987) *Discourse and Social Psychology: Beyond Attitudes and Behaviour*. London: Sage.

Potter, J. and Wetherell, M. (1988) Accomplishing attitudes: Fact and evaluation in racist discourse. *Interdisciplinary Journal for the Study of Discourse* 8: 51–68.

Reichard, S. and Tillman, C. (1950) Patterns of parent–child relationships in schizophrenia. *Psychiatry* 13: 247–257.

Reicher, S. D. and Haslam, S. A. (2011a) After shock? Towards a social identity explanation of the Milgram 'obedience' studies. *British Journal of Social Psychology* 50: 163–169.

Reicher, S. D. and Haslam, S. A. (2011b) Culture of shock: A fresh look at Milgram's obedience studies. *Scientific American Mind* 22: 30–35.

Reicher, S. D., Haslam, S. A. and Miller, A. G. (2014) What makes a person a perpetrator? The intellectual, moral, and methodological arguments for revisiting Milgram's research on the influence of authority. *Journal of Social Issues* 70: 393–408.

Reicher, S. D., Haslam, S. A. and Smith, J. R. (2012) Working toward the experimenter reconceptualizing obedience within the Milgram paradigm as identification-based followership. *Perspectives on Psychological Science* 7: 315–324.

Ringuette, E. L. and Kennedy, T. (1966) An experimental study of the double bind hypothesis. *Journal of Abnormal Psychology* 71: 136–141.

Roger, D. and Bull, P. (1989) Introduction. In D. Roger and P. Bull (eds), *Conversation: An Interdisciplinary Perspective*. Clevedon: Multilingual Matters, pp. 21–47.

Ross, C. (2006) The paradoxical bodies of contemporary art. In A. Jones (ed.), *A Companion to Contemporary Art Since 1945*. Oxford: Blackwell Publishing, pp. 378–400.

Royal College of Physicians (1962) *The Report on Smoking and Health* https://www.rcplondon.ac.uk/projects/outputs/smoking-and-health-1962. Accessed 3 March 2017.

Russell, N. J. C. (2009) Stanley Milgram's obedience to authority experiments: Towards an understanding of their relevance in explaining aspects of the Nazi Holocaust. http://researcharchive.vuw.ac.nz/handle/10063/1091. Accessed 1 March 2017.

Rutter, D. R. and Stephenson, G. M. (1979) The functions of looking: Effects of friendship in gaze. *British Journal of Social and Clinical Psychology* 18: 203–205.

Sacks, H. (1963) Sociological description. *Berkeley Journal of Sociology* 8: 1–16.

Sacks, H. (1974) An analysis of the course of a joke's telling in conversation. In J. Sherzer and D. Baumann (eds), *Explorations in the Ethnography of Speaking*. Cambridge: Cambridge University Press, pp. 337–353.

Sacks, H. (1984) On doing 'being ordinary'. In J. M. Atkinson and J. Heritage (eds), *Structures of Social Action: Studies in Conversation Analysis*. Cambridge: Cambridge University Press, pp. 413–429.

Sacks, H. (1992) *Lectures on Conversation*. 2 vols. G. Jefferson (ed.). With introductions by Emanuel A. Schegloff. Oxford: Blackwell.

Sacks, H., Schegloff, E. A. and Jefferson, G. (1974) A simplest systematics for the organization of turn-taking for conversation. *Language* 4: 696–735.

Scheflen, A. E. (1965) *Stream and Structure of Communicational Behavior: Context Analysis of a Psychotherapy Session*. Eastern Pennsylvania Psychiatric Institute.

Schegloff, E. A. (1984) On some questions and ambiguities in conversation. In J. M. Atkinson and J. Heritage (eds), *Structures of Social Action.* Cambridge: Cambridge University Press, pp. 28–52.

Schegloff, E. and Sacks, H. (1973) Opening up closings. *Semiotica* 8: 289–327.

Schelde, T. and Hertz, M. (1994) Ethology and psychotherapy. *Ethology and Sociobiology* 15: 383–392.

Schuham, A. I. (1967) The double-bind hypothesis a decade later. *Psychological Bulletin* 68: 409–416.

Searle, J. R. (1969) *Speech Acts: An Essay in the Philosophy of Language.* Cambridge: Cambridge University Press.

Sears, D. O. (1986) College sophomores in the laboratory: Influences of a narrow data base on social psychology's view of human nature. *Journal of Personality and Social Psychology* 51: 515–530.

Selye, H. (1976) *The Stress of Life.* New York: McGraw-Hill.

Shadish, W. R. and Carlson, L. H. (2007) *When Hell Froze Over: The Memoir of a Korean War Combat Physician Who Spent 1010 Days in a Communist Prison Camp.* Indiana: iUniverse.

Shakespeare, W. (1992) *The Tragedy of Hamlet, Prince of Denmark.* B. A. Mowat and P. Werstine (eds). New York: Washington Square Pocket.

Sheatsley, P. B. (1965) White attitudes towards the negro. *Daedalus* 95: 217–238.

Shepherd, I. L. and Guthrie, G. M. (1959) Attitudes of mothers of schizophrenic patients. *Journal of Clinical Psychology* 15: 212–215.

Steiner, F. (1986) Differentiating smiles. In E. Branniger-Huber and F. Steiner (eds), *FACS in psychotherapy research.* Zurich: Department of Clinical Psychology, Universität Zurich, pp. 139–148.

Stiles, W. B. (1995) Disclosure as a speech act: Is it psychotherapeutic to disclose? *Journal of Clinical Psychology* 15: 212–215.

Sullivan, H. S. (1927) The onset of schizophrenia. *American Journal of Psychiatry* 84: 105–134.

Takooshian, H. (2000) How Stanley Milgram taught about obedience and social influence. In T. Blass (ed.), *Obedience to Authority: Current Perspectives on the Milgram Paradigm.* Mahwah, NJ: Lawrence Erlbaum, pp. 9–25.

Tedeschi, J. T., Schlenker, B. R. and Bonoma, T. V. (1971) Cognitive dissonance: Private ratiocination or public spectacle? *American Psychologist* 26: 685–695.

The Independent (1996) Eysenck took £800,000 tobacco funds. www.independent.co.uk/news/eysenck-took-pounds-800000-tobacco-funds-1361007.html. Accessed 27 February 2017.

The Guardian (2011) 14,000 British professors – but only 50 are black. https://www.theguardian.com/education/2011/may/27/only-50-black-british-professors. Accessed 27 February 2017.

The Scotsman (2008) 'I really know what I'm talking about. I'm a brilliant f***ing artist' www.scotsman.com/lifestyle/i-really-know-what-i-m-talking-about-i-m-a-brilliant-f-ing-artist-tracey-emin-interview-1-1434721. Accessed 19 April 2017.

The Star (2015) Brendan Ingle rejects reunion approach from Nazeem Hamed. www.thestar.co.uk/news/no-thanks-naz-brendan-ingle-rejects-reunion-approach-from-naseem-hamed-1-7310471. Accessed 3 March 2017.

Trower, P., Bryant, B., Argyle, M. and Marzillier, J. (1978) *Social Skills and Mental Health*. London: Methuen.

U.S. Department of Education (2007) https://nces.ed.gov/pubs2007/2007064.pdf. Accessed 27 February 2017.

Watzlawick, P. (1963) A review of the double-bind theory. *Family Process* 11: 132–153.

Watzlawick, P., Beavin, J. H. and Jackson, D. D. (1967) *Pragmatics of Human Communication: A Study of Interactional Patterns*. London: Faber and Faber.

Wetherell, M. and Potter, J. (1992) *Mapping the Language of Racism: Discourse and the Legitimation of Exploitation*. London: Harvester Wheatsheaf.

Wierzbicka, A. (1995) Kisses, handshakes, bows: The semantics of nonverbal communication. *Semiotica* 103: 207–252.

Willis, J. and Todorov, A. (2006) First impressions: Making up your mind after a 100-ms exposure to a face. *Psychological Science* 17: 592–598.

Wiseman, R. (2012) The truth about mind control. *New Statesman*. www.newstatesman.com/blogs/lifestyle/2012/07/truth-about-mind-control. Accessed 3 March 2017.

Wittgenstein, L. (1953) *Philosophical Investigations*. Oxford: Blackwell.

Zimbardo, P. (2007) *The Lucifer Effect: Understanding How Good People Turn Evil*. New York: Random House.

INDEX